D1560095

PARADOX AND TRANSFORMATION

**BALLINGER SERIES
ON
INNOVATION AND ORGANIZATIONAL CHANGE**

Series Editors:
Michael Tushman and Andrew Van de Ven

HD 58.8 .P36 1988

Paradox and transformation

PARADOX AND TRANSFORMATION
Toward a Theory of Change in Organization and Management

Edited by
ROBERT E. QUINN
KIM S. CAMERON

Ballinger Publishing Company • Cambridge, Massachusetts
A Subsidiary of Harper & Row, Publishers, Inc.

RITTER LIBRARY
BALDWIN-WALLACE COLLEGE

Copyright © 1988 by Ballinger Publishing Company. All rights reserved. No part of this publication may be reproduced, stored in a retrieval system, or transmitted in any form or by any means, electronic, mechanical, photocopy, recording or otherwise, without the prior written consent of the publisher.

International Standard Book Number: 0–88730–156–8

Library of Congress Catalog Card Number: 88–6220

Printed in the United States of America

Library of Congress Cataloging-in-Publication Data

Paradox and transformation.

   (Ballinger series on innovation and organizational change)
   Includes index.
   1. Organizational change.   I. Quinn, Robert E.   II. Cameron, Kim S.
III. Series.
HD58.8.P36   1988   658.4′06   88–6220
ISBN 0-88730-156-8

RITTER LIBRARY
BALDWIN-WALLACE COLLEGE

CONTENTS

v

LIST OF FIGURES

LIST OF TABLES

PREFACE

In our analyses of organizational phenomena, we have found that paradoxical observations attract our attention. These observations capture some dynamic tension, opposition, or contradiction. When someone points out the presence of such a paradox, we have been required to think more carefully because the statement invariably entails some creative insight that implies understanding beyond the obvious. Becoming aware of paradoxes in organizations has led us to insights that have enriched, and often exceeded, our previous understanding.

The literature in organizational studies, however, seldom contains examples or explanations of paradoxes. Even though organizations are complex, dynamic systems, our descriptions and models of them are often superficial. Our explanations of complicated phenomena are sometimes limited by assumptions of linearity (i.e., one-way, cause-and-effect relationships) and equilibrium. They tend to ignore contradictions, oppositions, and incongruities or quickly resolve them by labeling one side of the contradiction good and the other bad. The literature reveals difficulty accepting simultaneous opposites that are positively defined, mutually-causal relationships, functional incongruities, and paradigm shifts. In short, authors have often not successfully tolerated paradoxical thinking.

Our intent in this book is to introduce and explore the implications of paradox in organizations. We are convinced not only that organizational paradox provides a rich metaphor for understanding organizational phenomena, but that it can lead to a more comprehensive and complex view of organizations and their management than has been previously available.

GENESIS OF THE BOOK

We have wrestled for several years with the problem of defining the construct of organizational effectiveness. Several empirical investigations, book chapters, and journal articles on the subject have helped us appreciate the complexity of that construct. Reflecting on that past work and progressing in our own thinking, we began to uncover the inherent paradoxes in effectiveness. The presence of oppositions began to illuminate the central place of contradiction in the effective performance of organizations. For example, we realized that effective organizations are usually characterized by stability but also by change. An emphasis on automation, efficiency, and production is consistent with effectiveness, but so is the development and maintenance of caring, meaningful relationships among employees. Effective managers, too, not only act logically and rationally but also illogically and irrationally.

Our observations in organizations and among managers, however, were not well reflected in the models and frameworks in the organizational literature. Contradiction was often interpreted as disconfirmation, and opposition was frequently dismissed as an aberration or an outlier.

While grappling with this problem we read Andy Van de Ven's 1983 review of Peters and Waterman's *In Search of Excellence*. Van de Ven pointed out the authors' insightful observation that the best managers and the best organizations are paradoxical and argued that traditional organizational theory, with its need for internal consistency, could not cope well with this observation. Indeed, Peters and Waterman's discussion of paradox was quite brief. The emphasis on linear, consistent models of organization in the literature, and the lack of frameworks that incorporated paradox, seemed to inhibit a more in-depth analysis on their part.

This motivated us to expand our search beyond the boundaries of organizational theory for insights about paradox in organizations. We were influenced by several books, among them Charles Hampden-Turners's *Maps of the Mind*, Mitroff's *Stakeholders of the Organizational Mind*, and the work of Siegfried Streufert on cognitive complexity. During this time, we became aware that several of our colleagues—among them were people who eventually contributed chapters to this book—were examining similar issues. In an attempt to provide a forum for the discussion of these ideas on organizational paradox, we sponsored a symposium at the 1985 meetings of The Academy of Management. Several papers and many lively discussions emerged from that session, and subsequent exchanges of papers and critiques led to our organizing this book.

THE OBJECTIVE

For us, paradox is not a dependent variable to be explained. It is a framework or metaphor similar to open systems, loosely coupled systems, or bureaucracy. Our intent in this book is to explore the utility of that metaphor. A fundamental question is: Will paradox help us to understand organizational phenomena in richer and more insightful ways?

The primary focus is on the illustration, explanation, and initiation of discussions of organizational paradox and its relationship to transformation and change in organizations. On one hand, all of the contributors admit that their chapters are more thoughtful explorations than well-developed or refined expositions. The rejoinders are designed specifically, in fact, to pinpoint blind spots as well as implications and elaborations. On the other hand, because paradox has not been incorporated into mainline organizational theory, the chapters do take giant steps toward explaining organizational phenomena that have been largely ignored or misunderstood. The book, then, provides a stimulus, a groundwork for further work on organizational paradox and transformation.

ORGANIZATION

This book is organized around two main emphases. After our initial chapter, which introduces the concept of paradox, writers of the next three chapters explore the theoretical issues surrounding paradox and transformation. Van de Ven and Poole (Chapter 2) provide an analysis of paradox and the requirements for an accompanying theory of change. Ford and Backoff (Chapter 3) review the literature and suggest some provocative ideas for new ways of thinking about paradox. Bartunek

(Chapter 4) explores the notion of reframing and its role in the dynamics often associated with paradox.

The remaining chapters focus on the applications of paradox. Eisenhardt and Westcott (Chapter 5) explore the power of paradoxical demands in the implementation of just-in-time manufacturing. Siporin and Gummer (Chapter 6) review the use of paradoxical interventions in family therapy and raise questions about such applications in organizations. Morgan (Chapter 7) shows how paradoxical or transformational thinking might be taught in an MBA program. And Argyris (Chapter 8) writes about the role of paradox in our own practice of crafting organizational theories. Finally, we summarize some of what we as editors have learned about the meaning of paradox, and we explore the potential of the paradox metaphor to explain dynamic organizational processes such as vicious and virtuous cycles.

ACKNOWLEDGMENTS

There are many people who have greatly influenced this effort. We would first like to thank each of the authors for both the material they have written and the cooperative attitude they have shown in the production of this volume.

We would like to thank Andy Van de Ven and Mike Tushman. They were the first to encourage us to pursue a book project on this topic. In our early efforts we were particularly enlightened by conversations with Van de Ven, Bob Backoff, Lou Pondy, Bill Starbuck, and Karl Weick.

The staff people at the University of Michigan Business School have been very helpful. We particulary thank Marie Bien and Dianne Haft, who worked long hours on the manuscript. The staff at Ballinger has also been both helpful and patient.

Our families have been understanding. We particularly thank Melinda and Delsa. Their love and sacrifice is most appreciated.

Finally we would like to express our sense of loss in the passing of Lou Pondy. As mentioned above, he had much to say about this topic. He not only informed us, he inspired us. We miss him greatly, and to him we dedicate the book.

1 ORGANIZATIONAL PARADOX AND TRANSFORMATION

Kim S. Cameron and Robert E. Quinn

> In formal logic a contradiction is the sign of defeat; but in
> the evolution of real knowledge it marks the first step in
> progress towards victory.
>
> —Whitehead

An emerging awareness of the inevitability of paradox is evident in recent literature in the organizational sciences. Observers are becoming more sensitive to the presence of simultaneous opposites or contradictions in effective management and organizational behavior. More and more writers recognize that paradoxes are indigenous to effective organizational functioning and, in particular, to individuals, organizations, and industries facing a modern post-industrial environment. Up to now, however, discussions of paradox have varied greatly in their precision and depth. What paradox is (and isn't) and how it fits with current organizational and management theory have not been clearly defined.

Unfortunately, organizational theorists and researchers are not yet very sophisticated in understanding the nature of paradox. Maruyama (1976) pointed out that the traditional ways in which organizational scientists think are inappropriate for analyzing such complex organizational phenomena as paradox. He described this thinking as

1

unidirectional, uniformistic, competitive, hierarchical, quantitative, classificational, and atomistic. The requirement for understanding complex phenomena, he asserted, is mutualistic, heterogenic, symbiotic, interactionist, qualitative, relational, and contextual thinking. Similarly, Van de Ven (1983) asserted that organizational and management theories match analytic thinking in narrowness and unidirectionality. Organizational theories, he argued, still do not generally consider the presence of paradox. Instead, they are based largely on linearity and consistency. The simultaneous presence of incongruent and contradictory patterns is seldom explained or even acknowledged. A need for internal consistency drives out contradictory thinking.

This book aims not only to bring the concept of paradox more centrally to the attention of organizational scholars and practitioners, but also to stimulate the formulation of management and organization theories that account for the presence of paradox.

DEFINITIONAL ISSUES

As suggested, some ambiguity exists regarding the definition of paradox in organizations. Fundamentally, paradox embraces clashing ideas. The Latin root, in fact, denotes "apparent contradiction" (Slaatte 1968). On the one hand, a relatively well-defined usage of paradox has emerged in philosophy. Paradox in that literature involves contradictory, mutually exclusive elements that are present and operate equally at the same time. Paradoxes differ in nature from other similar concepts such as dilemma, irony, inconsistency, dialectic, ambivalence, or conflict. For example, a dilemma is an either-or situation where one alternative must be selected over other attractive alternatives. An irony exists when an unexpected or contradictory outcome arises from a single alternative. An inconsistency is merely an aberration or discontinuity from past patterns. A dialectic is a pattern that always begins with a thesis followed by an antithesis and resolved by a synthesis. Ambivalence is uncertainty over which two or more attractive (or unattractive) alternatives should be chosen. And a conflict is the perpetuation of one alternative at the expense of others. In precise terms, paradox differs from each of these concepts in that no choice need be made between two or more contradictions. Both of the contradictory elements in a paradox are accepted and present. Both operate simultaneously. The key characteristic in paradox is the simultaneous presence of contradictory, even mutually exclusive elements.

On the other hand, paradox is generally used in everyday language, as well as in the organizational literature, synonymously with concepts such as dilemma, irony, inconsistency, or dialectic. Unexpected or discontinuous elements in analysis have often been labeled paradoxical (for example, Benne 1964; Martin, Feldman, Hatch, and Sitkin 1983), and the criterion of contradictory, mutually exclusive elements has not always been applied. Paradox's precise definition and attributes are not yet common components of organizational analysis. Another purpose of this book, therefore, is to help define more precisely the meaning of paradox in organizational settings and to identify applications of the paradox metaphor in organization and management theory.

THE EMERGENCE OF PARADOX

Perceptions of paradox occur more frequently in turbulent times. Reports of paradoxical conditions appear almost daily in the popular press. For example, despite record-breaking sales and profits in the past year, the three major auto companies in the United States recently announced plans to lay off almost 150,000 more employees. The banking industry, which once was protected from competition, now faces encroachment in the marketplace from insurance agencies, brokerage houses, and even retailing firms. Well over 100 banks failed this past year with over 900 branches closing, yet at the same time, record profitability has been reported in the industry and overseas expansion is underway. Over a third of a million jobs have been lost in the computer and microcircuit industries since 1980, yet those industries are clearly viewed as sunshine areas of the economy that will provide continued growth. While the federal deficit remains at an all-time high and the balance of payments holds at multibillions in the red, inflation remains low and more people are employed than ever before in America's history.

These seemingly paradoxical conditions are more likely to be perceived in a modern post-industrial environment characterized by more and increasing information, more and increasing complexity, more and increasing turbulence, and more and increasing competition (Huber 1984; Cameron 1986b). Drucker's (1980: 1) prediction at the beginning of the decade that this kind of environment would permeate American organizations, and his suggestions for management action, seem appropos:

> The one certainty about the times ahead, the times in which managers will have to work and to perform, is that they will be turbulent times. And in

turbulent times, the first task of management is to make sure of an institution's capacity for survival, to make sure of its structural strength and soundness, of its capacity to survive a blow, to adapt to sudden change, and to avail itself of new opportunities.

Other authors have labeled this type of environment a third wave (Toffler 1980), an information society (Masuda 1980), a telematic society (Martin 1981), and a techtronic era (Brezinski 1970). In each case, authors identify new management challenges presented by an environment that is both rich in opportunity yet highly constrained, flexible yet rigid, munificent yet constrictive.

PSYCHOLOGICAL PARADOX

Fundamentally, paradox is a mental construct. It exists only in the thoughts or interpretations of the individual. The capacity to perceive and think about paradox, however, can be very important to the scientific process.

Investigators have discovered that paradoxical thinking is associated with creative insights and scientific breakthroughs (i.e., the transformation of old ways of thinking about a problem to new ways). For example, Rothenburg (1979) introduced the concept of "Janusian thinking" while investigating the creative achievements of individuals such as Einstein, Mozart, Picasso, and O'Neill, as well as fifty-four highly creative artists and scientists in the United States and Great Britain. Janusian thinking occurs when two contradictory thoughts are held to be true simultaneously. The explanation or resolution of the apparent contradiction is what leads to major breakthroughs in insight.

> In Janusian thinking, two or more opposites or antitheses are conceived simultaneously, either as existing side by side, or as equally operative, valid, or true. In an apparent defiance of logic or of physical possibility, the creative person consciously formulates the simultaneous operation of antithetical elements and develops those into integrated entities and creations. It is a leap that transcends ordinary logic. What emerges is no mere combination or blending of elements: the conception does not only contain different elements, it contains opposing and antagonistic elements, which are understood as coexistent. As a self-contradictory structure, the Janusian formulation is surprising when seriously posited in naked form. (Rothenburg 1979: 55)

The surprising nature of Janusian formulations results from the preconception that two opposites cannot both be valid at the same time.

However, holding such thoughts engenders the flexibility of thought needed for individual creativity.

For example, Einstein's conception of the theory of relativity emerged from what he described as "the happiest thought of my life." He conceived of a man jumping off a tall building, and on the way down, taking from his pocket a wallet, placing it in front of himself, and letting go. It occurred to Einstein that relative to the man, the wallet would remain stationary in the air. At that instant, therefore, the wallet (and the man) was simultaneously moving and at rest. That is, two conditions that seem to be mutually exclusive were present at the same time. Einstein's paradox led to a complete revolution in the accepted laws of physics. Rothenburg's study uncovered similar paradoxes in composers who conceived of simultaneous dissonance and harmony in a chord, artists who painted tension and rest in the same scene, and athletes who experienced both exhaustion and exhilaration at a point of peak performance.

This relationship between paradox and excellence, and between paradox and quantum leaps in knowledge and insight, is also illustrated by Schumacher (1977), who distinguished between two types of problems—convergent problems and divergent problems. Convergent problems deal with distinct, precise, quantifiable, logical ideas that are amenable to empirical investigation. Convergent problems are solvable problems; as they are studied more rigorously and more precisely, answers tend to converge into a single accepted solution. Divergent problems, on the other hand, are problems that are not easily quantifiable or verifiable and that do not seem to have a single solution. The more rigorously and precisely they are studied, the more the solutions tend to diverge, or to become contradictory and opposite. For example, the problem of world peace seems to necessitate security and protection on the one hand, and reducing the threat of war by disarmament on the other. The education of children is a process of passing on past knowledge and culture—a process requiring those who know to tell those who don't know—as well as a process of allowing freedom, autonomy, and self-development—where an absence of authority, constraints, and "telling" exists. Governments (at least in the Free World) face the problem of insuring liberty—where, left to themselves, those who have, get, and those who don't have, don't get—as well as equality—where the haves and the have-nots divide resources equitably.

In normal organizational science, "good scientists study the most important problems they think they can solve" (Medawar 1967: 1).

Consistency and control take priority in defining problems. Bernard (1957: 55, 77) suggested:

> When faced with complex questions, physiologists and physicians, as well as physicists and chemists, should divide the total problem into simpler and more and more clearly defined partial problems. They will thus reduce phenomena to their simplest possible material conditions and make application to the experimental method easier and more certain.

Schumacher (1977: 126), on the other hand, argued that unlike convergent problems, divergent problems deal with "higher faculties" and "higher levels of being."

> I have said that to solve a problem is to kill it. There is nothing wrong with killing a convergent problem. . . . Divergent problems cannot be killed; they cannot be solved in the sense of establishing a correct formula; they can, however, be transcended. A pair of opposites . . . cease to be opposites at the higher level, the really human level, where self-awareness plays its proper role. It is then that such forces as love and compassion, understanding and empathy, become available. . . . Opposites cease to be opposites.

According to Schumacher, wrestling with divergent problems, because of their inherent paradoxes and incompatibility with linear methods, is more likely to produce breakthroughs of the kind studied by Rothenburg than are convergent problem solutions. Excellence in science seems to be inherently linked to the tension of paradox.

Without the tension that exists between simultaneous opposites, unproductive "schismogenesis" occurs (Bateson 1936; Morgan 1981). Schismogenesis is a process of self-reinforcement where one action or attribute perpetuates itself until it becomes extreme and therefore dysfunctional. For example, consider the situation where one person's dominance produces submissiveness in another, which in turn reinforces even more dominance on the part of the first person and more submissiveness on the part of the second. A negatively reinforcing cycle is produced. One person's actions produce more extreme reactions in the other until the system becomes so out of balance that it disintegrates. Bateson referred to this condition as complementary schismogenesis. Or consider the situation where dominance in one person produces a reaction of dominance in another, which sets up a cycle of escalating competition and eventual mutual destruction. (The current international arms race is a good example.) Bateson called this symmetrical schismogenesis. Similar forces accelerate one another until system disintegration occurs.

Most existing theories are schismogenic. Theories are always tied to values, and most values have a perceptual opposite. The need for logic and internal consistency, however, drives out contradictory notions (Van de Ven 1983). One value is implicitly chosen over another. Order is assumed over change; ends over means, individual over collectivity, or vice versa. A paradoxical perspective would make contradictory notions, like loose and tight coupling, for example, explicit, and would consider their simultaneous presence and dynamic balance. A paradoxical perspective would consider how both could be simultaneously pursued.

ORGANIZATIONAL PARADOX

Paradoxical characteristics in organizations have been identifiable in the literature of the last decade, even though inherent contradictions have seldom been explicated by authors. Contradictions have seldom been labeled as paradoxical. For example, authors have identified the following as characteristic of effective organizations, even though the paradoxical nature of these attributes has been ignored.

1. Loose-coupling—which encourages wide search, initiation of innovation, and functional autonomy—as well as tight-coupling—which encourages quick execution, implementing innovation, and functional reciprocity (for example, Morgan 1981; Zaltman, Duncan, and Holbeck 1973).
2. High specialization of roles—which reinforces expertise and efficiency—as well as high generality of roles—which reinforces flexibility and interdependency (for example, Lawrence and Lorsch 1967).
3. Continuity of leadership—which permits stability, long-term planning, and institutional memory—along with infusion of new leaders—which permits increased innovation, adaptability, and currency (for example, Chaffee 1984).
4. Deviation-amplifying processes—which encourage productive conflict and opposition that energize and empower organizations—as well as deviation-reducing processes—which encourage harmony and consensus needed to engender trust and smooth information flows (for example, Maruyama 1963).
5. Expanded search in decisionmaking—which allows for wider environmental scanning, access to more information, and divergence of input—as well as the creation of inhibitors to information

overload—which reduce and buffer the amount of information reaching decisionmakers and lead to convergence in decisionmaking (for example, Huber 1984).

6. Disengagement and disidentification with past strategies—which foster new perspectives and innovation and inhibit defining new problems simply as variations on old problems—as well as reintegration and reinforcement of roots—which foster commitment to a special sense of organizational identity and mission and past strategies (for example, Tichy 1983).

INVESTIGATIONS OF
ORGANIZATIONAL PARADOX

More recently, several authors have explicitly acknowledged in their research the presence of paradoxes associated with organizational effectiveness. For example, Cameron (1986b) reported research on colleges and universities in which the presence of paradox was found to be central in explaining how institutions overcame decline and improved in effectiveness. He argued, "Organizational effectiveness is inherently paradoxical. To be effective, an organization must possess attributes that are simultaneously contradictory, even mutually exclusive." By way of illustration, a study was summarized of fourteen small colleges in which each had experienced decline in both revenues and enrollments during the 1970s. Half of those schools successfully recovered; half did not. The question of interest was, "What distinguishes the successful recoverers from those that continued to slide?" The following conclusions were drawn.

1. Recovering institutions engaged in proactive, entrepreneurial, and innovative actions that were oriented toward long-term recovery. Simultaneously, they initiated conservative, self-protection mechanisms (for example, efficiency measures) oriented toward short-term survival.

2. Management strategies were simultaneously oriented toward both enacting and manipulating the external environment (for example, changing suppliers and markets), and ignoring the environmental constraints by establishing environmental buffers and concentrating on internal human resource and allocation decisions.

3. Top leadership paid a great deal of attention to symbol as well as substance. On the one hand, structural, personnel, and curricular changes were instituted, so that the basic fiber of the institution was altered. On the other hand, substance was ignored in favor of image. Much energy went into helping constituencies interpret events favorably. The management of symbols and interpretations was a critical difference between successful managers and others who failed (Cameron and Ulrich 1986).

4. Institutions engaged in domain defense along with domain offense (Miles and Cameron 1982). That is, energy was spent in defending the institution against the encroachment of external environmental events and stakeholders, while at the same time, aggressive strategies were initiated to influence the external environment and important stakeholders outside the institution's boundaries.

5. The core culture or "saga" of successful institutions was reinforced and perpetuated (that is, institutional roots were strengthened), but at the same time innovations and creative activity helped change the character of the school. The simultaneous destruction and creation processes typical of successful innovations were typical in these institutions (Cameron 1983, 1984; Chaffee 1984).

These conclusions are similar to those that were drawn from another study of 334 four-year colleges and universities throughout the United States (Cameron 1985, 1986a). One of the questions under investigation in that study was, "What accounts for the improvement of organizational effectiveness over time in colleges?" The following are some of the main findings.

1. Institutions that improve in effectiveness over time have an infusion of new leaders at the top as well as continuity and stability among top administrators. The necessity for both new ideas and fresh perspectives exists simultaneously with the requirement for an enduring sense of history among the institution's leadership.

2. Improving institutions emphasize and reinforce internal morale issues among institution members, while at the same time, they react to external demands and are sensitive to market issues. Institutions that do not improve often have leaders that neglect to reinforce the value of human resources inside the organization and to stay "close to home." On the other hand, staying close to home

at the expense of adapting to market conditions inhibits organizational effectiveness.
3. Overwhelmingly, the major predictors of improving effectiveness are factors under the control of managers (for example, strategic actions) rather than context or demographic factors. On the other hand, turbulent and hostile environmental conditions act as inhibitors to effectiveness; supportive conditions enhance the probability of improvement.

Other authors have similarly identified paradoxical characteristics in organizations that perform effectively. For example, Quinn and Rohrbaugh (1983) developed a model of organizational effectiveness that organized the criteria upon which effectiveness judgments are made. They labeled it "the competing values model" because it points out the simultaneous opposition in the criteria that individuals use to judge effectiveness. Figure 1–1 reproduces that model.

These authors used a listing of criteria claimed in the literature to be a comprehensive set of indicators of effectiveness (Campbell 1977), and submitted it to various statistical procedures. Two dimensions emerged from these statistical analyses that help organize the criteria. One dimension ranged from an emphasis on decentralization and flexibility on one end (top of Figure 1–1) to centralization and stability on the other (bottom of Figure 1–1). The second dimension ranged from an emphasis on internal, individualistic elements on one end (left side of Figure 1–1) to an emphasis on external, macro-level elements on the other (right side of Figure 1–1). The power of that model lies in displaying empirically the paradox that exists inherently in notions of effectiveness in organizations. Subsequent research based on the model by Quinn and Cameron (1983), Rohrbaugh (1981), and Cameron (1985) found that organizations do not pursue a single set of criteria. Rather, they pursue competing, or paradoxical, criteria simultaneously.

For example, in a study of organizational effectiveness in the U.S. Employment Service, Rohrbaugh (1981) identified eight major criterion sets that indicated highly desirable performance. These criterion sets were compatible with the competing values model in Figure 1–1. He discovered that some Employment Service offices tried to achieve effectiveness by being innovative as well as conservative; other organizations tried to be both clannish and personal as well as tough and hard-driving. Every office had weaknesses, but every office also displayed high performance on contradictory criteria. Paradoxical performance was a central characteristic of effective performance.

Figure 1-1. The Competing Values Framework: Effectiveness.

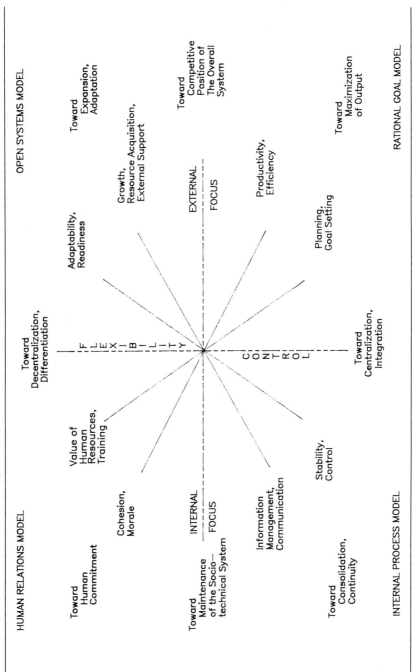

HUMAN RELATIONS MODEL

OPEN SYSTEMS MODEL

Toward Decentralization, Differentiation

Toward Expansion, Adaptation

Toward Competitive Position of The Overall System

Adaptability, Readiness

Growth, Resource Acquisition, External Support

EXTERNAL FOCUS

Productivity, Efficiency

Toward Maximization of Output

Value of Human Resources, Training

Cohesion, Morale

FLEXIBILITY

CONTROL

Planning, Goal Setting

Toward Centralization, Integration

INTERNAL FOCUS

Information Management, Communication

Stability, Control

Toward Human Commitment

Toward Maintenance of the Socio—technical System

Toward Consolidation, Continuity

INTERNAL PROCESS MODEL

RATIONAL GOAL MODEL

In another study of leader effectiveness based on the competing values model, Quinn, Dixit, and Faerman (1987) found that the most effective leaders were described by their subordinates as exhibiting seemingly contradictory behaviors or styles. That is, the most effective leaders did not display a single or unitary style, as most of the leadership literature concludes. Rather, they were characterized as possessing paradoxical styles and displayed behaviors that seemingly were contradictory. The authors argue that the presence of contradictory characteristics had not been discovered earlier because existing theoretical frameworks did not allow it. Contradiction is dismissed before the analysis even begins.

Peters and Waterman's (1982) analysis of corporate performance in America also suggested that today's excellent firms possess a variety of paradoxical characteristics such as simultaneous loose and tight coupling, productivity through participation along with a bias for action (non-participation), autonomy and entrepreneurship along with "sticking to the knitting," and so on. They concluded, "The excellent companies have learned how to manage paradox" (1982: 100).

Other investigators have identified the power of paradox in explaining the success of organizational transformations in the context of new ventures and innovations. Macmillan's (1985) review of literature dealing with the emergence and effectiveness of new ventures in corporations identified a variety of inherent paradoxes in that process. For example, successful new ventures require both high commitment to current products and the status quo in an organization (which establishes a firm groundwork for launching new ventures) as well as radical change and questioning of the status quo, which is needed to launch innovative ventures, (Schon 1966). Specialization in roles enhances the probability that new ideas and new products will emerge, yet compartmentalization also creates hierarchy and restriction of communication flows needed for new ideas to emerge (Kanter 1983). Top management support for new ventures is a critical factor in their success, yet that support tends to alienate those engaged in core organizational activities. Too much support also isolates the new venture and makes it difficult to integrate back into the firm's core business (Fast 1979). Failure in new venture activity produces rigidity, protectionism, and restriction, yet failure is required in order to work out bugs in innovative activities and make them resilient (Roberts 1980). New ventures need to be related closely enough to the firm's core businesses that they can rely on resource transfer, yet related ventures are generally seen as draining away or deflecting resources needed by core businesses and infringing upon established domains (Fast 1979). Venture teams need maximum discretion in development, yet milestones and strict accountability are required; a broad mission is functional in developing new ventures, yet so are specific targets (Hill and Hlavacek 1972).

These examples of paradox in recent research are provided merely to exemplify the increasingly common occurrence of paradox in effective organizations. It is our contention that organizational theory and research can no longer ignore this phenomenon if they are to explain organizational and managerial behavior adequately. However, many issues and much ambiguity surround the paradox construct that must be addressed if progress is to be made. We suggest several principles that might prove fruitful in future research and theory building.

1. *Ignoring the contradictory nature of organizations may be dysfunctional for managers and researchers.* Many effective organizations demonstrate both proactivity and entrepreneurship as well as stability and control. However, too much action and innovation can create a loss of direction, wasted energy, and a disruption of continuity. An overemphasis on control and coordination can produce stagnation, loss of energy, and abolition of trust and morale (Quinn and Kimberly 1984). Most theories do not consider such contradictory elements—they simply assume away one of the competing elements. In so doing they attribute actions to managers that may be dysfunctional. Similarly they lead researchers to see only part of the phenomena that are before them.

2. *Theories of congruence have an order bias.* Synthesis is desirable but not required in organizations. Paradox need not always be resolved. Rothenburg proposed that the resolution of paradox led individuals to produce quantum leaps in insight and creativity. When they were able to reconcile two contradictory elements, remarkable advances resulted. On the other hand, Schumacher suggested that the mere recognition that two opposite elements are simultaneously true and present in a system creates flexibility and freedom that are not present in totally linear systems. Contradictions need not be reconciled to enhance effectiveness because paradoxes are not necessarily dialectical. Achieving perfect fit or congruence may lead to a tensionless state in which the system becomes static. Not all paradoxes need be resolved.

3. *Paradoxes are paradoxical.* Most of the models and theories of organization assume consistency and symmetry (for example, structural, leadership, or motivational contingency theories). According to these

models, characteristics or behaviors are matched with particular contexts in order to produce effectiveness. Congruence, it is assumed, leads to effectiveness. However, the principles of paradox emerging from several of the studies cited above suggest that disconfirmation, contradiction, and nonlinearity are inherent in all organizations—a direct contradiction of many current models and theories. Paradoxes also are predictable and symmetrical by themselves. They are both confusing and understandable, common and surprising. This paradoxical characteristic of paradoxes in organizations is illustrated by two different studies of effectiveness in higher education institutions and government organizations.

In one study (Cameron 1985b), an attempt was made to assess some of the basic propositions of the multiple constituencies model of organization effectiveness. A variety of different constituencies were assessed to obtain their preferences and expectations relative to an organization's performance. As might be expected, different constituencies held different, and sometimes opposite, preferences and expectations for organizations. The actual performance was then measured on a variety of dimensions for a set of organizations in order to obtain their effectiveness levels. One important result showed that the organizations that achieved the highest levels of effectiveness scores were also those that satisfied the most separate constituency group expectations, even when different constituencies held contradictory expectations. Highly effective organizations were paradoxical in that they performed in contradictory ways to satisfy contradictory expectations (a somewhat surprising conclusion given current perspectives on effectiveness).

A second study by Quinn and Cameron (1983) used the competing values model to identify changes in criteria of effectiveness over organizational life cycle stages. Effective organizations do not emphasize activities in only one of the quadrants, but maintain some balance or capacity among all four. Effectiveness criteria in different quadrants were emphasized in different life cycle stages. What was defined as effective performance in one stage was contradictory to effectiveness in another stage. However, a predictable pattern of change was found: criteria in stage one preceded criteria in stage two, which preceded stage three criteria, and so on. The competing values model helped organize the criteria so that what contradictory criteria would be valued in the next stage can be predicted. Paradox was predictable, despite its surprising nature.

4. *Paradoxical criteria are not indicated merely by both high and low scores on an attribute.* The complexity of paradoxes in organizations cannot be evaluated without considering simultaneous opposites. That is, investigators in the future may want to measure both the extent to which the element "a" is present as well as the extent to which the opposite of "a" is present. Low scores on "a" may not necessarily indicate the presence of its opposite (Cameron 1984).

For example, consider a condition of excellent physical health called wellness, and its opposite, illness. Indicators of wellness might include low percentage of body fat, low levels of serum lipids in the blood, high tolerance for stress, low blood pressure, cardiovascular fitness, and so forth. High scores on these indicators would suggest excellent health (wellness), but low scores would not necessarily indicate illness. Completely different, even independent, criteria would be required to indicate illness, such as fever, bleeding, nausea, congestion, and so forth. Assessments of health should include both sets of criteria in order to avoid linearity, since wellness and illness could exist simultaneously in the same individual. Similarly, in organizations, criteria of effectiveness may be independent of criteria of ineffectiveness, so both should be measured. Paradoxes are not indicated merely by the presence of high and low scores (bimodal distributions) on the same attribute.

5. *Many inferential statistical procedures mask rather than uncover the presence of paradox in organizational research.* It is common to use means, medians, and linear trends as the basis for statistical analyses and inferences. Unfortunately, taking averages and finding midpoints may mask the presence of paradox, as might the reliance on linear trends in regression equations. Not only might investigators want to be sensitive to nonlinearity and variation in their data, but they may not want to neglect or explain away as aberrations the outliers and contradictions in their analyses. This suggests that Tukey's (1977) advice to manipulate and explore data in non-statistical ways before submitting it to standard programs of analysis should be taken seriously. In addition, giving consideration to variances and unexplained discontinuities may lead to interesting insights that are normally outside the realm of most current theories.

6. *Hypotheses should be generated that do not consider merely the rejection of the null or not.* Contradictory hypotheses, or antitheses, are required for investigators to be sensitive to the presence of paradox. Data supporting two mutually exclusive points of view should not be

interpreted merely as disconfirmation of a single hypothesis. On the other hand, instead of simply including random contradictions in a search for indicators of effectiveness, care must still be taken to bound and justify the criteria selected in assessments. Models should be developed and used to organize and help interpret the relationships among paradoxical criteria.

REFERENCES

Bateson, G. 1936. *Naven.* Cambridge: Cambridge University Press.

Benne, Kenneth. 1964. "From Polarization to Paradox." In *T-Group Theory and Laboratory Methods,* edited by Leland Bradford, Jack Gibb, and Kenneth Benne. New York: Wiley.

Bernard, C. 1957. *An Introduction to the Study of Experimental Medicine.* New York: Dover.

Brzezinski, Z. 1970. *Between Two Ages: America's Role in the Techtronic Era.* New York: Viking.

Cameron, K.S. 1983. "Strategic Responses to Conditions of Decline: Higher Education and the Private Sector." *Journal of Higher Education* 54: 359–80.

———. 1984. "The Effectiveness of Ineffectiveness." In *Research in Organizational Behavior,* Vol. 6, edited by B.M. Staw and L.L. Cummings. Greenwich, Conn.: JAI Press.

———. 1985. "Cultural Congruence, Strength, and Type: Relationships to Effectiveness." Working paper, Graduate School of Business Administration, University of Michigan.

———. 1986a. "A Study of Organizational Effectiveness and Its Predictors." *Management Science* 32: 87–112.

———. 1986b. "Effectiveness as Paradox." *Management Science* 32: 539–53.

Cameron, K.S. and Ulrich, D.O. 1986. Forthcoming. "Transformational Leadership in Colleges and Universities." In *Higher Education: A Handbook of Theory and Research,* edited by J.R. Smart. New York: Agathon.

Cameron, Kim. 1985. "An Empirical Test of the Multiple Constituencies Model of Organizational Effectiveness." Working paper, University of Michigan.

Campbell, John. 1977. "On the Nature of Organizational Effectiveness." In *New Perspectives on Organizational Effectiveness,* edited by Paul Goodman and Johannes Pennings. San Francisco: Jossey-Bass.

Chaffee, E.E. 1984. "Successful Strategic Management in Small Private Colleges." *Journal of Higher Education* 55: 212–41.

Drucker, P. 1980. *Managing in Turbulent Times.* New York: Harper & Row.

Fast, N.D. 1979. "The Future of Industrial New Venture Departments." *Industrial Marketing Management* 8: 264–73.

Hill, R.M., and J.D. Hlavecek. 1972. "The Venture Team: A New Concept in Marketing Organization." *Journal of Marketing* 36 (July): 44–50.

Huber, G.P. 1984. "The Nature and Design of Post-Industrial Organizations." *Management Science* 30: 928–51.

Kanter, R.M. 1983. *The Change Masters.* New York: Simon and Schuster.

Lawrence, P.R., and J.W. Lorsch. 1967. *Organizations and Environment.* Homewood, Ill.: Irwin.

MacMillan, Ian. 1985. "Progress in Research on Corporate Venturing." Research Report Series, Center for Entrepreneurial Studies, New York University.

Martin, J. 1981. *Telematic Society: The Challenge for Tomorrow.* Englewood Cliffs, N.J.: Prentice-Hall.

Martin, Joanne; Martha Feldman; Mary Jo Hatch; and Sim Sitkin. 1983. "The Uniqueness Paradox in Organizational Stories." *Administrative Science Quarterly* 28: 438–53.

Maruyama, M. 1963. "The Second Cybernetics: Deviation-Amplifying Mutual Causal Processes." *American Scientist* 51: 149–64.

———. 1976. "Toward Cultural Symbiosis." In *Evolution and Consciousness: Human Systems in Transition,* edited by E. Jantsch and C.H. Waddington. Reading, Mass.: Addison-Wesley.

Masuda, Y. 1980. *The Information Society.* Bethesda, Md.: World Future Society.

Medawar, P.B. 1967. *The Art of the Solvable.* London: Oxford.

Miles, R.H., and K.S. Cameron. 1982. *Coffin Nails and Corporate Strategies.* Englewood Cliffs, N.J.: Prentice-Hall.

Morgan, G. 1981. "The Schismatic Metaphor and Its Implications for Organizational Analysis." *Organizational Studies* 2: 23–44.

Peters, T.J., and R.H. Waterman. 1982. *In Search of Excellence: Lessons from America's Best-Run Companies.* New York: Harper & Row.

Quinn, R.E., and K.S. Cameron. 1983. "Organizational Life Cycles and Shifting Criteria and Effectiveness." *Management Science* 9: 33–51.

Quinn, R.E.; N. Dixit; and S.R. Faerman. 1987. "Some Archtypes of Managerial Performance." Working paper, Institute for Government and Policy Studies, SUNY Albany.

Quinn, Robert, and John Kimberly. 1984. "Paradox, Planning, and Perseverence: Guidelines for Managerial Practice." In *Managing Organizational Transitions,* edited by John Kimberly and Robert Quinn. New York: Dow Jones-Irwin.

Roberts, E.B. 1980. "New Ventures for Corporate Growth." *Harvard Business Review* (July-August): 134–42.

Rohrbaugh, J. 1981. "Operationalizing the Competing Values Approach." *Public Productivity Review* 5: 141–59.

Rothenburg, A. 1979. *The Emerging Goddess.* Chicago: University of Chicago Press.

Schön, D.A. 1966. "The Fear of Innovation." *International Science and Technology* (November): 70–78.

Schumacher, E.F. 1977. *A Guide for the Perplexed.* New York: Harper & Row.

Slaatte, H.A. 1968. *The Pertinence of the Paradox.* New York: Humanities Press.

Tichy, N.M. 1983. *Managing Strategic Change: Technical, Political, and Cultural Dynamics.* New York: Wiley.

Toffler, A. 1980. *The Third Wave.* New York: Morrow.

Tukey, J.W. 1977. *Exploratory Data Analysis.* Reading, Mass.: Addison-Wesley.

Van de Ven, A.H. 1983. "Review of *In search of excellence.*" *Administrative Science Quarterly* 28: 621–24.

Zaltman, G.; R. Duncan; and J. Holbeck. 1973. *Innovations and Organizations.* New York: Wiley.

2 PARADOXICAL REQUIREMENTS FOR A THEORY OF ORGANIZATIONAL CHANGE

Andrew H. Van de Ven and Marshall Scott Poole

How and why does change occur in organizational structure and behavior over time? This question is central to understanding collective behavior. However, a formal theory that adequately addresses this question has not yet been devised. Hernes (1976), Dahrendorf (1969), and others have suggested that a theory of change in social structure should meet four requirements:

- It should include properties of individual motives and collective structure, and show links among them—part-whole relations among structure and action are basic to any theory of organizational change.
- It should identify and explain the sources of change from both within the social structure (for example, due to dialectical contradictions and tensions within the organization) and outside the structure (for example, due to purposive actions of individuals or extra-organizational events);

The authors appreciate helpful comments while preparing this paper from David Bastien, Edward Freeman, Joseph Galaskiewicz, Ann Goodell, Raghu Garud, Gudmund Hernes, Douglas Polley, and S. Venkataraman, as well as from participants at presentations of this paper at Harvard University, Stanford University, and the University of Minnesota. The preparation of this paper was supported (in part) with a grant to study the management of innovation to the Strategic Management Research Center by the Program on Organizational Effectiveness of the Office of Naval Research under contract No. N00014-84-K-0016.

- It should explain both stability (pressures toward unity, consensus, order) and change (pressures toward conflict, pluralism, and disruption); and
- It should include time as the key historical accounting system.

These four requirements are interdependent, and must be attained jointly in a theory of organizational change. The theory should link system structure with purposive action at micro and macro levels of the organization because the dominant paradigm of management and organization theory rests on the firm belief that any macro-organizational structure must be grounded in the purposive actions of individuals. If one denies this assumption (as does Mayhew 1980), much of the management profession with its elaborate educational, consulting, and research industries would become irrelevant. Moreover, a theory of change must spell out the relationships between structure and action with some precision, rather than implicitly assuming they are independent. This forces theorists to consider micro-macro linkages: the purposive actions of individuals are best understood as micro phenomena, whereas structural dynamics are best understood at collective, macro levels (Knorr-Cetina and Cicourel 1981).

If one accepts the premise that such a theory should link system structure with purposive action, then one must also explain how change is produced both by the internal functioning of the structure and by the external purposive actions of individuals, who can alter the system's direction in response to external events or in service of their own interests. If one concludes that organizational change is totally controlled by forces immanent to the social system, no room is left for individual purpose and no theory of action can result. Conversely, if one concludes that organizational change is totally controlled by purposive individual action unconstrained by nature or structural forces, only a teleological or utopian theory can result.

But system dynamics and action do not always change. They can also preserve or maintain current structures or processes. The third requirement is that the theory should explain both organizational stability and instability in the same conceptual framework. As March (1981: 564) has commented, "In its fundamental structure, a theory of organizational change should not be remarkably different from a theory of ordinary action." Without this requirement, any theory of organizational change would explode and be unable to explain the amazing persistence and fixity observed in common organizational life.

Finally, a theory of organizational change should include time as its key historical metric, because, by definition, change is a difference that can only be noted over time in an organizational unit. Different change theories may adopt different conceptions of time. Chronos (or calendar time) tends to predominate in studies of system structure, while kiros (time gauged in terms of peak experiences—as in the planting and harvesting periods of a growing season) appears to be the most common metric of time in studies of purposive action. A theory of change that links structure and action must therefore reconcile chronos and kiros time metrics.

To our knowledge these four requirements have not been synthesized in any theory of organizational change. Perhaps one reason for this failure is that social theorists have, in effect, treated the first three requirements as paradoxical. Paradox is the simultaneous presence of two mutually exclusive assumptions or statements; taken singly, each is incontestably true, but taken together they are inconsistent. If unacknowledged and unresolved, a paradox can drive theorists to emphasize one pole over the other, in an attempt to maintain an elusive consistency. Organization and management theorists have not been immune to this tendency. Most efforts to build theories of organization change have emphasized either action or structure, stability or change, external or internal causality, and have subordinated the other terms. In part, this tendency to deny the existence of paradox may be due to the common quest to achieve coherent, consistent, and parsimonious theories. But this quest often appears to minimize appreciation of the paradoxes inherent in human beings and their social institutions. Moreover, and most important, a theory that incorporates paradox need not, itself, be paradoxical. However, achieving such a theory requires adopting new methods for systematically addressing paradox inherent in organizational life.

The concern of this chapter is not with a particular theory of organizational change; it is with the implications of the four requirements for constructing such theories. We will explore the paradoxes apparent in the requirements. In so doing, we will also explain why they are essential to a theory of change. We will apply four basic methods for dealing with each paradox: live with paradox; switch levels of analysis; use time; and adopt new concepts to address the paradox. Along the way, we will examine how the four requirements have been treated in some of the major theories of organization structure and action. Taken individually, each theory emphasizes certain aspects of the four requirements. But if the theories could be combined and juxtaposed in some way, or if new integrative theories evolve, we believe they could achieve the four requirements for a theory of organizational persistence and change. We make some suggestions for developing such theories—in the hope that they will either stimulate further work in this direction, or upon reflection, provide a better understanding of the pitfalls of this direction.

Achievement of this agenda will require some theoretical pluralism on the part of the reader, and a willingness not to jump to premature conclusions or denials of the paradoxes. For, as we will see, although it may be easy to say that a theory of organizational change should be balanced and should incorporate the four requirements, such an "obvious" surface conclusion is difficult to work out in a logically coherent way.

PARADOXES AND THEIR RESOLUTION

A paradox, also called antinomy, is a real or apparent contradiction between equally well-based assumptions or conclusions. When considered separately, the arguments supporting paradoxical propositions appear sound. However, considered together, the arguments appear contrary or even contradictory. One famous paradox is the Liar, studied by the Megaric philosophers around 400 B.C. If someone says, "I always lie," how are we to understand this statement? It seems both true and false. Nielsen (1967: 622) summarizes four different ways that the Liar paradox has been resolved:

> (1) that the man's remarks can be called both true and false, but in different respects (Aristotle); (2) that it makes no sense at all (Chrysippus); (3) that in a covert manner it embodies two statements having different levels of reference, and when these are kept separate no paradox arises (Bertrand Russell); and (4) that the offending sentence would normally be used as an outpouring of remorse or self-disgust, not as an occasion for drawing inferences, and its paradoxical aspect troubles us only when we fail to notice its normal use (Wittgenstein).

Much effort has been devoted to resolving or understanding paradoxes, because they reveal inconsistencies in our logic or assumptions. Paradoxes can arise from either theoretical inconsistencies or from limited frames of reference. They require us to alter our assumptions, to shift perspectives, to pose problems in fundamentally different ways, and to focus on different research questions. Four general strategies will be used in this chapter to deal with paradoxes. Each represents a different way of transforming our theories and ways of thinking.

The first response is to accept the paradox and learn to live with it. Aristotle's response to the Liar's paradox is an example of living with paradox. We can learn a great deal from juxtaposing contradictory propositions and assumptions, even if they are incompatible. As theorists we may feel a strain toward cognitive consistency, but that does not mean that the world is consistent. Paradoxes remind us of this inconsistency, and enable us to study the dialectic between opposing levels and forces.

However, living with paradox has its costs as well. Contrary perspectives are generally pursued by different researchers; this may result in fragmentation of knowledge and counterproductive bickering among proponents of the "correct" horn of the dilemma. And it is not always clear just what sort of relationship "tensions between opposing positions" constitutes. This relationship must be clearly defined, or analysis can become sloppy. Notwithstanding these ambiguities, to accept a paradox is an enlightened conceptual stance. It is to acknowledge that things need not be consistent; that seemingly opposed viewpoints can inform one another; that our models are, after all, just models, incapable of fully capturing the "buzzing, booming confusion" no matter how strongly our logical arrogance tries to convince us otherwise.

The remaining three strategies for dealing with paradoxes attempt to resolve paradox. They attempt to spell out the nature of the "tensions" between contrary positions.

The second response to paradox follows Russell's approach—it resolves paradoxes by clarifying levels of reference and the connections among them. Level distinctions such as part-whole, micro-macro, or individual-society have proven extremely useful for social research. To carry out this analysis, it is necessary to specify as precisely as possible how the levels interrelate. This has not been as easy for social scientists as it was for Russell in his theory of logical types. Despite much work on aggregation of individual acts into social action (for example, Coleman 1973, 1986), there is still no satisfactory solution (Arrow 1970). The same can be said for other level distinctions. In the face of the difficulty of spelling out inter-level relations, many researchers have let them stand while advancing only partial and tentative solutions. However, many of the most powerful insights in social science have resulted from attempts to sort out levels and their relationships. Ethnomethodology (Garfinkel 1968; Cicourel 1971), Parsonian sociology, and exchange theory (Homans 1961; Blau 1964) all developed out of their originators' desires to clarify phenomena by distinguishing levels of analysis.

A third way to address paradoxes is to take the role of time into account. In this resolution, one horn of the paradox is assumed to hold at one time and the other at a different time. The two contrary assumptions or processes each exert separate influence, and each may influence the other through its prior action. Several types of temporal relationships may exist among contradictory forces.

1. One side of the paradox may influence the conditions under which the other will operate, as in Reese and Overton's (1973) formulation, in which behavioral learning sets the stage for cognitive acquisitions.
2. One side may create the conditions necessary for the existence of the other, as in Smelser's (1962) theory that individual activity serves as the "precipitating event" for collective beliefs to develop.
3. There may also be mutual influence over time, with swings from one side to the other, as in Buckley's (1968) morphogenesis theory of system development.

The difficulty of achieving a clear temporal separation of contrary assumptions, theories, or processes remains to be solved. When does behavioral theory stop holding and cognitive theory begin? At what point does individual motivation end and collective action begin? One may find the paradox unavoidable at transition points. Most attempts at temporal resolution have glossed over these issues of transition points, and focused instead on periods of relatively pure action on either side of the paradox.

The resolution of paradoxes by level distinctions or temporal analysis leaves each set of assumptions or processes basically intact. Both sides of the paradox are assumed to be fundamentally sound, and the paradox is resolved by separating them and spelling out how one side feeds into or composes the other. However, it is also possible that the paradox may stem from a logical flaw in theory or assumptions. To overcome this flaw it is necessary to introduce new terms or a new logic. Contradictions among terms can be eliminated by advancing theories and constructs representing a more encompassing perspective. These theories resolve paradoxes by eliminating logical problems or suggesting a new set of concepts, as Wittgenstein (1953) did in his solution to the Liar paradox.

However, such advances come slowly, and many apparent resolutions may lead to dead ends. When perspectives radically shift, we may lose as well as gain. The new perspective may oversimplify points described in exquisite detail by traditional views. It may also lack solutions for problems that originally gave rise to previous positions. As the new perspective is worked out, there is always a period of ambiguity that may hide many faults and flaws. Much time and effort may be wasted pursuing "will-o-the-wisps," as Perrow's (1986) discussion of the history of organizational population ecology models suggests. These risks are the price one pays for theoretical advances. Without risks and investments of intellectual energy and commitment, we must accept paradoxes as they are.

No matter which of the four responses we choose, working with paradoxes is a difficult and long-term effort. None of the four responses has been fully developed. How to manage the dialectic between positions if we choose to live with paradoxes is unclear. And if we attempt to resolve paradoxes we face formidable obstacles.

Put baldly, very few scholars have given these issues very much thought. There are many ringing denunciations of opposing viewpoints, but too few attempts at bridging or synthesis. Hence, addressing organizational paradoxes is an exciting and challenging effort. It is an issue on the cutting edge of organization and management theory, and one that will spawn new ideas and creative theory. Looking at paradoxes forces us to ask very different questions and to come up with answers that stretch the boundaries of current theories. The resulting formulations are likely to be of interest not only to organizational scholars, but to all scholars of social processes.

In the next three sections, we will consider the paradoxes apparent in three requirements for a theory of organizational change—action versus structure, stability versus instability, and internal versus external sources of change. We will discuss the problems each presents for current theory and research, and will apply each of the four methods for dealing with paradox. To maintain continuity, we use one specific theory to exemplify each method throughout the chapter. Obviously, the four methods for addressing paradox are applicable to many other theories that cannot be covered here.

ORGANIZATIONAL STRUCTURE AND ACTION

The Action::Structure Paradox

Most readers will subscribe to the following definition: an organization is a social action system constructed by people to achieve their goals and ambitions. This definition emphasizes that the central objects of study are the structural properties of a social system, the purposive actions of people, and the relationship of system and action. Individuals are viewed as purposeful and goal-directed, guided by interests or values, and by the rewards and constraints that are both created by individuals and imposed upon them by the social environment. Individuals interact with others to achieve their self- and other-regarding interests. These interactions are structured by social relationships consisting of interrelated and recurrent patterns of social ordering. One important source of social ordering is the organization itself, whose structural properties channel individual activity and shape members' perspectives and perceived options.

These statements are deceptively simple and satisfying. However, they are imbedded with contrary assumptions regarding action and structure. Individuals are free, purposeful actors, in control of their own behavior. The organizational structure imposes constraints on action, even shaping desires and purposes. Individual actors create and maintain organizations. An organization is a powerful social institution with a life of its own; an organization can outlast a complete personnel turnover and can control—even crush—individual actors.

Attempts to encompass these contradictory assumptions in a single coherent theory have gone awry. The path of least resistance often taken has been to emphasize either system structure or individual action; many theories originally intended to deal with both terms gradually move in this direction. For example, as Coleman (1986) discusses, Parsons (1937), in his early work, attempted to balance action and structural emphases. However, as he elaborated his theory, Parsons increasingly focused on structure. Action became largely determined by structure in Parsons' later work (Garfinkel 1968; Giddens 1976).

Traditionally, action has been conceptualized as a micro-level phenomenon, while social structure has been construed at the macro level. Making the theoretical linkage between micro motives and actions of individuals and the macro structure of social systems has historically been important for social theorists, from Hobbes and Rousseau through Weber and Parsons, because it connects the individual to society, links "positive social theory and normative social philosophy," and implies how action might change society (Coleman 1986: 1310).

This form of methodological individualism continues to be a firmly entrenched assumption in most theories of organization and management. Even those who take the more pessimistic view that individuals are merely products of their environments do not deny a role to individual motives and actions. Accordingly, the functioning of an organization, as well as the engine of organizational change, must be grounded in the purposive actions of individuals confronted by particular institutional and environmental settings that shaped incentives and, thus, the actions.

The problem, however, is that social and organizational theorists have not been successful in developing a theory of action that connects individual interests with social structure. This is, in part, because of the difficulty posed by the action::structure paradox.* This paradox can best be understood in three aspects.

First, ambiguity surrounds the genesis of action and structure. Most theories of action view individual purpose and action as the source of organizational structure. In this script of an Organizational Creation Story, organizations evolve from recurrent patterns of individual interaction that gradually become formalized (Blau 1964). However, the script is different for structuralists focusing on issues of power and how coordination is achieved (Perrow 1981, 1986). In this version, action is impossible without such resources as authority, shared rules, and information—resources that stem from organizational structure. Explanations for coordinated action depend on common goals and structural features that facilitate coordination, which, again, are provided by the organization's structure. Hence, an equally good argument can be made that structure is prior to action in most ordinary cases. Thus, we are confronted with a potential paradox: action requires structure, yet structure only exists through action. Although it is easy to assert the common sense solution that action and structure are reciprocals of each other, it has been difficult to develop a systematic theory capable of encompassing the two assumptions.

A second aspect of this paradox derives from contrary ontological assumptions about structure and action. Organizational structures are generally assumed to be concrete and measurable. They seem to be tangible objects because their traces reside in organizational records, rules, buildings, and outputs, and because their members orient to them as objects. On the other hand, action is more subjective and ephemeral. To document actions it is necessary to identify motives or purposes; many scholars have acknowledged the difficulties inherent in grasping the meaningful connections actors perceive and the practical reasoning that precedes behavior (Mills 1940; Weber 1947; Parsons 1951).

*The symbol :: indicates opposition.

This contributes to the paradox. Organizational change must be seen as change in concrete, measurable properties; yet organizational change is best understood as a result of intersubjective processes of intentionality and practical reasoning.

The third paradoxical aspect derives from how action and structure enter into social scientific explanations. Traditionally, a deterministic explanation has been given for structure. Organizational structure is conceived of and measured as variables (formalization, decision centralization, complexity), and researchers study how structure accounts for variance in behavior (Hall 1963; Hage and Aiken 1967; Pugh 1981). This approach provides little room for purposive action; it emphasizes cause-effect connections in which meaning is irrelevant except as it is reduced to variables measuring subjects' "perceptions" or "attitudes" about the structure (Starbuck 1981).

Explanations couched in terms of action theory emphasize reconstructing the meaningful connections that underlie individuals' choices. Such reconstruction relies on interpretive methods. Seldom can it be represented in "variance-explained" terms, because each action ensues through a process of practical reasoning and choice-making that is unique within the context—although it may be understood in terms of typical interpretive schemes and reasoning procedures (March and Simon 1958; March 1981; Lindblom 1981). In Mohr's (1982) terms, structural explanations are variance theories, while action explanations are a type of process theory. The split between structural and action explanations contributes a final pair of contraries: organizational change must be explained deterministically if changes in structure are studied. Yet it must be explained interpretively, as a function of meaningful connections between events, if the active force behind change is taken into account.

Resolving the Action::Structure Paradox

Method 1: Live with Paradox and Make the Best of It. As stated above, one way to address paradox is to accept its existence explicitly and use it constructively for understanding organizational change. This is the approach adopted in earlier work by Van de Ven and Astley where they juxtaposed contradictory assumptions and theories to identify the sources of conflict and tension that may stimulate change in organizational structure and action (Van de Ven and Astley 1981; Astley and Van de Ven 1983).

Van de Ven and Astley distinguish between deterministic structural forms and voluntaristic personnel actions at macro and micro levels of organizational analysis. Figure 2–1, for example, illustrates that the action::structure paradox can exist at multiple levels of organizational analysis. In terms of Figure 2–1, we will briefly discuss the insights that can be gained by living with the tensions or contradictions inherent in the horizontal and diagonal relationships between structure and action, and the vertical relationships between parts and wholes of structure, or the self versus collective orientations of personnel actions.

As stated before, structural forms and personnel action are central issues of interest to organization and management theory. Organizations, after all, are neither purely deterministic nor purely voluntaristic. The interesting questions and problems, then, turn on how structural forms and personnel actions at each level of analysis interrelate and produce tensions that stimulate changes over time.

For example, at the individual level there are the system problems of selecting, socializing, and controlling individuals for roles and positions in the structure, on the one hand. On the other hand, the problem is examining how the purposive actions of people over time restructure these roles and positions. As personal aspirations and values of individuals change, and career options for promotion and mobility among roles and positions in the organizational structure change, misfits may occur. At the group or departmental level, how the structural division and integration of labor and resources among subunits influence and are influenced by the social-psychological emergence of collective norms,

Figure 2–1. Structural Forms and Personnel Actions at Micro to Macro Levels of Organizations.

MACRO LEVEL (Whole, collective orientation)	Industry/Community structure	Industry/interorganizational collective action
	Organization design	Board of directors executive committee
. .		
MICRO LEVEL (Part, self orientation)	Department/division	Task force management committee
	Roles and Positions	Individual
	Structural Forms	Personnel Actions

interaction patterns, conflict, and power relations within and between groups is a key issue. At the organizational level, there is the problem of how system structure both influences and reflects environmental shifts and strategic choices of powerful individuals within and outside the organization over time. Finally, at the population or interorganizational level, there are questions about how organizational niches or market structure are both the product and constraint of collective working rules determined by a series of political contests and bargains among pluralistic interest groups, each pursuing its partisan ambitions and values.

These issues lead to useful insights because they:

1. admit to the existence of both deterministic and voluntaristic aspects of social systems;
2. juxtapose these aspects by reciprocally relating structural forms and personnel actions at comparable levels of analyses; and
3. focus on how these relationships unfold over time in complementary and contradictory ways (Van de Ven and Astley 1981: 455).

It is these reciprocal relations between structural forms and personnel actions that make tension and conflict a pervasive characteristic of organizational life.

The vertical relationships among micro and macro dimensions in Figure 2–1 deal with the conflict and tension inherent in part-whole or self versus collective ("me-we") frames of reference in an organization. Considering these levels is useful, because many problems and solutions apparent at one level of the organization manifest themselves in different and contradictory ways at other levels.

For example, relying on the concept of requisite variety, Weick (1979) argued that with increasing environmental complexity, uncertainty, and variety, the overall structure of the organization becomes more complex, loosely coupled, decentralized, particularistic, and anarchistic. If this is so at the macro level, then at the micro level the structure of the individual parts or groups within the organization will become more simple, tightly coupled, hierarchical, universalistic, and cohesive. The whole tries to become more adaptive, but this results in the parts exhibiting characteristics that lead to nonadaptiveness, narrowness, and "group think." This unintended consequence is the result of a basic principle of contrary part-whole relationships established in 1909 by Georg Simmel: "The elements of differentiated social circles are undifferentiated, those of undifferentiated ones are differentiated" (Blau translation 1964: 284). Conant and Ashby's (1970) principle of requisite variety at the macro level turns out to be a law of requisite simplicity at the micro level. This principle of contradictory part-whole relationships was further developed by Blau (1964).

These and other dialectical relationships between parts and wholes of organizations are not adequately taken into account by many organizational theories. This is unfortunate because many macro theories of order and consensus include micro theories of conflict and coercion, and vice versa. For example, structural-functional theories have been attacked for their inability to explain change because of the emphasis on order, consensus, and unity (Silverman 1970). While this is true at the macro-organizational level, it is only possible because of coercion, domination, and control of disruptive tendencies at the micro level. If this were not so, there would be no need for rules, indoctrination, socialization, and control mechanisms—concepts that are central to structuralists' views of organizations. On the other hand, radical change theories (Burrell and Morgan 1979) overemphasize conflict, coercion, and disruptive tendencies in organizations without admitting that these tendencies can only occur by having order, consensus, and unity at the micro level. Thus, it can be seen that although Marx posited conflict and struggle between classes, insufficient attention has been given to the forces of cohesion and unity within the classes. As Coser (1956) suggested, "out-group conflict" is associated with "in-group cohesion."

In summary, much can be learned about organizational change by explicitly accepting the action::structure paradox at micro and macro levels of organizational analysis. Organizational change can be understood as arising from two basic ways that this paradox manifests itself in organizational life: (1) in the tensions that emerge over time between personnel action and structural forms which are created by and constrain purposive action at each level of organizational analysis; and (2) in the forces of conflict, coercion, and disruption at one level of organization, and forces of consensus, unity, and integration at another level—forces that are prerequisites and reciprocals of each other.

Method 2: Clarify Connections between Organizational Levels. A second way to address the action::structure paradox is to distinguish levels of reference in the contrary propositions and to spell out the connections between them. Recent theories of social action by Arrow (1970) and Coleman (1973; 1986) show promise in applying this method. Basically, this approach assumes individuals can act but organizations cannot, and attempts to specify models by which individual actions can combine to create collective outcomes. These system-level outcomes, may, in turn, impose constraints on individual actions (Coleman, 1986: 1312). Coleman (1986) suggests that such a model should consist of (a) a set of assumptions about how the interests and goals of actors stand in relation to one another vis-à-vis the action system, and (b) a set of combinatorial rules for merging individual actions into collective acts. (Potentially there could also be mapping rules that specify how collective structures "feedback" to affect individual action.)

With regard to component (a) of the model, Coleman discusses three types of interdependent relationships among individual interests, which lead to different types of social organizations and change processes:

A *pure market* is a configuration in which there are "independent actors, each with differing private interests and goals and each with resources that can aid others' realization of interests. The actions that purposive actors will engage in when this configuration of interests and resources exists is social exchange, and when a number of these exchange processes are interdependent, we describe the whole set as a market institution" (p. 1324).

A *hierarchy* is a set of relations "in which one actor's actions are carried out under the control of another and advance the other's interests." The associated institution is the formal organization or authority structure (pp. 1324–25).

A *federation* (our term) is set of independent actors linked by common interests. They are connected by a constitution embodying a set of norms regarding rights and obligations (p. 1326).

With regard to component (b), Arrow (1970), Coleman (1973), and others have proposed sets of mathematical or logical rules for combining individual interests and actions into collective action and macro-structural forms.

This direction, while promising, must overcome several problems. First, this approach assumes that only individuals can have purposes, that individuals are the prime motive force in any change. This leads to an overemphasis on the micro (action) to macro (structure) relation, and an underemphasis on the opposite direction. The approach devotes much attention to combinatorial rules, but much less to disaggregation rules that show how structure influences action.

Second, this approach also runs the risk of confounding the action-structure dimension with macro-micro dimension. Coleman only admits to purposive action at the micro level and structural forms at the macro level. But purposive action can also exist at the macro level in collective decisionmaking bodies or committees, and structural forms are also present at the micro level in the roles and positions individuals occupy. Thus a more complex scheme, like that illustrated in Figure 2–1, is necessary.

Finally, it is hard to specify in precise mathematical terms how social actions are combined. Most formal systems require simplifying assumptions about individuals akin to those in classical economics to model social action. Whether these capture the subtleties and many variations of action is open to question. It may take an unmanageably complex rule system to capture all of the nuances of a social choice system.

Method 3: Use Time to Relate Structure and Action. Time offers a third method to resolve the action::structure paradox. Action and structure can be related through an alternating temporal order. Buckley's (1967) morphogenetic system theory follows this strategy to articulate a coherent relation between action and structure. The theory of morphogenesis proposes that action and structure influence each other, but in alternating cycles over time. The cycles are composed of three phases:

1. a period in which preexisting structures dominate behavior;
2. a period where action begins to articulate alternative arrangements, which sets the stage for structural change; and
3. a period of structural elaboration, in which changes in structure are institutionalized. Then the cycle can start over again.

Tushman and Romanelli's punctuated equilibrium model of organizational evolution follows a pattern similar to Buckley's theory. They posit alternating cycles of *convergence,* "which elaborate structures, systems, controls, and resources toward increased coalignment," and reorientation, "periods of discontinuous change where strategies, power, structure, and systems are fundamentally transformed towards a new basis of alignment" (1985: p. 173). Convergence seems to be predominantly influenced by structure, whereas reorientation is driven by purposive actions of executive leaders.

The key problems these approaches must resolve relate to the boundaries between periods and to a tendency toward structural bias. The problem of establishing boundaries between periods is not a trivial one. A crisis that upsets existing structural arrangements presents a relatively

RITTER LIBRARY
BALDWIN-WALLACE COLLEGE

clear boundary. But problems can also develop incrementally, and incremental adjustments can cumulate to produce qualitative change (Lindblom 1965). When structural and action influences shade together, this approach is not particularly informative because it relies on temporal sequencing.

In these temporal models, structure is easier to portray than action because structure is more easily observed than individual motives and behavior. As a consequence, theories that assume alternating influence between structure and action over time tend to reflect a bias for structure. For example, Buckley accords much more space to an analysis of structures and their effects on action than vice versa. Action is not left out of this theory, but its operations are left opaque. While processes of organizational convergence and equilibrium are richly described by Tushman and Romanelli (1985) in the punctuated equilibrium model, the punctuation process itself remains underdeveloped (Van de Ven and Garud forthcoming). These theories have to perform a balancing act; it is necessary to pay close attention to articulating the relation between structure and action and between time periods. Tushman and Romanelli's punctuated equilibrium model does a good job of balancing structural and action influences.

Method 4: Advance a New Conception of the Structure-Action Relationship. A final attack on the action::structure paradox involves developing a new concept of the action-structure relationship. Giddens (1976; 1979; 1985) has advanced a theory of structuration that expresses such a new approach (see also Barthes 1979; Touraine 1977; Ranson, Hinings, and Greenwood 1980; Bartunek 1984; Poole, Seibold, and McPhee 1985, 1986; Barley 1986). *Structuration* refers to the process of production and reproduction of social systems via members' application of rules and resources. Implicit in this definition is a distinction between *system* and *structure*. Structure refers to the rules and resources people use in acting and interacting. System is the outcome of the application of rules and resources, the observable patterns of relations between people and groups. For example, the status hierarchy of an organization is a system. The structure underlying this system include rules, such as norms of superior-subordinate interaction, and resources, such as formal authority or superior knowledge. The system exists because it is structured: members use rules and resources to create and maintain status relationships, and the

RITTER LIBRARY
BALDWIN-WALLACE COLLEGE

hierarchical pattern can be explained by differences in the rules and resources available to different individuals.

The theory of structuration assigns a dual nature to structures: they are both the medium and outcome of action. Structures make action—and hence the existence of social systems—possible. But structures only exist as they are produced and reproduced in interaction; they have no independent, objective existence, but instead are continuously produced and reproduced. Thus structure and action mutually entail each other. Giddens's advance consists of explaining how this entailment comes about and what its significance is.

In the terminology of Figure 2–1, Giddens introduces a new intervening column between structural forms and personnel actions, which he terms *modalities of structuration*. A modality of structuration represents the individual actors' appropriation of structure for use in a particular action context. For example, in a conflict situation, an individual might use a workflow diagram as a norm to justify her claim that orders should be routed to another person. In doing this the individual, according to her own motives and within the limits of her interaction skills, is using the institution in action. Hence, institutions determine the structural features available for appropriation; they limit the possible ways in which an individual can act.

In drawing on structures, individuals reproduce the structures. The structures they draw on constantly become more important, whereas those they use less "decay." In addition, how people use structures determines how they are reproduced and whether they remain stable or change (Barley 1986). However, despite the central role individuals play in producing and reproducing structures, the complexity of social systems means that people do not wholly control structuration. Systems may be very complex, and apparently straightforward actions may lead to consequences unintended by individuals trying to control the system.

This brief summary shows how the theory of structuration cuts through the action::structure paradox. It posits that structure and action coexist, in a mutual process of production and reproduction. Action draws on structure; structure only exists in action; they "connect" in modalities of structuration. If the operation of modalities can be specified, the theory of structuration represents a significant conceptual advance for addressing the action::structure paradox.

Conclusion

The approaches discussed here are representative of the four ways to deal with paradox. But, in themselves, they do not represent complete theories of change. They simply state ways in which action and structure relate. They must be supplemented by explanations for change (or lack thereof) and the internal and external forces that drive change. The theories discussed here as examples of each of the four ways to address paradox will be covered in the next two sections.

INTERNAL AND EXTERNAL SOURCES OF CHANGE

Basic to the following discussion are definitions of change and the process of change. Organizational change is an empirical observation of differences in time of a social system. As Nisbet (1970) argued, all three elements in this definition are necessary. A mere array of differences is not change, only differences. Time is critical because any difference necessarily involves earlier and later points of reference. Mere mobility, motion, or activity is not change, even though each is in some degree involved in change. As mentioned above, we focus here on the structural forms and personnel actions of an organization as the objects being transformed. Change without reference to an object is meaningless. The process of change adds the more abstract idea of an inference or a presumed relationship among differences noted in time. Hence, while organizational change can be directly observed empirically, it is important to emphasize that the process of change is a latent inference; that is, it is a theoretical explanation for the pattern of changes observed.

The Roots of the Internal::External Paradox

Two basic theories of the process of change have long historical roots in the literature, and each admits to only one source of change. *Developmentalism* argues that change is set in motion from within the system that is undergoing change, while *accumulation* theories posit that change comes from outside the system. While common sense might suggest that internal and external sources of organizational change are equally plausible, historically the literature has polarized into "nature versus nurture" camps regarding whether the process of change is stimulated and governed by forces internal or external to the unit undergoing change. And as Nisbet (1970) notes, theories of internally driven change tend to undervalue external causes, while explanations in terms of exogenous variables generally deny immanent processes in social systems. To understand the nature of this paradox, it is helpful to consider the two positions in more detail.

By far, the most traditional and firmly entrenched theory of the change process is *developmentalism,* which has its roots in Greek thought, and according to Nisbet (1970: 176), has become "a master principle of Western philosophy." Nisbet points out that fundamental to Greek science was the concept of *physis,* meaning "the way things grow." *Physis* was central because the Greeks believed that "everything is either coming-into-being or going-out-of-being; nothing is fixed." The pattern of growth or change was held to be driven by forces inherent within the nature or structure of the thing being studied, and not as the consequence of external forces. To understand growth or change it is necessary to identify:

1.   the origin of a phenomenon;
2.   its cycle or pattern of change, from origin to end;
3.   "the end, goal or *telos* of the process, for in growth all changes are, by definition, relative to a specific end or result"; and
4.   the mechanism or forces through which the developmental process operates (Nisbet 1970: 175–76).

Developmentalism is based on two central assumptions of *immanence* and *continuity.* Developmentalism assumes change is immanent; that is, the social system contains within it an underlying logic, program, or code that regulates the process of change and that moves from a given point of departure toward a subsequent end which is already prefigured in the present state. What lies latent, rudimentary, or homogeneous in the embryo or primitive state, becomes progressively more complex and differentiated. External events and processes can influence how the immanent form expresses itself, but they are always mediated by the logical necessity of the internal developmental process.

The assumption of continuity stems from the Leibnizian principle that "nothing happens all at once; nature never makes leaps. . . . Everything goes by degrees" (Nisbet 1970: 179). For example, in *The*

Origin of Species, Darwin (1936: 361) wrote "as natural selection acts solely by accumulating slight, successive, favourable variations, it can produce no great or sudden modifications; it can act only by short and slow steps." So too, revolution for Marx was not a discontinuous process; "he saw revolution as the product of a line of development quite as continuous as the line of embryonic growth leading up to birth" (Nisbet 1970: 180).

In his critique, Nisbet emphasizes that development is not in itself a social fact; it is a *conceptual inference* that stresses the immanent and incremental processes of change. However, many studies cannot support the immanence and/or continuity premises of developmentalism because major changes and creations of totally new social activities rarely emerge incrementally and deterministically from within social systems. There are many organizations whose creation and change more nearly resemble a process of accumulation where new units or parts are discontinuously added from outside of the unit or replace existing ones until the entire unit is assembled or transformed.

The *accumulation* theory of social change (alternatively labeled "epigenesis" by Etzioni, 1963), examines how existing social systems are expanded or new ones are established as a means of achieving individual or collective goals. In this case the emphasis is on processes external or independent of the developing form. New organizations can be started from "scratch," but more commonly they develop as several existing organizations or individuials merge to form a larger and more inclusive social entity (Olsen 1978). For example, an entrepreneur may develop a new technological product and start a new business, workers may form a labor union through which to bargain with their employer, or an association may begin to address the plight of farmers. In each of these examples, the change is not directed by an immanent logic or internal plan; rather, it is driven by forces external to the system, specifically, by purposive individual actions. The accumulation theory argues that social change occurs as individuals or groups of people, especially powerful elites, purposefully expand existing organizations and activities or create new ones to achieve their interests through collective action. Change does not occur according to underlying logics, but is driven by particularistic events, changes in the organization's environment, or human intervention.

The concepts of initiation, take-off, and start-up are useful to describe the accumulation process. *Initiation* is the time when people decide to form a new unit and *take-off* is the time when the unit can do without the support of its initiators and can continue growing "on its own," functionally independent. The period between initiation and take-off could be called *start-up*, where the new unit must draw its resources, staff, and power from the founding leaders and groups in order to accumulate followers and contributors directly committed to developing and sustaining the new unit.

Etzioni (1963: 490) points out that important relations of *timing* exist between initiation and take-off points. For example, the longer the start-up period, the lower the perceived urgency and probability of actualizing goals and ambitions for a new venture, and the more difficult it is to mobilize commitment of resources and involvement of key stakeholders. On the other hand, if the time lapse is very small, there may be insufficient time during start-up to establish competencies, tangible products, or a constituency to sustain the new venture at take-off.

Resolving the Internal::External Paradox

In summary, developmentalism and accumulation represent two traditional and mutually-exclusive theories of the process of change. Attempts to consider both explanations simultaneously create a theoretical tension that often presses researchers toward one pole or the other. Attempts to graft external causality onto an immanent developmental model often violate the integrity of the immanent explanation. If external changes are mediated by an immanent logic, the importance of the external force tends to diminish, and it becomes a source of qualifications and small deviations from the necessary immanent path.

On the other hand, a theory that emphasizes external causality focuses on the multitude of paths change can take in response to a wide range of external events. Rather than an underlying logic or form, accumulation theories emphasize the process of purposeful construction and adaptation. It is hard to combine developmentalism with accumulation because immanence and continuity deny or constrain explanations in terms of external intervention and discontinuity.

Common sense tells us the two theories ought to be reconciled. Indeed, this is necessary to achieve the requirement that a good theory of organizational change should include both internal and external sources of change. As we have done for the action::structure paradox, we will explore the four ways that can be used to reconcile this internal::external paradox.

Method 1: Live with the paradox.   One response to the internal::external paradox is to accept it and learn to live with it constructively. In fact, that is what most mainstream organization theories are doing. Developmentalism is most evident in natural selection and structural-functional contingency theories, while accumulation underlies strategic choice and collective action models of change. This is illustrated in Figure 2–2, where we revise our earlier typology of central perspectives in organization theory (Van de Ven and Astley 1981; and Astley and Van de Ven 1983). The figure emphasizes the different change processes inherent in each perspective, whereas earlier treatments focused more on

Figure 2–2. Processes of Change in Central Organizational Perspectives: An Extension of Typology by Van de Ven and Astley (1981) and Astley and Van de Ven (1983).

MACRO LEVEL (Global or relational properties of populations or collectives) · · · · · · ·	NATURAL SELECTION VIEW An evolutionary process of variation, selection, and retention of structural forms in a population of organizations. A single member's fate is the result of a random probability of being selected at a given time.	COLLECTIVE ACTION VIEW A political and conflictural process of partisan mutual adjustment and coercion circumscribed by collective "working rules" among interest groups with pluralistic bases of power. Collective action controls, liberates and expands individual action.
MICRO LEVEL (Structural or absolute properties of parts or members)	STRUCTURAL CONTINGENCY VIEW An evolutionary process of progressive internal structural differentiation and integration modified by adaptations to internal tensions and external constraints.	STRATEGIC CHOICE VIEW An intendedly rational process of choice and action by one or a few elite individuals or leaders who initiate and socially construct their environment and organizations.
	STRUCTURAL FORMS DEVELOPMENTALISM - immanent[a] - continuous/persistent	PERSONNEL ACTION EPIGENESIS - exogenous - discontinuous

[a]Immanence is that which is part of the structure. When acting independently individuals are exogenous to the structure; when acting as role occupants they are endogenous.

a static description of each perspective. Moreover, with reference to the structure::action paradox, it is evident that natural selection and structural contingency theories focus on structure, while collection action models emphasize purposive action.

Developmentalist perspectives. Developmentalism is clearly reflected in three contemporary organization theories: natural selection, structural-functionalism and contingency theories. While these theories focus on different organizational aspects at different levels of analysis, they commonly focus on changes in structural forms of organizations, and view these changes as immanent and continuous processes. Furthermore, they explain changes in organizational forms as a function of structural or environmental forces which are mediated by immanent processes and which omit the role of purposive individual or collective action.

Organizational natural selection focuses on changes in the structural and demographic characteristics of populations of organizations across communities, industries, or society at large (Campbell 1969; Hannan and Freeman 1977; Aldrich 1979). Relying on biological evolution, change proceeds in an immanent (to the population) and continuous process of *variation, selection, and retention.* Whether planned or unplanned, the population ecology model is indifferent to the source of variations in organizational forms; they just happen (Aldrich 1979). Selection occurs principally through the competition among forms, and the environment selects those forms which optimize or are best suited to the resource base of an environmental niche (Hannan and Freeman 1977: 939). Retention involves the forces (including inertia and persistence) that perpetuate and maintain certain organizational forms. Retention serves to counteract the self-reinforcing loop between variations and selection. As Weick (1979) and Pfeffer (1982) note, whereas variations stimulate the selection of new organizational forms, retention works to maintain those structures and practices that were selected in the past.

Structural-functional theories focus more on the overall structural configuration of individual organizations (for example, Parsons 1951; Merton 1968; Homans 1961), and posit that a social system, if it is to survive, must fulfill a set of interrelated functions—those of instrumental adaptation, resource allocation, social and normative integration. These interrelated functions are immanent to all organizations. With increasing age, size, and technological sophistication organizations become structurally differentiated because functionally specialized units are held to perform activities more effectively. In other words, structural-functionalism is another form of evolutionary development, where change is an immanent and continuous process of structural differentiation, integration, and adaptation.

This is even more evident in *structural contingency theory,* a particular "social engineering" application of the structural-functional model concerned with the problem of adapting the most appropriate (efficient or effective) organizational structural designs that fit changing organizational contexts (Woodward 1965; Thompson 1967; Lawrence and Lorsch 1967). Organization structure is viewed as a set of interrelated components that must instrumentally achieve organizational goals, and are therefore "functional." Organizational change occurs through a process of adaptation, which is necessary to adjust the organization's structural form to respond to internal tensions or to shifts in the more macro social systems of which the organization is a part. While these "contingent" factors are constraints to which the system must adapt, the process of organizational change is fundamentally viewed as a continuous imminent progression over time toward achieving the functions of the system through greater structural differentiation.

Accumulation perspectives. Accumulation appears to be the underlying change explanation in two contemporary models of organization: strategic choice and collective action. Both models emphasize the purposive action of individuals who, by themselves or in interaction with others, choose and construct their social institutions. The two theories differ in unit of analysis and in locus of power that controls the change process.

Strategic choice models view organizational change as created by one or a few elite powerful leaders who are assumed to make decisions that either everyone agrees with or who then coerce others to follow. These simplifying assumptions permit theorists to take a micro individual or small group perspective on collective decisionmaking. Decisionmaking is the basic process model underlying strategic choice models. This has been construed as a proactive, rational process by some theorists (for example, March and Simon 1958) and as an anarchistic, reactive, sensemaking process by others (March 1981; Lindblom 1981; Nutt 1984). However construed, decisionmaking processes are the basic vehicle by which both organizational environment and structure are enacted (Weick 1979) to embody the purposive meanings and actions of strategic individuals.

Collective action models take a more macro-level perspective of the accumulation process. They assume the existence of a pluralistic or eglitarian power structure among partisan individuals, who can be either members of one organization or representatives from different organizations and interest groups. As a consequence, voluntary and normative means are used to mobilize independent people and resources in a collective change effort. Conflict theory and political decisionmaking underly most conceptions of the change process in the collective action view. Conflict theory views tension and change as ubiquitous; all social organization is inherently unstable, and any unity is due largely to the action and coercion by powerful interest groups (Dahrendorf 1959: 161–62). While change can occur through a revolt, most organizational theorists view change as a political process of collective bargaining, negotiation, compromise, and mutual adjustment among partisan interest groups (Lindblom 1965). The potential for domination and coercion by powerful interest groups over powerless groups is circumscribed by norms, customs, and laws of reasonable value and practice, which are the "working rules" of collective action (Commons 1950).

Juxtaposing the two perspectives.   Just as with the action::structure paradox, fruitful insights into organizational change can be gained by examining the tensions between developmental and accumulation processes at micro and macro organizational levels of personnel action and structural forms. Hrebiniak and Joyce (1985), for example, have derived four mutually exclusive types of organizational adaptations by reformulating the two dimensions that underly the four cells in Figure 2–2—degree of strategic choice and degree of environmental determinism. Each type implies different generic strategies, different types of search, decision, and political processes, and differing degrees of innovative potential. They conclude:

> simple models relying on the conceptual construction of mutually exclusive, competing explanations of cause and effect may not be sufficient to capture the complexity and richness of organizational behavior. The discussion of the research implications of the present typology suggests the complexity and interdependence of important variables and decision processes as a function of both choice and determinism (Hrebiniak and Joyce 1985).

Method 2: Use time to relate internal and external causality. A punctuated equilibrium model (Tushman and Romanelli 1985) uses *time* as one avenue for incorporating both developmentalism and accumulation change process models in a theory of action. In a punctuated equilibrium model, accumulation best describes the process of occasional discontinuous *reorientations* in part or all of a social system, while developmentalism characterizes the periods of continuous *convergence.* *Accumulation* (through either strategic choice or collective action) appears to be the basic process underlying discontinuous organizational changes because the resulting transformation represents a metamorphic or radical change that no longer includes representations of the earlier organization. *Developmentalism* (through either natural selection or structural contingency processes) describes morphogenic change, that is, where an organization converges over time toward increasing order, complexity, unity or operational effectiveness in response to disruptive forces that are introduced into the system. Thus, change in a given social unit may be empirically observed either to result from institutional "embodiments" of old functions, or to serve totally new functions.

Developmentalism and accumulation change processes occur at different times in the same organizational unit. Tushman and Romanelli argue that most of the time an incremental, continuous and immanent process of development occurs, which is punctuated by occasional discontinuous periods of externally stimulated accumulation. In no instance would we expect to find both developmentalism and epigenises processes to operate at the same time in a given organizational unit because they are mutually exclusive, as defined by Tushman and Romanelli. Thus, *time* provides the vehicle for incorporating contradictory change processes in a punctuated equilibrium model that explains both internal and external sources of change.

However, we should caution that while relations among developmentalism and accumulation change processes may be chronological, they may or may not be causal. Tushman and Romanelli posit that reorientations may result from internal inconsistencies during convergence or from major changes in the environment or from acts of leadership. Careful longitudinal observations of specific cases of organizational changes are needed to infer whether temporal relations between periods might be causal. Further, prediction of future changes, as opposed to explanation of past changes, may be difficult with a punctuated equilibrium model. Like its counterparts in biology, the organizational punctuated equilibrium model permits a wide variety of options that it cannot predict with much precision, though it does provide predictions regarding how effective an organization will be based on how it deals with convergence and reorientation. This conclusion conforms with Durkheim's (1950: 117) admonition that "all scientific causal prevision is impossible." There may not be a causal relationship between antecedent and subsequent periods. Durkheim makes us realize that study of past and present conditions yields us but one thing alone: knowledge of the past leading up to the present condition.

Method 3: Clarify levels to determine what is internal and external. Of course, what is viewed as macro versus micro and internal versus external is always a matter of one's frame of reference when comparing and contrasting different theories. As Figure 2–2 is currently drawn, the natural selection and collective action views are classified as macro because they respectively pertain to global and relational properties of collectives, while structural contingency and strategic choice views pertain to structural and absolute properties of parts or members of a social system (as defined by Lazarsfeld and Menzel 1968). In addition, what is internal or external is designated as that which is immanent or exogenous to the social structure. Thus, individuals or collectives are viewed as exogenous to the structure when they act autonomously, but are immanent to the structure when they act as occupants of organizational roles and positions. This classification is in keeping with the distinction between individual actors and role occupants made in most social system theories.

But complex organizations can be viewed as consisting of multiple, quasi-independent subunits of structure and action. We could therefore productively shift the frame of reference from changes in the overall complex organization to that of changes within these organizational subunits. From this subunit perspective, we can examine how changes within units are related to changes in other subunits and how they, in turn, relate to changes in the overall organization. By shifting levels of analysis in this way, we should expect to observe developmentalism and accumulation change processes to be operating at different micro and macro parts of the organization at the same time. A change in one subunit may set off a domino effect of changes in those other parts of the complex organization which are interdependent with the unit undergoing change.

Thus, one way to reconcile the internal::external paradox is to clarify one's frame of reference. This leads one to recognize that the issue is not so much whether change is stimulated by internal versus external sources. Instead, the more discriminating issue for explaining change processes within and between organizational units is *the degree of interdependence or coupling between organizational units*. For an autonomous organizational unit, change may arise from either internal or external sources and may reflect either a developmental or accumulation progression. However, when the units are tightly coupled, the source of change in any one of the interdependent units is both internal and external by virtue of the fact that internally stimulated changes within one unit are also external sources of changes for other units in the interdependent network. Moreover, what may appear to reflect an accumulation process of discontinuous and externally driven changes within individual units, may appear to be nothing more than a continuous and immanent process of routine changes for the total network of interdependent units. It depends upon one's frame of reference and where the organizational boundaries are drawn.

Method 4: Introduce new concepts to reconcile internal and external causality.   The final method builds on the theory of structuration discussed earlier. It attempts to eliminate the internal::external paradox by reconceptualizing it as an issue of whether an individual or a group is an active controlling, or passive manipulated agent of organizational change processes. Sztompka (1979) argues that:

> An individual may be a slave of instincts or a slave of social norms; in either case he is a slave, and hence passive, even though his slavery originates "inside" in the first case and "outside" in the second. On the other hand, an individual can be a master of his drives or a master of social situations; in either case he is a master, hence autonomous, even though his mastery is exercised over internal factors in the first case, and external ones in the second. It follows that passivism has something to do with a subjugation to pressures, whether internal or external, and autonomism has something to do with a control over them. The question of internality or externality of pressures is irrelevant to the main issue (Sztompka 1979: 266).

What is at issue is whether things are done *to* or *by* a person. The core difference is between an image of an individual as an active subject or as a passive object. And the factor that distinguishes an active from passive agent is the degree of control one exercises over one's activities—not whether the activities are endogenously or exogenously stimulated. Internal and external causality are thus mediated—and potentially integrated—by actors' degree of control.

By transforming the internal-external stimulus for change question into "Who has control over what?" Sztompka (1979: 269) suggests two further crucial questions: "What is the control exercised over?" and "What is the substance of control?" There are several situations in which individuals can (or can not) exercise control:

1. control over a singular act or episode, such as sending a report of a production irregularity to a supervisor;
2. control over a sequence of acts, such as developing and implementing a new production system in a factory; and
3. control over a multiplicity of acts extending over a whole life, such as striving to produce the highest quality and lowest cost products in the industry.

In each of these various situations, the *content* of control can also vary:

1. some level of self-conscious attention and application of skills and abilities to the actual situation presented to the individual;
2. some level of planning or foresight of the possible courses of action that can be taken in the recognized situation; and
3. some degree of decisionmaking or choice in undertaking a course of action from among the alternatives foreseen.

The question, then, is the degree to which these actions are controlled or not controlled by a human agent. The strongest formulation of the active agent perspective would require demonstrating that the individual has control of each situation and is self-conscious, able to plan, decide, and implement the chosen course of action. Conversely, a strong form of the passive agent perspective would claim all aspects of control to be absent in all situations.

These distinctions can be combined usefully with the structuration model outlined previously. Actors or units are under varying degrees of constraint in structuring organizations. In some structurational processes, the actors or units are largely "trapped" by the system. There is little latitude for external influence, because the logic and momentum of the system itself overwhelm actors, as illustrated in Perrow's (1984) description of "normal accidents." Other structuration processes are controlled to a great extent by actors or units, which understand the operation of the system and can control it. Structurational processes will differ according to the various combinations of control situations and contents outlined by Sztompka.

It is also important to note that actors or units themselves can restructure the nature of control in a given situation—thus altering the mix of internal and external causality. They can increase their capacities for control by learning about the system, environments, and the forces shaping structuration (McPhee 1985). And they can alter the system and the environment so that they are more controllable. The dilemma of internal versus external causality is less daunting when we recognize that both are continuously produced and reproduced in a structurational process. They are mediated in a common process and their relative influence is determined by actor or unit control over this process (which is itself continuously structured, waxing or waning).

To succeed, this analysis must overcome the barriers mentioned previously. An additional problem is in the possibility of conflating actor or unit with the environment. Since all are viewed as outcomes of structuration as well as its instruments, boundaries tend to blur, creating analytical problems.

ORGANIZATIONAL STABILITY AND CHANGE

The Stability::Instability Paradox

In order to develop a viable theory of change, we must address the problem of system stability and instability. As we noted above, the desideratum is to develop theories that explain stability and change in the same terms. The paradox between stability and instability can be traced back to the dispute between the Greek philosophers Democritus and Heraclitus. Democritus argued that being was, in essence, stable and fixed. Heraclitus maintained that the essence of reality was change, that the whole universe was in continuous flux. These two polar positions remain strong in contemporary social theory. For example, classical functionalism has often been criticized as too conservative because of its emphasis on stability and equilibrium states. Marx explicitly drew upon Heraclitus to emphasize change in his early work.

Once again, common sense suggests stability and instability are two sides of the same coin. And it would seem that stability and instability can be explained as outcomes of the same social action process under different conditions. Yet, contrasting explanations that emphasize either stability or change continue to polarize researchers. Even theories that set out to include both stability and change often evolve so that they emphasize one over the other. Functionalism is a case in point, for although it promised to deal with both stability and change (Parsons 1937), it gradually came to emphasize stability. Its biological metaphor pushed it toward homeostasis and its normative orientation of a "healthy" organization as one with no tensions or strains.

Any attempt to grapple with the stability-instability relationship must build on the theories of the action-structure and internal-external relationships which we have explored in previous sections. Theories of social action articulate the influence of action on structure and vice versa in such a way that stability can be seen as a result of structure constraining actors, or of action preserving structure. In the same way, change can be explained as a function of action or of structural forces. So, in principle, a social action theory is a framework for the simultaneous explanation of stability and change. However, to merely advance a social action theory does not guarantee an adequate representation of stability and change. What is necessary is an *explicit framework* for dealing with the stability-instability relationship. A second problem must also be addressed. Any theory of organizational stability and instability must acknowledge the role of *system complexity*. Action is not totally under the control of individuals; complicated systems have their own laws of effect; that is, they are "action generators" (Starbuck 1983). Once these complex systems are set in motion, actions often "escape" their purposes and result in unintended consequences.

Resolving the Stability::Instability Paradox

In the remainder of this section, we will extend the four theoretical perspectives previously to illustrate how the stability::instability paradox might be handled.

Method 1: Live with the stability::instability paradox.   A fruitful extension of our discussions of the action::structure and internal::external paradoxes can be obtained by contrasting organizations as both stable and continuously changing entities. For example, shifting between a structural-functionalist analysis and conflict theory (for example, Coser 1956) can divulge two sides of organizations, both of which have much to say about change. The implications of conflict theory for change are obvious. But there are also insights from stable state analysis. Stable systems gradually evolve toward complexity that sets the parameters for change and may contain the seeds of change, as Hage and Aiken's (1972) analysis of change in a hospital illustrates.

Another way to juxtapose organizational stability and instability is to examine relationships either between various organizational levels as shown in Figure 2–1, or perspectives, as shown in Figure 2–2, of personnel action and organizational structure. Stability and instability might be found at different levels of analysis. For example, contingency theory can be interpreted as explaining how organizations achieve a stable state with respect to their environment. Within this system equilibrium, individual actors and units that enter into the strategic choice process can be viewed as continuously changing and jockeying for political advantage (Pfeffer 1982). A richer understanding of organizational systems can be achieved by considering the reciprocal roles these levels have in a part-whole relationship. Other cross-level or action-structure contrasts could also be examined.

Method 2: Clarify levels of reference. This approach attempts to model how stability and instability are determined by individual actions aggregated into collective forces. In an insightful paper that supplement's Coleman's approach, Hernes (1976) provides a dynamic logic for setting various action-structure configurations in motion so as to systematically explain stability or change in the same terms. He also addresses the problem of social system reproduction discussed earlier.

Hernes's basic argument is that any system, stable or changing, has a process that generates its stability or instability. If a system is stable, it is because some process maintains the system in a steady state. If the system is changing, these changes are mediated by the same process, or the process itself is changing. Moreover, to be an adequate explanation of the system, the process must link micro (action) and macro (structural) levels, and it must be capable of dealing with both endogenous and exogenous sources of change. Thus Hernes's perspective meshes well with the ideas raised in the previous section. Any process describing the stability or change in a system must incorporate some assumptions regarding the action-structure linkage.

Hernes describes social system change in terms of three structures:

> The first is the *output structure* or a distribution of results, such as that given by a population pyramid. The second is a specification of the logical form of the process generating these results, which I will call a *process*

structure. The simplest and most compact way of expressing a process structure is by a mathematical model or formulas which give its functional form, such as the equations for birth and death processes of a population. But many process structures, for example that for the generation of a compulsive neurosis, are intractable to mathematical expression and may also be hard to express precisely in verbal terms. Finally the parameters governing the process, such as age-specific birth and death rates, take on definite values in concrete situations, and their configurations may have a certain constancy. Hence, it is natural to speak of a *parameter structure* (Hernes 1976: 519).

Examples of the three structures in theories of innovation diffusion are illustrated in Figure 2–3. For instance, the model of contagious diffusion is described by the process equation in the first column; verbally this equation may be expressed as, "The rate of diffusion of an innovation is a function of how quickly those who have adopted the innovation contact those who have not adopted it and persuade them to do so. The rate of contact and persuasion is indicated by *kn*, where *k* is a diffusion cooeficient and *n* is the number of potential adopters (N) who have already adopted the innovation." Note that this mathematical

Figure 2–3. Two Examples of Process Structure, Parameter Structure, and Output Structure.

PROCESS STRUCTURE	PARAMETER STRUCTURE	OUTPUT STRUCTURE
Contagious Diffusion $\dfrac{dN}{dt} = Kn\,(N-n)$	$K = ?$	Time Trajectory
Constant Source Diffusion $\dfrac{dN}{dt} = c\,(N-n)$	$c = ?$	Time Trajectory

Source: Adapted from Hernes (1976).

formula simply restates a verbal theory. The components of such theories can be divided into those dealing with output structure (the results), those pertaining to process structure (the motor of change), and those pertaining to the parameters (which govern the rate at which the system operates).

Hernes goes on to argue that stability and change can be understood as results of the forces—aggregate individual actions and environmental pressures—acting on these structures to maintain or change parameters, processes, and outputs. A system is stable when forces keep the output structure constant (or oscillating about an equilibrium value), and do not change the parameter or process structures. The system will change when forces cause outputs, parameters, or processes to change. Table 2–1 shows four possible configurations underlying the stability or change in a system, based on forces that might hold stable or change output, process, or parameter structures. The four macro-level processes are:

- *Simple Reproduction* (which corresponds to system stability) is a situation when the process, parameter, and output structures do not change. It is exemplified by Kanter's (1975) homosocial reproduction, in which managers select and promote people like themselves and train them to do things as they always have been done, thereby reproducing the system.
- *Expanded Reproduction* is a situation when the process and parameter structures hold constant, yet output changes. An example would be growth in the capital base allowing a firm to reinvest and further enhance capital growth.

Table 2–1. Four Possibilities for Change or Stability at Three Levels.

	Type			
Item	*1*	*2*	*3*	*4*
Does the output structure change?	No	Yes	Yes	Yes
Do the parameter values change?	No	No	Yes	Yes
Does the process structure change?	No	No	No	Yes

1 = simple reproduction
2 = expanded reproduction
3 = transition
4 = transformation

- *Transition* is a situation in which the process holds constant, yet parameters and (therefore) output structures change. For example, growth may actually change the rate of investment, hence changing the parameters governing growth. Hernes notes that theories of micro-level behavior are necessary to explain parameter change at the macro level.
- *Transformation* is a case in which there is alteration in process structure, giving rise to alterations in parameters and outputs. For example, in their study of diffusion of medical innovations, Coleman, Katz and Menzel (1966) found that a contagion theory of diffusion held up to a point and then a constant source process took over (see Figure 2–3). At the individual level they explained this as reduction of uncertainty; professional connections were more important at the outset when limited information on the drug was available, but once the drug had been used enough to test it, network connections were not as important. A different model based on simple likelihood of having encountered the drug and having a use for it was more appropriate.

The conceptual structure Hernes provides for linking these four different orders of stability and change is similar to that often used in economic and demographic modeling. A global assumption is made about the types of relations that hold among actors, which describes an ideal type of actor. For example, in Coleman's (1986) description of market relations, actors are assumed to be independent, have resources that can meet each others' needs, and will form stable exchange relationships because they are economically rational. This ideal actor allows one to make predictions about the outputs of social action processes in the aggregate. Given the standard model, there is no need to look at action per se, but merely apply the ideal type, given certain levels of inputs and contextual constraints. This output of action then becomes a set of variables that determines the stability or instability of process and parameter structures. These variables operate on the structures at the macro level and are therefore mediated by the nature of the macro system, which may be designed to amplify or dampen their effects.

This approach treats actors as ideal types and aggregates their actions to yield emergent properties that operate as variables on the macro level. However, from the perspective of the next two approaches to be discussed—structuration and morphogenesis—this approach makes overly simplistic assumptions about action and reduces it to a uniform, standard actor. Structuration and morphogenesis can use Hernes's distinctions between output, parameter, and process structures, but they incorporate action processes directly rather than by transforming them into variable outputs of the aggregate individual action system. In general, theories of the action-structure relation that advance synthetic concepts or give action a separate time will incorporate more diverse, less "demographic" models of action, than will global aggregation approaches. It would, in principle, be possible to generate an aggregated model with a diverse theory of action, but this would result in multiple outcomes, and therefore multiple ideal-type actors. This would make aggregation procedures very complex and the resulting models difficult to work with and solve.

Method 3: Use time to relate structure and action.   To link morphogenetic theory with Hernes's model would involve dividing the influences on output, parameter, and process structures into sequential phases that alternate in a cycle of social action. In the first phase, effects on parameter and process structures would be influenced by the macro-level factors only, because action would be constrained by existing structure. During the second phase, the actor appropriates institutions with some innovations or adaptations. In this phase the forces that constrain the abilities of people to adapt institutional structures are crucial. The degree of latitude the individual has determines whether the system remains stable or changes. In the third phase, the system is reproduced. At this point the connections involved in the reproduction of system and structure come into play. Depending on the system configuration, either the system is reproduced or change is institutionalized in this phase. Having completed the third phase, the process cycles back to phase one and continues. Tushman and Romanelli's (1985) punctuated equilibrium model can be further elaborated in light of these ideas. Phase one corresponds to a middle to late convergence period, phase two to reorientation (in which the executive leaders are the key actors), and phase three to an early convergence period. By articulating Tushman and Romanelli's model with the morphogenetic model additional insights emerge. For example, the morphogenetic model implies that there may be several attempts at reorientation before convergence finally "takes." Only if conditions are right for reproducing the reorientation will the second phase end, signalling a transition from instability to stability.

In essence, this approach separates the processes of appropriation and reproduction and puts them in an alternating sequence, rather than considering them simultaneously, as the structuration model does. The resulting theory would have separate phases in which models of structural influence, appropriation and adaptation, and reproduction would hold. Weick's (1979) model of organizing is another example of this approach.

Method 4: Introduce a new conception of stability and instability.   As stated before, the theory of structuration implies that action in the system is continuously producing and reproducing the process and output structures. Therefore, a model must show how particular structural features enter into action and thereby maintain or change the process and parameter structures. Because action is context-bound, this model must allow for different outcomes, depending on the particular actors involved, the context, and how action unfolds.

Barley (1986) provides a good example of the multiple routes action may follow in his study of CT technology implementation. In two similar hospitals, with similar constellations of actors and similar power distributions, the CT technology led to quite different organizational structures. In one case, the new technology led to a hierarchical structure dominated by physicians—essentially, a reproduction and reinforcing of status quo relationships, a continuation of a stable state. In the other case, the CT technology provided lower participants with a way to gain some control; it resulted in a flatter structure in which physicians and lab technicians were more nearly equal in power, generating instability and change. The action system in one lab operated to reproduce traditional status and power relationships; in the other lab traditions were not preserved, but rather the innovation altered system processes.

As this example suggests, an account of the structuration of stability and change in systems requires focusing on the effects of action on structure, and the influences of structure on action.

First, Berger and Luckmann (1966) and Weick (1979) have discussed how individuals socially construct their realities. Through a process of "enactment," actors appropriate (i.e., make attributions) about their institutions and act accordingly. This phenomenological view of structure raises a new set of questions for analysis. What forces shape how people use institutions and structures available to them? Does the actor perceive the structure to impose itself on the individual and severely constrain action, as in ritual? In this case there would be simple reproduction. Or does the actor perceive self to be able to construct and adapt the structure? In this case instability and change may result, if actors so choose. For example, a new school superintendent might borrow a model of business organization and apply it to a school system. This would require the superintendent to adapt the school structure to that of economic institutions, which, in turn, might result in a hybrid structure that significantly alters operations in the school system. Transition or transformation could result. Of course, whether such a novel structure influences the organization depends on whether the school system internalizes and perpetuates the new model, which anticipates the second issue.

The second issue to consider is whether an enacted social structure takes hold. As structuration theory suggests, the reproduction of the system and structure determine whether innovations persist or are extinguished. For example, NIH ("not invented here") attitudes of existing administrators and teachers would probably prevent the model of business organization from "taking" in a school system, and the instabilities produced by the changes would be temporary; gradually the system would return to its initial stable state. However, if present principals and administrators were replaced with new people who believed in the policy and who changed school reward and promotion practices, the new policy might survive. Thus, with structuration theories the entire configuration of the action system must be considered, including the inclinations of individuals, the constraints the system puts on them, and the nature of the macro-level process.

CONCLUSIONS

In this essay, we assumed that a good theory of organizational change should achieve four basic interdependent requirements; we examined the paradoxical nature of three of these requirements; and we applied four methods to address the paradoxes. To provide a common thread we chose theories that represented good examples of each mode of paradox resolution—Van de Ven and Astley (1981) for method 1, Coleman's social action theory for method 2, Tushman and Romanelli's (1985) punctuated equilibrium model for method 3, and the theory of structuration for method 4—and attempted to expand and elaborate them throughout the essay. The four methods represent progressively more sophisticated ways to investigate a wide array of paradoxes.

Our application of these methods to paradoxical requirements for a theory of change suggests that much of contemporary organizational theory is still struggling to live with paradoxes—and with productive results. As we discussed, the typical approach to living with paradox is to juxtapose and compare how competing theories of organizational structure and action deal with various organizational problems. Through this analysis, organizational change can be understood to arise from two basic sources:

1. tensions that emerge over time between personnel action and structural forms which are created by and constrain purposive action at each level of organizational analysis; and
2. forces of conflict, coercion, and disruption at one level of organization, and forces of consensus, unity, and integration at another level—forces that are prerequisites and reciprocals of each other.

In addition, significant advances in organizational theory are being made to address paradoxes directly with the other three methods. The themes developed in this essay weave through the three paradoxes to create more or less consistent pictures of how organizational change should be analyzed.

If we attack a paradox by clarifying levels of analysis, we are led to theories that specify how individual actions combine into collective actions. These combinatorial models describe how structure determines the impact individual actions have on collective processes; they also specify how structure limits the options individuals have. Which change forces are internal and which are external depend on the particular collective under analysis. For example, if we are interested in work units, organizational structure is an external force; if we focused on the organization as our unit of analysis, it is an internal force. The degree to which internal versus external forces predominate in driving change is determined by the degree of interdependence or coupling between the focal unit and its environment.

This way of addressing paradox can be modeled as a linkage between unit and environment. To carry off these models of linkages between action and collective and between focal unit and micro or macro levels, it is necessary to advance an ideal-typical model of the actor. This step enables us to characterize individual actions more or less uniformly, in such a way that they can serve as inputs to the models that map one level onto another. The hallmark of this approach is careful specification of levels and of how one level maps onto another. Such precision requires us to adopt a model of action that is perhaps simpler than that of other approaches.

If temporal sequence is used to resolve a paradox, we must work out a theory with alternating cycles of action dominance and structural dominance. It is especially important to discuss, as does Buckley (1968), how the transitions between action and structural phases are accomplished. There must also be an alternation between the dominance of external and internal forces, as depicted by the punctuated equilibrium model. A temporal approach would also imply that the process and parameter structures in Hernes's formulation would be affected by different forces, depending on where in the action cycle we are.

Finally, if paradoxes are addressed by advancing new concepts or distinctions, it is necessary to create a new conception of the action-structure relationship, such as that advanced by the theory of structuration. By adding the concept of modality of structuration, this approach attempts to bridge action and structure and to show their intimate connections. In this approach, any distinction between action and structure is for analytical purposes only; retaining it as an assumption about the nature of organizations unnecessarily bifurcates a holistic phenomenon. The theory tries to provide an analytical volcabulary that enables us to study action and structure in a fundamentally new way.

This approach also bridges the distinction between internal and external change forces. In the structuration of organizations, processes classified as "internal" or "external" for analytical purposes are simultaneously produced and reproduced as a single moment of action. As Sztompka notes, this conception is of a unity rather than of distinct identifiable internal and external forces. And stability or change can be modeled as products of the actors' appropriation of institutional structures constrained by the connections governing reproduction of the system. This approach leads to a richer model of action because it assumes an active agent with great latitude of response to the action context. However, it also puts us on new and shaky conceptual ground. Much remains to be worked out about this novel position.

In choosing one method of addressing a given paradox, one must also deal with the other paradoxes using the same method. As shown, the action::structure, internal::external, and stability::instability paradoxes are highly interdependent. As a consequence we see no alternative at the moment but to adopt a consistent response to each paradox.

Several extensions of this paper are evident here. First, the essay does not pay sufficient attention to the role of system complexity in organizations. Organizational systems are often so complex that actors cannot grasp all their connections. As a result, social action often has unforeseen and unintended consequences. Several theorists have argued that complex systems have laws of their own, quite different from those governing simple systems (Weick 1979; Forrester 1968). And, as Masuch (1985) notes, such systems often "escape" from their human creators.

> It often appears impossible to trace the behavior of such systems back to the actions of individuals. . . . Supposedly, individuals act with some degree of purpose, yet the sum total of their interactions is often at variance with their intentions. In short, their activities have side effects. Such side effects may create nothing but random outcomes. Frequently, however, social systems display regularities that make little sense in terms of individual intentions. Side effects sometimes follow a logic of their own. . . . They are in concert, although neither a conductor nor a score appears to be present. (Masuch 1985: 14)

The implications of models such as Masuch's vicious cycles for the four theories should be considered.

Second, this essay has not adequately considered different conceptions of time. Clearly, the model of time researchers adopt—whether chronos or kiros, continuous time or granular time, reversible or irreversible time—will have a major impact on both the description and explanation of development. Development of these issues should represent high priorities for further work.

REFERENCES

Aldrich, H. 1979. *Organizations and Environments*. Englewood Cliffs, N.J.: Prentice Hall.

Arrow, K. 1970. *Social Choice and Individual Values,* 2d ed. New Haven, Conn.: Yale University Press.

Astley, W.G., and A.H. Van de Ven. 1983. "Central Perspectives and Debates in Organization Theory." *Administrative Science Quarterly* 28: 245–73.

Barley S. 1986. "Technology as an Occasion for Structuring: Evidence from Observations of CT Scanners and the Social Order of Radiology Departments." *Administrative Science Quarterly* 31: 78–108.

Bartunek, J.M. 1984. "Changing Interpretive Schemes and Organizational Restructuring: The Example of a Religious Order." *Administrative Science Quarterly* 29, no. 3: 355–72.

Berger, P.L., and T. Luckmann. 1966. *The Social Construction of Reality* Garden City, N.Y.: Doubleday.

Barthes, R. 1979. *S/Z*. New York: Hill and Wang.

Blau, P.M. 1964. *Exchange and Power in Social Life*. New York: Wiley.

Buckley, W.S. 1968. *Sociology and Modern Systems Theory*. Englewood Cliffs, N.J.: Prentice Hall.

Burrell, G., and G. Morgan. 1979. *Sociological Paradigms and Organizational Analysis*. London: Heinemann Educational Books.

Campbell, D. 1969. "Variation and Selective Retention in Socio-Cultural Evolution." *General Systems* 16: 69–85.

Cicoural, A.V. 1971. *Cognitive Sociology*. New York: Free Press.

Coleman, J.S., E. Katz, and H. Menzel. 1966. *Medical Innovation*. Indianapolis, Ind.: Bobbs-Merrill.

——— . 1973. *The Mathematics of Collective Action*. Chicago: Aldine.

——— . 1986. "Social Theory, Social Research, and a Theory of Action." *American Journal of Sociology* 16 May: 1309–35.

Commons, J.R. 1950. *The Economics of Collective Action*. Madison, Wis.: University of Wisconsin Press.

Conant, R.C., and W.R. Ashby. 1970. "Every Good Regulator of a System Must Be a Model of That System." *International Journal of Systems Sciences* 1, no. 2: 89–97.

Coser, L.A. 1956. *The Functions of Social Conflict*. New York: Free Press.

Dahrendorf, R. 1959. *Class and Class Conflict in Industrial Society*. Stanford, Calif.: Stanford University Press.

——— . 1979. *Life Chances: Approaches to Social and Political Theory*. Chicago: University of Chicago Press.

Darwin, C. 1936. *The Origin of Species*. New York: Modern Library.

Durkheim, E. 1950. *The Rules of Sociological Method*. Edited by G.E.C. Catlin, Glencoe, Ill.: Free Press.

Etzioni, A. 1963. "The Epigenesis of Political Unification." In *Social Change: Sources, Patterns, and Consequences,* edited by A. Etzioni. New York: Basic Books.

Forrester, J.W. 1968. *Principles of Systems*. Cambridge, Mass.: MIT Press.

Garfinkel, H. 1968. *Studies in Ethnomethodology*. Englewood Cliffs, N.J.: Prentice-Hall.

Giddens, A. 1976. *New Rules of Sociological Method*. New York: Basic Books.

——— . 1979. *Central Problems in Social Theory*. Berkeley, Calif.: University of California Press.

——— . 1985. *The Constitution of Society*. Berkeley, Calif.: University of California Press.

Hage, J., and M. Aiken. 1967. "Relationship of Centralization to Other Structural Properties." *Administrative Science Quarterly* 12 (June): 72–92.

——— . 1972. *Social Change in Complex Organizations*. New York: Random House.

Hall, R.H. 1963. "The Concept of Bureaucracy: An Empirical Assessment." *American Journal of Sociology* 69 (July): 32–40; note erratum in 69 (November): 291.

Hannan, M.T., and J. Freeman. 1977. "The Population Ecology of Organizations." *American Journal of Sociology* 82: 929–64.

Hernes, G. 1976. "Structural Change in Social Processes." *American Journal of Sociology* 82, no. 3: 513–45.

Homans, G.C. 1961. *Social Behavior: Its Elementary Forms.* New York: Harcourt, Brace, and World.

———. 1958. "Social Behavior as Exchange." *American Journal of Sociology* 63: 597–606.

Hrebniak, L., and W. Joyce. 1985. "Organizational Adaptation: Strategic Choice and Environmental Determinism." *Administrative Science Quarterly* 30: 336–49.

Kanter, R.M. 1975. *Men and Women of the Corporation.* New York: Harper and Row.

Knorr-Cetina, K., and A.V. Cicourel, eds. 1981. *Advances in Social Theory and Methodology: Toward an Integration of Micro- and Macro-Sociologies.* London: Routledge & Kegan Paul.

Lawrence, P.R., and J.W. Lorsch. 1967. *Organizations and Environments.* Cambridge, Mass.: Harvard Business School, 1967.

Lazarsfeld, P.F., and H. Menzel. 1968. "On the Relation Between Individual and Collective Properties." In *A Sociological Reader in Complex Organizations,* edited by A. Etzioni. New York: Holt, Rinehart and Winston.

Lewin, K.; T. Dembo; L. Festinger; and P. Sears. 1944. "Level of Aspiration." *Personality and the Behavior Disorders,* Vol. 1, edited by J. McV. Hunt. New York: Ronald Press.

Lindblom, C.E. 1965. The *Intelligence of Democracy: Decision Making Through Mutual Adjustment.* New York: Free Press.

———. 1981. "Comments on Decisions in Organizations." In *Perspectives on Organization Design and Behavior,* edited by A. Van de Ven and W. Joyce, pp. 245–48. New York: Wiley.

McPhee, R.D. 1985. "Formal Structure and Organizational Communication." In *Organizational Communication: Traditional Themes and New Directions,* edited by R.D. McPhee and P.K. Tompkins. Beverly Hills, Calif.: Sage.

March, J.G. 1981. "Decisions in Organizations and Theories of Choice." In *Perspectives on Organization Design and Behavior,* edited by A. Van de Ven and W. Joyce, pp. 205–44. New York: Wiley.

———. 1981. "Footnotes to Organizational Change." *Administrative Science Quarterly* 26: 563–77.

March, J.G., and H.A. Simon. 1958. *Organizations.* New York: Wiley.

Masuch, M. 1985. "Vicious Circles in Organizations." *Administrative Science Quarterly* 30, no. 1 (March): 14–33.

Mayhew, B.H. 1980. "Structuralism Versus Individualisms: Part I, Shadow Boxing in the Dark." *Social Forces* 59: 335–75.

Merton, R.K. 1968. *Social Theory and Social Structure.* Glencoe, Ill.: Free Press.

Mills, C.W. 1940. "Situational Actions and Vocabularies of Motives." *American Sociological Review* 5: 940–13.

Mintzberg, H.; D. Raisinghani; and A. Theoret. 1976. "The Structure of 'Unstructured' Decision Processes." *Administrative Science Quarterly* 21, no. 2 (June): 246–75.

Mohr, L.B. 1982. *Explaining Organizational Behavior: The Limits and Possibilities of Theory and Research.* San Francisco, Calif.: Jossey-Bass.

Nielsen. H.A. 1967. "Antinomies." *New Catholic Encyclopedia.* New York: McGraw-Hill.

Nisbet, R.A. 1970. "Developmentalism: A Critical Analysis." In *Theoretical Sociology: Perspectives and Developments,* edited by J. McKinney and E. Tiryakin, pp. 167–204. New York: Meredith.

Nutt, P.C. 1984. "Types of Organizational Decision Processes." *Administrative Science Quarterly* 29: 414–50.

Olsen, M.E. 1978. *The Process of Social Organization: Power in Social Systems.* 2d ed. New York: Holt, Rinehart and Winston.

Parsons, T. 1937. *The Structure of Social Action.* New York: McGraw-Hill.

———. 1951. *The Social System.* New York: Free Press.

———. 1962. *Toward a General Theory of Action.* New York: Harper and Row.

———. 1964. *The Social System.* New York: Free Press.

Perrow, C. 1981. "Markets, Hierarchies and Hegemony." In *Perspectives on Organization Design and Behavior,* edited by A. Van de Ven and W. Joyce, pp. 371–86. New York: Wiley.

———. 1984. *Normal Accidents.* New York: Basic Books.

———. 1986. *Complex Organizations: A Critical Essay,* 3d ed. Glenview, Ill.: Scott, Foresman.

Peters, T., and R. Waterman. 1982. *In Search of Excellence: Lessons from America's Best-Run Companies.* New York: Harper and Row.

Pfeffer, J. 1982. *Organizations and Organization Theory.* Marshfield, Mass.: Pitman.

Poole, M.S.; D.R. Seibold; and R.D. McPhee. 1985. "Group Decision Making as a Structurational Process." *Quarterly Journal of Speech* 71: 74–102.

———. 1986. "A Structurational Approach to Theory-Building in Group Decision-Making Research." In *Communication and Group Decision Making,* edited by R. Hirokawa and M.S. Poole. Beverly Hills, Calif.: Sage.

Pugh, D. 1981. "The Aston Program of Research: Retrospect and Prospect." *Perspectives on Organization Design and Behavior,* edited by A.H. Van de Ven and W. Joyce, pp. 135–67. New York: Wiley.

Ranson, S., B. Hinings, and R. Greenwood, 1980. "The Structuring of Organizational Structures." *Administrative Science Quarterly* 25, no. 1: 1–17.

Reese, H., and W.F. Overton. 1978. "Models of Development and Theories of Development." In *Life-Span Developmental Psychology: Methodological Issues,* edited by J.R. Nessleroade and H.W. Reese. New York: Academic Press.

Silverman, D. 1970. *The Theory of Organizations.* Exeter, N.H.: Heinemann.

Smelser, N. 1962. *Theory of Collective Behavior.* New York: Free Press.

Starbuck, W.H. 1981. "A Trip to View the Elephants and Rattlesnakes in the Garden of Aston." In *Perspectives on Organization Design and Behavior,* edited by A.H. Van de Ven and W. Joyce, pp. 167–99.

Sztompka, P. 1979. *Sociological Dilemmas: Towards a Dialectical Paradigm.* New York: Free Press.

Thompson, J.D. 1967. *Organizations in Action.* New York: McGraw-Hill.

Touraine, A. 1977. *The Self-Production of Society.* Trans. by D. Coltman. Chicago: University of Chicago Press.

Tushman, M.L., and E. Romanelli. 1985. "Organization Evolution: A Metamorphosis Model of Convergence and Reorientation." In *Research in Organizational Behavior,* Vol. 7, edited by B. Staw and L. Cummings, pp. 171–222. Greenwich, Conn.: JAI Press.

Van de Ven, A.H., and W.G. Astley. 1981. "Mapping the Field to Create a Dynamic Perspective on Organization Design and Behavior." In *Perspectives on Organization Design and Behavior,* edited by A.H. Van de Ven and W. Joyce, pp. 427–68. New York: Wiley.

Van de Ven, A.H., and R. Garud. Forthcoming. "A Framework for Understanding the Emergence of New Industries." In *Research on Technological Innovation, Management and Policy,* Vol. 4, edited by R.S. Rosenbloom and R. Burgelman. Greenwich, Conn.: JAI Press.

Weber, M. 1947. *The Theory of Social and Economic Organizations.* Trans. by A.M. Henderson and T. Parsons. New York: Free Press.

Weick, K. 1979. *The Social Psychology of Organizing,* 2d ed. Reading, Mass.: Addison Wesley.

Wittgenstein, L. 1953. *Philosophical Investigations.* New York: MacMillan.

Woodward, J. 1965. *Industrial Organization: Theory and Practice.* London: Oxford University Press.

SURMOUNTING OUR HUMAN LIMITATIONS

William H. Starbuck

> *Plus ça change, plus c'est la meme chose.*
> —Old French proverb

Van de Ven and Poole are making a major contribution to organization theory. Their chapter is thoughtful, learned, and encyclopedic. I am grateful to have had the privilege of reading it, and I commend it to all serious students of organizational behavior.

However, their chapter also makes tough reading. It offers few examples, and even these examples seem abstract; some of the examples are not actually described; the tone is philosophical; the writing incorporates a lot of esoteric jargon; and the basic topic is a knotty one. Nevertheless, the insights a reader gets do repay the effort of reading.

The chapter looks upon organization theory from a macroscopic viewpoint, and it speaks more to the overall enterprise of theory building than to specific theories. For instance, why have organization theories addressed change less often and less satisfactorily than stability? How does the study of organizing differ from the study of anything else? Why do theoretical paradoxes arise, and what purposes can they serve? What and how can organization theorists learn from observing the incongruous?

The chapter's introduction aimed my expectations in the wrong direction. As a result, I reacted to the introduction by posing several questions that cast doubt, I thought, on the approach being taken by Van de Ven and Poole. As I neared the chapter's end, however, I realized that it addresses almost all of my initial questions. It does not answer all of them, of course, for some have no answers; but I am impressed that Van de Ven and Poole see most of the major issues I see.

Fortunately for me, Van de Ven and Poole have left a couple of paradoxes unresolved.

CAN PARADOXES NOT BE PARADOXICAL?

In the spirit of this volume, Van de Ven and Poole present their readers with a major paradox. On the one hand, they state that paradoxical requirements "are essential to a theory of change" and they recognize that theorists can live with paradoxes; and on the other hand, they advise theorists how to resolve paradoxes. But is a paradox that can be resolved truly a paradox, or is it only fuzzy thinking? Should not a true paradox remain forever paradoxical?

Van de Ven and Poole prescribe three methods for resolving paradoxes: (1) clarify levels of analysis, (2) take time into account, and (3) introduce new terms to correct logical flaws. Each of these prescriptions addresses logical deficiencies in a theory that make it appear paradoxical . . . but falsely so. The three prescriptions may reveal inadvertent errors or oversights, and correcting logical deficiencies may improve a theory's rationality. But correcting errors and logical deficiencies does not actually resolve any paradoxes: it merely shows that no paradoxes existed in the first place.

Yet, true paradoxes do exist, and so theories should express and contain them. Driving all of the paradoxes out of theory would blind it to some phenomena and render it useless for sensemaking.

True paradoxes exist, in part, because processes that tend to change some characteristics of a social system also tend to evoke antithetical processes that affect these characteristics oppositely (Fombrun and Starbuck 1987). One such antithetical effect is that the handicaps of individuals elicit compensating social supports. For instance, business firms may become insolvent, so legislatures have enacted measures to help firms survive insolvency, and some firms have survived insolvency repeatedly. A second antithetical effect is that organizations' strategic choices create opportunities for competitors. For example, many industries encompass both suppliers of standardized products and suppliers of customized products; although these types of firms compete at the margin, they also support each other by meeting needs the other does not fill (Starbuck and Dutton 1973).

Antithetical processes make social systems complex and simple, ambiguous and clear, contradictory and logical, stable and changing. Processes tending to simplify a social system by eliminating some characteristics offset processes tending to proliferate characteristics; and processes tending to complicate the social system by adding relationships offset processes tending to destroy relationships. Processes tending to clarify relationships offset processes tending to muddy relationships, and conversely. Processes tending to displace the social system from its current state offset processes tending to preserve the current state, and conversely. Thus, the social system remains a complicated mixture of contending processes, hard to understand and hard to represent in formal theories.

It is no wonder that we people, facing such a world, create multiple sensemaking frameworks that are themselves complex and simple, ambiguous and clear, contradictory and logical, and stable and changing. Many social scientists have noted these multiple and contradictory frameworks. For example, Edelman (1977: 5) remarked that "In every culture people learn to explain chronic problems through alternative sets of assumptions that are inconsistent with one another; yet the contradictory formulas persist, rationalizing inconsistent public policies and inconsistent individual beliefs about the threats that are widely feared in everyday life." To illustrate this idea, he said that both the poor and the affluent learn two contrasting characterizations of the poor, one as victims of exploitative institutions and one as independent actors responsible for their own plight and in need of control to compensate for their inadequacies. Hewitt and Hall (1973) observed that societies offer their members numerous "quasi-theories," which are widely accepted recipes that can robustly explain observed events in diverse situations. The quasi-theory of time, for instance, asserts that events can be expected at certain times, and so an event can be explained by saying that its time has come, or a non-event can be explained by saying that its time has not yet come.

Multiple sensemaking frameworks are familiar elements of organizational life, and large organizations are paradox-tolerant: one part of an organization can engage in activities that work against the activities of another part. Simon (1957: 20) called attention to the fact that "principles of administration . . . , like proverbs, they occur in pairs. For almost every principle one can find an equally plausible and contradictory principle." For example, the injunction to minimize spans of control runs counter to the injunction to minimize the numbers of hierarchical levels. Simon pointed out that if one tries to render one of these injunctions more valid by narrowing its scope, the injunction no longer solves so many problems. More recently, Hedberg, Nystrom, and Starbuck (1976) argued that, to remain viable, organizations have to keep several dimensions in balance: Each of these dimensions is anchored by opposing concepts, such as consensus and dissension, or planning and opportunism; so keeping them in balance requires multiple processes that contest with one another. Starbuck, Greve, and Hedberg (1978: 122–23) urged:

> Organizations are right to receive prescriptions skeptically. Their complexities make organizations very difficult to manage as complete systems, whereas prescriptions for managing organizations have to be simple in order to be understandable. When prescriptions describe methods and strategies which are easily translated into actual behaviors, these prescriptions oversimplify, they ignore contingencies, and they state half-truths. When prescriptions specify methods and strategies applying to complete, complex systems, these prescriptions read like poems that express verities but that have obscure applications to actual behaviors. Both kinds of prescriptions induce the people who follow them to misinterpret what is prescribed. Thus organizations should never adhere strictly to any prescription . . . including this one. . . .
>
> One sensible operating rule is that whenever organizations adopt one prescription, they should adopt a second prescription which contradicts the first. Contradictory prescriptions remind organizations that each prescription is a misleading oversimplification that ought not be carried to excess.

Westerlund and Sjöstrand (1979) listed numerous myths that organizations harbor and can bring to forth frame problem analyses. Most, but not all, of these myths occur in mutually contradictory pairs. For instance, the myth of organizational limitations states that an organization has boundaries that circumscribe its abilities; this myth, however, contradicts the one of the unlimited environment, which claims that the organization's environment offers innumerable opportunities. Similarly, the fairy tale of optimization convinces organization members of their competence by asserting that the organization is acting optimally; but it contradicts the fairy tale of satisfaction, which says that satisfactory performances are good enough.

A good theory of organizations has to account for such phenomena. Van de Ven and Poole assert that "most important, a theory that incorporates paradox need not, itself, be paradoxical." At first, this remark struck me as wise; but on reflection, I am not sure what it means. Gödel's theorem shows that deductions from a system of axioms may yield correct inferences that contradict each other (Nagel and Newman 1958). Conant and Ashby's (1970) principle of requisite variety suggests that a theory about a paradoxical world must itself be paradoxical.

DO TRUE PARADOXES EXIST IN SPITE OF RATIONALITY OR BECAUSE OF IT?

It may indeed prove to be far the most difficult and not the least important task for human reason rationally to comprehend its own limitations. It is essential for the growth of reason that as individuals we should bow to forces and obey principles which we cannot hope fully to understand, yet on which the advance and even the preservation of civilization depends. Historically this has been achieved by the influence of the various religious creeds and by traditions and superstitions which made men submit to those forces by an appeal to his emotions rather than to his reason. The most dangerous stage in the growth of civilization may well be that in which man has come to regard all these beliefs as superstitions and refuses to accept or to submit to anything which he does not rationally understand. The rationalist whose reason is not sufficient to teach him those limitations of the powers of conscious reason, and who despises all the institutions and customs which have not been consciously designed, would thus become the destroyer of the civilization built upon them.—Friedrich A. von Hayek (1955: 92)

True paradoxes may also exist, in part, because rational logic is unrealistic. Rationality is defined by human physiology: To human brains, rationality makes sense and irrationality makes no sense. But from a less anthropocentric perspective, we people may not be capable of understanding our worlds in full, and rationality may not be able to comprehend the complexities and contradictions of our worlds.

Human brains are impressively complex; it would require a network of hundreds of millions of today's computers to simulate just one complete brain (Albus 1981; Starbuck 1987). Yet human brains are only somewhat more elaborate than the intellectual systems of other mammals that have evolved on earth, say chimpanzees or dolphins; and it is evident that small differences in intellectual abilities may translate into large differences in understanding. Consider what a small absolute difference in intellect probably led Jeremiah J. Callahan, President of Duquesne University, to say in 1931: "We certainly cannot consider Einstein as one who shines as a scientific discoverer in the domain of physics, but rather as one who in a fuddled sort of way is merely trying to find some meaning for mathematical formulas in which he himself does not believe too strongly, but which he is hoping against hope somehow to establish. . . . Einstein has not a logical mind." Was it Callahan or Einstein who was more rational?

On the one hand, we may be like chimpanzees swinging about in the rafters of the New York Stock Exchange and trying to articulate its laws. The paradoxes we see may look illogical to creatures with our limited reasoning capacities and our form of logic, yet they might make sense to creatures with more complex brains or with brains that employ a different form of logic. Based on a comprehensive study of scientific problem solving, Faust (1984: 153–54, 164) concluded:

> I would argue that scientists' cognitive limitations are widely underrecognized and that this stems from a fundamental attribution error. What scientists have not accomplished or solved is usually attributed to something other than cognitive limitations, whereas cognitive limitations may be the most parsimonious explanation. For example, scientific failures are often explained by such things as lack of sufficient data, a muddling of judgment by subjective factors or biases, or the nature of the questions that have been posed (e.g., that they are not appropriate scientific questions). Time and again, these are the factors that are used to account for the upper boundaries of scientific knowledge and for unsatisfactory progress on scientific problems. Although all of these factors may operate, the most fundamental one may be our insufficient cognitive ability to answer questions—or at least to reach satisfactory solutions at a satisfactory rate. This other explanation for the limits of science was perhaps best summed up by Einstein when he was asked why greater progress had not been made on certain physics problems. He replied that the problems were "too hard for the physicists". . . .
>
> If we were capable of greater cognitive complexity, we no doubt would have made far greater scientific progress than we have achieved. The question then is how far we can progress in the face of our cognitive limitations. This question goes beyond concerns raised about limits in our capacity to obtain revealing information about the world. It is more basic. One must ask, if nature were somehow revealed to us, how much would we be able to grasp of what we were shown?

On the other hand, rationality may invalidate itself. Because we people construct our worlds to substantial degrees, the complexities we confront lie partly within our individual and collective control; and we might be able to live in extremely simple and understandable social systems if that became our shared, primary goal. Indeed, ants may find their worlds more understandable than we do ours. But it seems that we people decline to seek simple and understandable worlds: When our lives grow too simple and too understandable, we inject them with more variety and more complexity and more uncertainty and more change. As individuals, we choose to take on more responsibilities or to learn new skills; and collectively, we search for social problems to solve or goals to pursue. Thus, we build worlds for ourselves that are slightly beyond our understanding.

The rationality we apply to theories is an ideal type, distilled from thousands of years of debate and analysis by mathematicians, philosophers, and scientists. The idealized rationality leaves no loose ends, it reduces all conditions to binary states—consistent or inconsistent, true or false, existent or nonexistent, good or evil—and it implies that all related beliefs aggregate into one or the other of two mutually opposed clusters (Cartwright and Harary 1956). Like other ideal types, this one may be so extreme that it cannot actually exist. Gödel's theorem implies as much, does it not? Scientific rationality is a fantasy that appeals to us aesthetically, but it violates its own rules, distorts our observations, and extrapolates incomplete knowledge to ridiculous extremes. Left alone, scientific rationality would assemble pristine structures of logical congruence, elegant in their parsimonious simplicity, and utterly at odds with all observable phenomena.

Because rationality distorts perception, it causes mistakes. One danger is that rationality may induce theorists to resolve true paradoxes in the misguided belief that these only represent confusion about levels of analysis or time or logic. Scientific rationality says that paradoxes cannot exist, even though it creates them; then believing that they cannot exist, it does what it must to render them false. Overprecision is a powerful tool for creating fallacies.

If rationality cannot fully comprehend our worlds, or if we are not sure whether it can, then improving a theory's rationality may be harmful: A theory should possess only enough rationality to render it understandable and satisfying to us, and it should retain as much irrationality as we can tolerate. Theorists should be striving to create theories that balance rationality against irrationality, not maximally rational ones. We people need fuzzy thinking, and we need to think amid disorderly hodgepodges of events that disrupt our efforts to adhere to the rational ideal. These real-life hodgepodges test our cognitive limits, and in doing so, protect us from our own self-destructive propensities (Starbuck 1983).

Microeconomic theory exemplifies a number of these points. It is a logically congruent and integrated system with accepted axioms and rules of inference; it both espouses and embodies rationality to such a degree that it closely approximates the ideal type of scientific rationality. However, microeconomic theory is more a religion than a science because, whenever economists are confronted with empirical evidence that contradicts it, they reject the evidence and refuse to modify the theory. Evidently, microeconomic theory cannot approximate reality closely and it could not be made to do so without sacrificing rationality, so it fails badly as an exemplar of social science. Nevertheless, I urge all doctoral students to study microeconomics because I have found that students who do not understand microeconomics also cannot think abstractly about relationships among many variables; I am unsure whether microeconomics teaches theoretical reasoning or whether it merely identifies those who possess it. The behaviors that microeconomics prescribes are arrogant, calculating, grasping, inconsiderate, and selfish; so its followers would create a mean and cruel world. Her studies of it convinced my wife, who values altruism and social relations, that microeconomics is unethical, because it is preoccupied with material things at the expense of all else, and impractical, because it constantly assumes "all things being equal" even though they never are. Yet economists find microeconomics a useful tool: This might be because they have no other; but it might also be precisely because the world does not satisfy the conditions that microeconomic theory assumes to be true, and so economists are forced to use it imperfectly.

HOW IS A THEORY LIKE A JOKE?
IN ALMOST EVERY WAY.

Lemma 1. *All horses are the same colour* (by induction).

Proof: It is obvious that one horse is the same colour. Let us assume the proposition $P(k)$ that k horses are the same colour and use this to imply that $k + 1$ horses are the same colour. Given the set of $k + 1$ horses, we remove one horse; then the remaining k horses are the same colour, by hypothesis. We remove another horse and replace the first; the k horses, by hypothesis, are again the same colour. We repeat this until by exhaustion the $k + 1$ sets of k horses have been shown to be the same colour. It follows

SURMOUNTING OUR HUMAN LIMITATIONS 73

then that since every horse is the same colour as every other horse, $P(k)$ entails $P(k + 1)$. But since we have shown $P(1)$ to be true, P is true for all succeeding values of k, that is, all horses are the same colour. —Joel E. Cohen 1961 (Weber 1973: 34)

The foregoing lemma follows a familiar recipe, and it looks much like a serious mathematical proof. Humor lies only a small distance from theoretical insight, and the line between them is fine. Both those who study humor and those who make it find that people must often be advised to interpret situations as humorous because, without such warning, they are inclined to miss the humor and to see the situations as problematic (Gruner 1978; Rothbart 1976); and known humorists report that their audiences refuse to take them seriously (Leacock 1938). Conversely, those who make theories find that they must often interpret situations in ways that resemble joking (Jones 1957; Koestler 1964).

Theorizing comes close to joking because theorizing is a mental exercise and a great deal of humor is mind play that entertains us by showing us peculiarities of our intellects. We laugh at our own mental reactions as much as at the stimuli that trigger them.

One such mental peculiarity is perceptual distortion. Our brains automatically filter information as they receive it: they emphasize some aspects and de-emphasize others; they separate foreground images from background images; and they analyze important stimuli consciously while handling unimportant stimuli automatically or ignoring them (Starbuck and Milliken 1988). We have to filter and focus because our brains cannot process the flood of data available to them. Of course, these distortions pose dangers, perhaps by causing us to overlook a real problem or to see a nonexistent one, so our humor celebrates perceptual distortion through caricature, exaggeration, and understatement. We chuckle, for example, at this rendition of testimony at an inquest because it caricatures British understatement.

I heard voices in altercation in a room near me. I thought that was likely to be the editor's. I opened the door and went in. The prisoner was in the room. He had the editor on the floor and was jumping on him. I said, "Is that the editor?" He said, "Yes." I said, "Have you killed him?" He said, "Yes," again. I said, "Oh!" and went away. That is all I remember of the affair.

Cross-examined: It did not occur to me to interfere. I thought very little of the affair at the time. I think I mentioned it to my wife in the evening; but I will not swear to that. (Barrie, 1896: 182)

But we rarely laugh at the perceptual distortions that infest our theories. We explain complex phenomena in stark terms, by referring to a handful of variables and even fewer causal relationships. We labor single-mindedly to answer minor questions while we ignore major ones; then we overgeneralize our findings and the extent of our knowledge, for example, by extrapolating observations of college freshmen to experienced executives. We do not laugh partly because it is not funny that the major questions lie beyond our reach, and partly because we know that effective theories have to be much simpler than reality.

Complex theories run up against Bonini's Paradox. Charles Bonini simulated a hypothetical business firm. His computer model was much more complex than the existing mathematical models, and it exhibited some interesting effects. But after many statistical analyses, he (1963: 136) concluded: "We cannot explain completely the reasons why the [theoretical] firm behaves in a specific fashion. Our model of the firm is highly complex, and it is not possible to trace out the behavior pattern throughout the firm. . . . Therefore, we cannot pinpoint the explicit causal mechanism in the model." Bonini's Paradox is this: As a model grows more realistic, it also becomes just as difficult to understand as the real-world processes it represents.

Another peculiarity of our intellects is associative memory. Human brains act as if they store and retrieve much information via discrimination nets that both link related chunks of information and distinguish between them (Feigenbaum and Simon 1963). Because any single chunk participates in several nets, it can be retrieved in more than one way; for example, a word or phrase might be retrieved on the basis of its sound, its spelling, its membership in a cliché, or its meaning (Pepicello and Weisberg 1983). Some of these retrievals can be interpreted as humorous, others as poetic, and others as insightful. Puns amuse us by disclosing confusions between words retrieved on the basis of sound; some puns only point out that two words sound alike, whereas other puns also juxtapose incongruous ideas: "A peer appears upon the pier, who, blind, still goes to sea" (*Ontario School Reader* 1876). Other jokes trick our memories with confused levels of analysis, confounded time periods, or ambiguous terms: "Where can you always find money? In the dictionary." "Mr. Fields, do you believe in clubs for young people? Only when kindness fails."

When we find such memory errors in our theories, however, we may laugh in derision but we regard them solemnly, and we tend to react by clarifying our theoretical levels of analysis, time periods, or terms. Yet it is not always that easy to distinguish humor from poetry or insight; and memory errors may lead us to fruitful analogies. For example, in 1905, a French mathematician, Jules Richard, propounded a renowned false paradox, the Richard Paradox (Nagel and Newman 1958). The Richard Paradox says that the deductive logic used in arithmetic reasoning may lead to a statement of the form: "The number n has the property R if, and only if, this number n does not have the property R." This is clearly a paradoxical statement, so, if it were correct, the Richard Paradox would strike at the heart of mathematics. However, the Richard Paradox is fallacious because it uses an assumption that it does not make explicit. One can expose its fallacy by clarifying levels of analysis; then, seeing what is wrong with it, one can laugh at the error. Almost all mathematicians did that. Alternatively, one can do what Kurt Gödel did: Gödel took the Richard Paradox as both a model and a challenge. He imitated its style, but found a way around its fallacy. The result, Gödel's theorem, is acclaimed as one of this century's major contributions to logic and mathematics.

Memory errors merge into inferential ones, and still another mental peculiarity is logical inference. Many jokes can be analyzed as syllogisms that make absurd assumptions or imply absurd consequences, or both. A case in point is the lemma that begins this section. Or, think of Tom Sawyer's inducing other boys to whitewash a fence and to pay him for the privilege; and a Greek named Hierocles wrote down one that has drawn groans for thousands of years: "A simpleton who heard that parrots live for two hundred years bought one to see if it was true." Very similar mental games with absurd assumptions or absurd consequences serve as tools for theory building; but one might well laugh if one did not know that theorizing requires a serious demeanor. For instance, a standard method of proving a proposition false is to assume that the proposition is true, and then to deduce absurd consequences from this. Many scientific theories make such patently absurd assumptions as "in the limit as n goes to infinity," or "no errors of measurement," or "perfect certainty and complete information."

> One might say that unrealistic assumption is the mathematical theorist's special skill. Nearly all of his assumptions distort reality by omitting aspects which he thinks are inessential. It is only by omission that he can achieve the simplicity on which comprehension hangs. The crucial skill lies in choosing assumptions which he and his readers can accept as fairly realistic and which, at the same time, render analysis feasible. (Starbuck 1965: 342–43)

Psychological theories about humor emphasize incongruity or its resolution. The incongruity theories say that laughter occurs when, in safe surroundings, people suddenly observe incongruities; whereas the incongruity-resolution theories hold that laughter occurs when people make sense of situations that did appear incongruous. While conceding that both of these processes do occur, Shultz (1976) and Suls (1983) argued that most adult humor has an incongruity-resolution structure. Both of these processes generate theoretical insights as well; but an unresolved incongruity can only disconfirm a current theory and the incongruity remains disorienting as long as it makes no sense, so satisfying insights come from processes with an incongruity-resolution structure. For instance, my colleagues and I believed that serious, existence-threatening crises are unusual events caused by abnormalities, either in organizations or in their environments (Starbuck 1988). We set out to discover these abnormalities, but we were inundated with examples. It gradually dawned on us that crises are prevalent and that we were seeing normality. Resolving this incongruity brought us to see that crises are caused by essentially the same processes that produce successes.

All perceptual frameworks have blind spots that prevent people from seeing some issues or solving some problems and that link behaviors into self-reinforcing cycles (Goleman 1985). People may discover these issues or problems because incongruous events call attention to themselves, or because the people go looking for incongruities. Recognizing the inevitability of blind spots, many theorists force incongruities to manifest themselves, and they use paradoxes, playful analogies, and metaphors as levers to break their minds free of imprisoning sensemaking frameworks. In particular, dialectic thinking cascades incongruous assumptions: a theorist states a proposition, next deduces its antithesis, and then asserts that both the proposition and its antithesis hold true. I frequently make use of a corollary idea: that all causal arrows should have two heads. Both rules start from the premises that an initial proposition is false and that the theorist's key problem is to discover some of the ways in which it is false. Both rules take nonparadoxical situations and insist that they must be paradoxical.

But incongruities make no sense within the perceptual frameworks that create those blind spots (Watzlawick, Weakland, and Fisch 1974). To make sense of incongruities, people need new perceptual frameworks that conceive the situations differently; they need "to pass from a piece of disguised nonsense to something that is patent nonsense" (Wittgenstein

1958: 464). Koestler (1964) argued that humor, artistic creativity, and theoretical insight are alike in that they all involve seeing a situation or an idea in two incompatible sensemaking frameworks. He said a climate of aggressiveness or anxiety evokes humor, a sympathetic or admiring climate elicits artistic creativity, and a neutral or detached climate fosters theoretical insight. McCall (1977: 120), on the other hand, remarked that "Perpetual seriousness reduces the number of frames of reference available to problem solvers." He advised problem solvers to punctuate their seriousness with playfulness. To make sense of McCall's advice, one has to discard the assumption that play connotes purposeless activity. Then one sees that play fosters experimentation with sensemaking frameworks, through suspension of reality, exaggeration, mental flexibility, exploration, and investigation. Taking a more instrumental approach, Watzlawick, Weakland, and Fisch (1974) prescribed diverse strategies for creating new sensemaking frameworks; these strategies fall into four basic categories: (1) redefine undesirable elements to make them appear desirable, or vice versa; (2) relabel elements so that they acquire new meanings; (3) ignore elements that one cannot change; and (4) try overtly to achieve the opposite of what one wants. That sounds not unlike the advice of Van de Ven and Poole.

Thus, theory building incorporates an alternation between sensemaking and incongruity hunting. A theorist who sees incongruities needs to find a sensemaking framework that resolves those incongruities. A theorist with a theory that makes sense needs to find incongruities that show the blind spots of that theory. Whereas resolving incongruities can involve the destruction of paradoxes, finding incongruities can depend upon the creation of paradoxes.

HOW CAN WE THINK BEYOND THE LIMITS OF LOGIC? AS WE REACH BEYOND THE ENDS OF OUR ARMS.

One can be aware of our cognitive limitations without abandoning hope that we can move beyond them. In achieving awareness of limitations, one gives up something, something about themselves and about others. But this loss may be the exchange of a false idol for greater enlightenment. —David Faust (1984: 165)

Although our limitations as human beings sometimes amuse us, they also cause us confusion, frustration, and disappointment because they keep us from understanding our worlds. Thus, they challenge us to surmount them.

We, the toolmakers, can attack this challenge as we have so many others, by finding or making tools that extend our capabilities. Computers are one such tool; they carry deductive logic beyond the limits of human rationality. Paradoxes are another such tool; they help us to grasp small chunks of irrationality. Paradoxes do this by being true and false at the same time.

REFERENCES

Albus, James S. 1981. *Brains, Behavior, and Robotics.* New York: McGraw-Hill.

Barrie, James M. 1896. *The Novels, Tales and Sketches of J.M. Barrie, Volume VIII: My Lady Nicotine, Margaret Ogilvy.* New York: Scribner's.

Bonini, Charles P. 1963. *Simulation of Information and Decision Systems in the Firm.* Englewood Cliffs, N.J.: Prentice-Hall.

Callahan, Jeremiah J. 1931. *Euclid or Einstein.* New York: Devin-Adair.

Cartwright, Dorwin, and Frank Harary. 1956. "Structural Balance: A Generalization of Heider's Theory." *Psychological Review* 63: 277–93.

Conant, Roger C., and W. Ross Ashby. 1970. "Every Good Regulator of a System Must Be a Model of That System." *International Journal of Systems Sciences* 1(2): 89–97.

Edelman, Murray. 1977. *Political Language: Words That Succeed and Policies That Fail.* New York: Academic Press.

Faust, David. 1984. *The Limits of Scientific Reasoning.* Minneapolis: University of Minnesota Press.

Feigenbaum, Edward A., and Herbert A. Simon. 1963. "Elementary Perceiver and Memorizer: Review of Experiments." In *Symposium on Simulation Models,* edited by Austin C. Hoggatt and Frederick E. Balderston, pp. 101–38. Cincinnati: South-Western.

Fombrun, Charles J., and William H. Starbuck. 1987. "Variations in the Evolution of Organizational Ecology." Working paper, New York University.

Goleman, Daniel. 1985. *Vital Lies, Simple Truths: The Psychology of Self-Deception.* New York: Simon and Schuster.

Gruner, Charles R. 1978. *Understanding Laughter: The Workings of Wit and Humor.* Chicago: Nelson-Hall.

Hayek, Friedrich A. von. 1955. *The Counter-Revolution of Science.* New York: Free Press of Glencoe.

Hedberg, Bo L.T.; Paul C. Nystrom; and William H. Starbuck. 1976. "Camping on Seesaws: Prescriptions for a Self-Designing Organization." *Administrative Science Quarterly* 21: 41–65.

Hewitt, John P., and Peter M. Hall. 1973. "Social Problems, Problematic Situations, and Quasi-Theories." *American Sociological Review* 38: 367–74.

Jones, R.V. 1957. "The Theory of Practical Joking—Its Relevance to Physics." *Bulletin of the Institute of Physics.* Reprinted in Weber (1973: 8–14).

Koestler, Arthur. 1964. *The Act of Creation.* London: Hutchinson.

Leacock, Stephen. 1938. *Humor and Humanity.* New York: Henry Holt.

McCall, Morgan W., Jr. 1977. "Making Sense with Nonsense: Helping Frames of Reference Clash." In *Prescriptive Models of Organizations,* edited by Paul C. Nystrom and William H. Starbuck, pp. 111–23. Amsterdam: North-Holland.

Nagel, Ernest, and James R. Newman. 1958. *Gödel's Proof.* New York: New York University Press.

Pepicello, William J., and Robert W. Weisberg. 1983. "Linguistics and Humor." In *Handbook of Humor Research, Vol. I,* edited by Paul E. McGhee and Jeffrey Goldstein, pp. 59–83. New York: Springer-Verlag.

Rothbart, Mary K. 1976. "Incongruity, Problem-Solving, and Laughter." In *Humour and Laughter: Theory, Research and Applications,* edited by Antony J. Chapman and Hugh C. Foot, pp. 37–54. London: Wiley.

Shultz, Thomas R. 1976. "A Cognitive-Developmental Analysis of Humour." In *Humour and Laughter: Theory, Research and Applications,* edited by Antony J. Chapman and Hugh C. Foot, pp. 11–36. London: Wiley.

Simon, Herbert A. 1957. *Administrative Behavior,* 2d ed. New York: Macmillan.

Starbuck, William H. 1965. "Mathematics and Organization Theory." In *Handbook of Organizations,* edited by James G. March, pp. 335–86. Chicago: Rand McNally.

———. 1983. "Organizations as Action Generators." *American Sociological Review* 48: 91–102.

———. 1987. "Sharing Cognitive Tasks Between People and Computers in Space Systems." In *Human Factors in Automated and Robotic Space Systems: Proceedings of a Symposium,* edited by Thomas B. Sheridan, Dana S. Kruser, and Stanley Deutsch, pp. 418–43. Washington, D.C.: National Research Council.

———. 1988. "Why Organizations Run into Crises . . . and Sometimes Survive Them." In *Information Technology and Management Strategy,* edited by Kenneth C. Laudon and Jon A. Turner. Englewood Cliffs, N.J.: Prentice-Hall.

Starbuck, William H., and John M. Dutton. 1973. "Designing Adaptive Organizations." *Journal of Business Policy* 3: 21–28.

Starbuck, William H., and Frances J. Milliken. 1988. "Executives' Perceptual Filters: What They Notice and How They Make Sense." In *The Executive Effect: Concepts and Methods of Studying Top Managers,* edited by Donald C. Hambrick. Greenwich, Conn.: JAI Press.

Starbuck, William H.; Arent Greve; and Bo L.T. Hedberg. 1978. "Responding to Crises." *Journal of Business Administration* 9(2): 111–37.

Suls, Jerry. 1983. "Cognitive Processes in Humor Appreciation." In *Handbook of Humor Research, Vol. I,* edited by Paul E. McGhee and Jeffrey Goldstein, pp. 39–57. New York: Springer-Verlag.

Watzlawick, Paul; John H. Weakland; and Richard Fisch. 1974. *Change: Principles of Problem Formation and Problem Resolution.* New York: Norton.

Weber, Robert L. 1973. *A Random Walk in Science.* London: The Institute of Physics.

Westerlund, Gunnar, and Sven-Erik Sjöstrand. 1979. *Organizational Myths.* London: Harper & Row.

Wittgenstein, Ludwig. 1958. *Philosophical Investigations, Part I.* New York: Macmillan.

3 ORGANIZATIONAL CHANGE IN AND OUT OF DUALITIES AND PARADOX

Jeffrey D. Ford and Robert W. Backoff

> You need not know where you're going as long as you're on your way.
>
> —Anonymous

Paradox is not something new to us; it is an inherent part of our life experiences. As children, we felt powerful because we could demand nurturing by crying, but our power to command was a tribute to our own helplessness. As adolescents we sought independence, but we did not want to be alone or rejected. As parents, we nurture through dependence, but destroy through overdependence. And throughout our lifetimes, we confront the more fundamental paradox that in living we are in the process of dying (Hampden-Turner 1981).

Nor is paradox new to organizational theorists and managers. Recent organizational writing and commentary have drawn attention to the apparent paradoxical nature of organizations and their management (e.g., Martin, Feldman, Hatch and Sitkin 1983; Peters and Waterman 1982; Quinn and Kimberly 1984). In his review of *In Search of Excellence*, Van de Ven (1983: 621) proposed that the "central contribution of the book is a better appreciation of the paradoxes inherent in the nature of man and organization." These paradoxes include individuals wanting control while seeking independence (Van de Ven 1983),

81

uniqueness from nonuniqueness (Martin, Feldman, and Sitkin 1983), flexibility through structure (Peters and Waterman 1982), centralization through decentralization (Pfeffer 1978), exclusion through involvement (Bales 1977), and order through fluctuation (Prigogine and Stengers 1984). In many respects, Van de Ven's observation is ironic given that current administrative and management theories do not explain or incorporate these oppositions, but eliminate them by ignoring one of the opposing values or positions.

Although paradox is not new, it is, nevertheless, only now emerging as an issue in the study of organizations. But why is it that organization theorists should be concerned with issues of paradox? What insights does it offer to the understanding of organizations that are not available or have not been available through existing "nonparadoxical" perspectives? For us, the answer to these questions is quite simple: paradoxes are important because they reflect the underlying tensions that generate and energize organizational change.[1]

Organizations are inherently paradoxical. In the acts of organizing, distinctions are drawn that are oppositional in tendency: differentiation and integration, collectivity and individuality, stability and change, uniformity and complexity, morphostasis, the maintenance of structure, and morphogenesis, creation of new structure (Gharajedaghi 1982). These oppositional tendencies, which frequently manifest themselves as paradoxes, provide the underlying tensions for change. A focus on paradox, therefore, moves us away from the concept of organizations as static systems coping with problematic environmental fluctuations through deviation counteracting processes to a concept of organizations as continually dynamic systems that carry the seeds of change within themselves.

This chapter is concerned with the role of paradox in organizational evolution and development. In particular, our concern is how organizations evolve to new forms. Our contention is that it is through the interplay of paradoxical tendencies that transformations occur. In developing this position, we explicate our assumptions of reality, offer a working definition of paradox, and discuss different approaches for conceiving of oppositional tendencies. We then describe the developmental logic stemming from these positions and discuss how managers can facilitate the process of organizational transformation.

ASSUMPTIONS OF REALITY

We regard reality as a human construction, that is, "the environment as we perceive it is our invention" (Foerster 1984: 42). From a constructivist point of view, the environment we face is not unlike that which a burglar confronts when faced with a lock that must be unlocked to get inside to the loot (Glasersfeld 1984). It is not possible for the burglar to know the exact characteristics of the lock to be picked. But, to gain entry, the burglar does not have to have the exact or matching key, only a key that fits, one that approximates the lock.

Although admittedly crude, Glaserfeld's metaphor of the burglar allows explication of a central point regarding constructed reality. It is not possible for us to know if our knowledge of reality matches some "true" reality, if the key we use is isomorphic to the lock. Even after gaining entry, the burglar still does not know the characteristics of the lock, only the characteristics of the key.

There are two reasons for our inability to "know" the "true" environment. Nerve cells do not encode the physical or qualitative nature of the agents that stimulate them, only the quantity of stimulation. The stimuli we encounter must be transformed, modified, rearranged, ordered, or converted through the process of cognition into the qualitative variety we experience (Foerster 1984). The electromagnetic radiation that stimulates a rod in the retina, for example, must be converted into a description of some "thing"—such as a rainbow—by the brain. It is this description of the rainbow that is understood as reality, not the electromagnetic radiation.

As a metaphor, this suggests that data (stimulation) coming into organizations must be converted by organizational participants into descriptions such as organizational performance or competitor activity, and that it is these descriptions which constitute their reality. Foerster (1984) proposes that the process of cognition is a recursive process of description constructing. Data, for example, is described as sales performance, which is described as organizational effectiveness, which is described as economic conditions, which are described as the quality of life, and so on.

Consistent with this position, Vico (as reported in Glasersfeld 1984) proposes that the only way of "knowing" a thing is to construct it: "Thus God knows his creation, but we cannot; we can only know what we ourselves construct" (Glasersfeld 1984: 28). The keys with which we open reality's door are our own constructions, our cognitive structures, our realities. To the extent that they appear to work, they are maintained. The fact that they appear to work tells us only that the key we have chosen is one way to get inside, not that it is "the" key.

Accordingly, what we experience is "a" reality of our own constructions rather than "the" reality. "A" reality is the description provided through one sense (e.g., touch or sight) in *correlation* with the description provided through another sense. This generates an experience that is given yet another description; for example, a dark sky (sight description) and a feeling of wet (touch description) give an experience that can be described as "raining" (correlated description). In contrast, "the" reality means that one sense is *confirmation* for another sense that it is raining (Foerster 1984).

We cannot know if our knowledge of reality matches some "true" reality because to know the "true" reality requires criteria by which it is possible to compare reality to our understanding of it. Otherwise, the criteria of comparison would be created according to our own constructions or understandings of reality. This requires us to somehow step outside of our minds (Morgan 1986; Watzlawick 1984). But, no matter what we try, we cannot check our perceptions and understandings independent of other perceptions, understandings, or methods of understanding that we have constructed. We can never check our understandings prior to their being percieved, nor can we know if our descriptions "match" some true reality, only that they "fit" (Glasersfeld 1984).

Together, these two reasons imply that it is impossible for us to be "objective discoverers" of reality (Glasersfeld 1984). We cannot assure ourselves that our view of reality is a true image outside of ourselves. Consequently, reality is regarded as a

> construction of those who believe they have discovered and investigated it. In other words, what is supposedly found is an invention whose inventor is unaware of his act of invention, who considers it as something that exists independently of him; the invention then becomes the basis of his world view and actions. (Watzlawick 1984: 10)

If, as suggested above, we cannot "know" an objective (i.e., prior to experience) environment, then how is it that we experience stable and reliable realities? Perhaps the realities we do experience are constructed so as "to make things correspond to one another in shapely proportion" (Vico, as quoted in Glasersfeld 1984: 29). Moreover, through interaction and deliberation, we establish intersubjective understandings of our realities (Holzner and Marx 1979), some of which we institutionalize.

According to Giddens (1984), structures (realities) have no objective existence of their own. They are not external to individuals, but are memory traces instantiated in social practices. They are produced and reproduced through social interaction. As they exist in individuals' understandings, structures are drawn on and, thereby, reproduced. Through social interactions, individuals produce and reproduce some level of shared understanding. But in their use, structures are also modified and new understandings are created, thereby being produced. In this respect, there is a duality of structure wherein structure (reality) is both the medium and outcome of the processes it recursively organizes.

Institutionalization, which provides for reality reproduction, occurs through the reciprocal typification of habitualized actions by different actors. Habitualized actions retain their meaning for individuals by becoming embedded as routines in actors' general stock of knowledge, taken for granted, and ready for future use (Berger and Luckmann 1966). Through institutionalization, individuals develop shared meanings that inform them of what they think and see. Habitualized actions act as deep, basic assumptions (Schein 1985); it is through institutionalization that constructions are objectified, resulting in our experience of an "objective" world as something other than our construction (Berger and Luckmann 1966).

As argued here, the concept of constructed realities implies that organizations are self-referential and self-reproductive systems (Hofstadter 1979; Morgan 1986).[2] They are self-referential in that distinctions between actor or operand, and that which is acted or operated upon, collapse (Varela 1975), resulting in the properties of the observer entering into the description of the observation (Howe and Foerster 1975). A property is defined in terms of itself (Schwartz 1981). This implies that the meanings and understandings given to stimulations occurring in organizations' environments are references back to, or reflections of, the organizations themselves, for, as Morgan (1986) suggests, systems cannot impose meaning without reference back to the constructing system that gives meaning—themselves. It is not possible, for example, to create or interpret biological or chemical tests for life apart from our constructed understandings of life. The fact that Mariner found no life *as we understand it* on Mars does not preclude the possibility of other life forms that we do not understand. The same is also true for organizations that fail to "see" the implications of technological developments to their businesses.

Because what organizations see is always in some reference to themselves, they cannot see what they are not without changing the reference, that is, their constructions.

This suggests that "environments," rather than independent and discrete entities, are really reflections and parts of the systems that constructed them (Morgan 1986). Because they are mirrors of the systems that constructed them, attributions to environments, such as uncertainty, turbulence, or competitiveness, or data collected about environments, are reflections of those looking in the mirror rather than a glimpse of some "true" environment.

Organizations are self-reproductive in that, through the process of social construction, they have the capacity to create copies of themselves (Hofstadter 1979). Self-reproduction in this case does not necessarily mean an exact duplicate, but reproduction through augmentation or translation wherein information about the species or class rather than the instance is reproduced (Hofstadter 1979). For example, organizations that grow differentiate themselves in such a way that the parts are reproductions of the parent, though not identical to the parent. This reasoning parallels Giddens' (1984) ideas that social interactions produce and reproduce structures.

DISTINCTIONS, DUALITIES AND PARADOX

The process of reality construction involves the drawing of distinctions (Foerster 1984; Gaines and Shaw 1985; Glasersfeld 1984; Voorhees 1986a), primitive concepts that cannot be analyzed formally. Distinctions are approximated by "one of the parts into which a whole is divided: a division, section, a class, category" (Gaines and Shaw 1985), except that no "whole" is presupposed nor is the notion of division (Gaines and Shaw 1985). A distinction is a difference drawn between or among things. To say that something is "A" is to draw a distinction between that which is "A" and that which is "not A."

Individuals evaluate and reflect on their experiences (Schon 1983). A consequence of reflection is that certain things are described retrospectively (Weick 1979) as stable, fixed, invariant, dynamic, turbulent, or uncertain. Such descriptions require that comparisons be made, that things be put *in relation to* other things (Glasersfeld 1984). Parents, for example, are understood by putting adults in relation to offspring. Similarly, competitors are understood by putting them in relation to noncompetitors. At a minimum, relations are established through the presence of the boundary "not" (Smith 1984). But "A" and "not A" are part of the same unity for, without one, the other would not exist. By defining "A," one is also defining what is "not A" (Smith 1984). *Any* action, any act of cognition, definition, or concept is based on and establishes distinctions (Smith 1984; Voorhees 1985a, 1986a). Thus, the very actions of organizing involve the drawing of distinctions; organization itself is a source of tension (Wilden 1980).[3]

Distinctions give rise to dualities, "systems composed of two distinct things united by a non-trivial binary relation. The two elements of a duality form a dual pair in which each member is dual to, or the dual of, the other" (Voorhees 1986a: 60). A specific duality, for example, differentiation/integration, is referred to as a polarity with the two poles forming the dual pair. Although projected as residing in forces acting from the outside, dualities actually are the result of reality construction and reside within individuals (Jantsch 1975; Voorhees 1985a). Stable, dynamic, differentiated, integrated are not characteristics of the world itself, but of how actors construct it. This does not deny that there is an external world, only that our constructions of that world are all secondary—they are in our mind (Voorhees 1985a). In this sense, when actors look into the environment, they gaze upon their own reflections (Morgan 1986).

There are numerous types of dualities (Voorhees 1986a). Four dualities of particular interest to our discussions here are synchronic, diachronic, vertical, and horizontal. *Synchronic* dualities are those where both poles are simultaneously present, occupying the same space and time. It is this type of duality that appears to underlie the concept of paradox provided by Cameron and Quinn in Chapter 1. *Diachronic* dualities, on the other hand, are those where there is a temporal separation between the poles. The debate surrounding strategic choice and natural selection (Hrebiniak and Joyce 1985) reflects a diachronic duality.

Horizontal, or "east/west," dualities are those that exist on the same level in a multi-level system. They are similar to what Bateson (1979) calls symmetric in that one can travel either east or west forever, never reaching the other pole. In terms of energy flows, horizontal dualities are continuous. *Vertical,* or "north/south" dualities, on the other hand, exist on different levels in a multi-level system. Similar to what Bateson (1979) calls complementary, they produce alternating sequences of energy flows because once the north (south) pole is reached, further travel is to the south (north) pole. In this respect, there is a limit to vertical dualities.

Dualities, regardless of their type, establish a tension field of opposites. It is the steering of a viable course through this field that is the primary issue confronting human systems (Jantsch 1975; Gaines and Shaw 1985; Troncale 1985). Organizations, for example, must continually balance differentiation and integration, morphogenesis and morphostasis, change and stability, collectivity and individuality. They must also dynamically balance the tensions of consensus-dissensus, contentment-discontentment, affluence-poverty, faith-disbelief, consistency-inconsistency, and rationality-irrationality (Hedberg, Nystrom, and Starbuck 1976). The steering of a viable course requires that opposites such as these be balanced dynamically, rather than holding to one bank or the other. *The potential for action depends on the tensions created by dualities* (Jantsch 1975).

Organizations, therefore, are full of tensions arising from the dualities constructed through actions of organizing. These actions involve, at a minimum, that decisions be made on what the organization is:

- "What business are we in?"
- "What is our product?"
- "What is our market?"
- "How will we be organized?"

But in making these decisions, distinctions are made between what the organization is and what it is not. The tensions created by the dualities of these distinctions provide an energy for organizational change. But they do not provide the only energy.

Organizations are embedded in multiple systems of higher order complexity, each of which involves its own set of distinctions in which organizations are but a part (Jantsch 1975). Thus, every organization is simultaneously a macro system to the parts within it and a micro system within a macro system (Braham 1973). Through these higher-order distinctions, dualities and their corresponding oppositional tendencies are created. The tensions from these higher-order dualities provide additional energy for organizational change. Thus, the energy for organizational change stems from the tensions created by organizations as wholes and as parts of wholes.

THE CONCEPT OF PARADOX

Working Definition

Although there have been numerous attempts to define paradox and to distinguish it from other terms (e.g., Cameron and Quinn, Chapter 1;

Watzlawick, Bavelas, and Jackson 1967; Seltzer 1986), it is our contention that these attempts all reflect the notions of constructed dualities discussed above. The *relativistic view* of paradox (Seltzer 1986), for example, regards paradox as a subjective phenomenon that exists in the minds of the beholders (Dell 1981). Efforts to define paradox as a "thing" that exists outside of or independent of individuals, therefore, are considered misguided. Because paradox is relativistic, depending on the premises, opinions, beliefs, and values of the beholder(s), the only way to "know" if something is paradoxical is to understand the existential reality or phenomenological world view of the beholder(s). What appears paradoxical to one, therefore, may not be paradoxical to another. In psychotherapy, for example, interventions do not appear paradoxical to therapists even though they do to clients (Seltzer 1986; Watzlawick, Bavelas, and Jackson 1967). According to this view, therefore, paradox is *individually* constructed.

The *interactional view* (Seltzer 1986) treats paradox as being located in interpersonal contexts. This is observed in psychotherapy where therapists direct clients to engage in activities that appear in opposition to, but are in fact designed to achieve the goals of therapy. According to this perspective, if therapists did not deny clients' assumptions and expectations in behalf of fulfilling those suppositions, no paradox would occur. Paradox, therefore, has relational prerequisites wherein the paradox surfaces in the relationship itself when messages exist on different levels of abstraction and are oppositional in nature. Paradox, therefore, is *socially* constructed.

The *dialectical view* is based on the principle that ideas and events generate their own opposites, demanding some form of resolution (Seltzer 1986). This suggests that a paradox is made manifest when opposites, which have heretofore been denied or ignored, are put side by side and "show" themselves simultaneously. This may occur through self reflection (the relativistic view) or through interaction (the interaction view).

Together, these three perspectives suggest our working definition of paradox: *some "thing" that is constructed by individuals when oppositional tendencies are brought into recognizable proximity through reflection or interaction.* Such construals may be individually or collectively created. This definition implies that paradox can be dissolved through reframing (Bartunek, Chapter 4) or the revision of conceptual schemes wherein the apparent paradox is transcended. Waltzlawick, Bavelas, and Jackson (1967), for example, indicate that the paradox of Achilles' inability to overtake the turtle was dissolved once it was established that infinite converging series have a finite limit.

Forms of Paradox

Paradoxical constructions occur in mathematical or symbolic (i.e., artificial) systems as well as in natural language systems (Watzlawick, Bavelas, and Jackson 1967). *Antinomies,* which exist in logical and mathematical systems, are provable contradictions. If there is a Statement S_i and its negation $-S_i$, both of which are provable through deduction, then the two can be combined to form a third statement S_j, which is also provable. Paradoxes stemming from differences in logical types are of this form (Bateson, 1979).

Semantic paradoxes differ from antinomies in that they do not occur in logical or mathematical systems, but arise from hidden inconsistencies in levels of thought structures, that is, in language. The Cretan who says "All Cretans are liars" is an illustration of this form of paradox. When carried to its logical conclusion, we find this statement is true only if it is not true; the man is lying if he is telling the truth and is truthful if he is lying (Watzlawick, Bavelas, and Jackson 1967). The riddle of the Sphinx, "What creature is it that walks on four legs in the morning, two legs at noon-time, and three legs in the evening?", also illustrates this semantic paradox. The solution, "Man. He crawls on all fours in infancy, stands upright in maturity, and leans on a stick in old age," stems from Oedipus's realization that language has a hierarchical structure with multiple levels of meaning (Hampden-Turner 1982). Semantic paradoxes and antinomies are paradoxical because they are self-referential.

But, because language does not have a logical-type hierarchy, the theory of logical types cannot be used to eliminate the contradiction in semantic paradoxes (Watzlawick, Bavelas, and Jackson 1967). Rather, a distinction in language levels is needed: the object level, the language of description that is as near as possible the description of physical objects, and the meta-level of language, which is about language itself and of which metaphor is the usual form (Hampden-Turner, 1982).

Pragmatic paradoxes occur where injunctions that must be obeyed are given within the context of a strong complementary interpersonal relationship and where the injunction must be disobeyed to be obeyed. Moreover, the person confronting the paradox is unable to step outside the situation and dissolve the paradox by communicating about it at a meta-level (Watzlawick, Bavelas, and Jackson 1967). For example, in the Barber's paradox, the soldier is ordered to shave all the soldiers in the company who do not shave themselves, but no others. But to obey this order, the soldier must disobey it by defining himself as a self-shaver if and only if he doesn't shave. Pragmatic paradoxes, therefore, put persons in untenable positions because "it simply is not possible to behave consistently and logically within an inconsistent and illogical context" (Watzlawick, Bavelas, and Jackson 1967: 196). Ultimate goals such as zero defects may create pragmatic paradoxes in just-in-time manufacturing situations (Eisenhardt and Westcott, Chapter 5).

As shown in Figure 3–1, the three preceding paradoxical constructions can be viewed in terms of the four dualities (synchronic, diachronic, horizontal, and vertical) discussed previously. Antinomies are paradoxes that apparently occur within the same system level at the same time. Semantic paradoxes, on the other hand, occur at the same point in time, but involve different system levels. Pragmatic paradoxes also appear to involve different levels, but at the same time and with the added restriction that the person cannot move to the meta level.

Figure 3–1 suggests that current concepts of paradox are framed as synchronic dualities. However, this may be more the function of individuals' tendencies to collapse time frames than the limitation of paradox to that form. Wilden (1980: xxxiii), for example, suggests that the environment of a given open system is of a different and more inclusive level of relation (or logical type) than the system it supports, but that we generally put " 'system' and 'environment' into a bilateral

Figure 3–1. Forms of Dualities.

Time Dualities	Directional Dualities	
	Horizontal	Vertical
Synchronic	same level same time e.g., antinomies	different level same time e.g., semantic & pragmatic paradox
Diachronic	same level different time e.g., contingency theory paradoxes	different level different time e.g., developmental paradoxes

and one dimensional either/or opposition with each other." In a sense, we flatten dimensions (Abbott 1983), invert, and symmetricize non-symmetrical relations (reducing logical typing found in antinomies), thereby losing the relational aspect of system and environment and treating them as entities rather than relations. Wilden argues, for example, that the descending hierarchy of land (photosynthesis), labor potential (creative capacity), and capital has been inverted (capital, labor, land) and that both of these hierarchies have been symmetricized into the flattened three factors of production found in capitalism.

When different levels (e.g., logical types, language) collapse, inter-cross, or otherwise become entangled, producing strange loops and snarled hierarchies (Hofstadter 1979), individuals experience a sense of paradox; what is held to be separable is revealed as inseparable (Varela 1984). These loops may be seen as vicious (Masuch 1985) or virtuous (Varela 1984). If individuals collapse time frames as well as levels, paradoxes may arise not only from the intercrossing of levels, but also from the intercrossing of temporal distinctions. If this is the case, our concepts of paradox may be limited by the assumption that they appear in the same time frame.

The controversy regarding natural selection and strategic choice perspectives (e.g., Hrebiniak and Joyce 1985) appears to stem, at best, from the collapse of a diachronic duality into a synchronic duality, and, at worst, from the collapse of a diachronic and vertical duality into a synchronic and horizontal duality. In a similar but reverse process, prescriptions for dealing with paradox of one form have been to treat the paradox as another form. For example, it has often been suggested that successful innovation requires simultaneously a mechanistic and organic structure—a synchronic and horizontal duality. To deal with this need, however, organizations have been advised to oscillate between organic and mechanistic structures (a diachronic and horizontal duality) or to create separate structures (a vertical and synchronic duality) (Duncan 1976).

Regardless of the paradox type, dissolution often involves movement to a different level (time?), that is, transcendence by "jumping out of the system" (Hofstadter 1979). In this respect, paradox cannot be understood without leaping beyond those levels tangled in the structure of the paradox to a different level of complexity (Goguen and Varela 1979; Troncale 1985; Varela 1984).[4] In the example of the Cretan liar, the phrases remain paradoxical unless one lets go of the need to choose between true or false, and "sees" the sentence's circularity as its own way of specifying its meaning. "The sentence sits in a larger domain and only becomes paradoxical when projected to the flatter domain of either true or false" (Varela 1984: 313). It is the ensemble of circularity of mutual specification and self-reference that constitutes the larger domain to which Varela refers.

POINTS OF VIEW AND PARADOX

A central component in our working definition of paradox is the notion of oppositional tendencies or dualities. But how one conceives of oppositional tendencies depends on one's points of view regarding identity (What is something?) and change (How does something become something else?). As used here, points of view refer to "the underlying assumptions, deeply held, often unexamined, which form a framework within which reasoning takes place" (Horn 1983a: 1). Points of view, which are also referred to as "logics" (Horn 1983a), paradigms (Kuhn 1970), or frames (Bartunek, Chapter 4; Torbert 1985) inform how and what we perceive, how we think about ourselves and others, and how we think about other points of view.

Oscar Ichazo (as discussed in Horn 1983b) suggests there are three points of view regarding identity and change. These are formal logic, dialectics and trialectics.[5] The axioms of these points of view are summarized in Table 3–1 and discussed below.

Formal Logic

As evidenced in its three axioms, formal logic is concerned with identity—the determination of what or who something is or is not. In the case of organizations, the operation of formal logic is evidenced in such questions as "What is an organization's structure?" or "What is its strategy?" How does formal logic answer these questions of identity? Formal logic looks for the entity's unchanging essence; a fixed or permanent quality (Lebeck and Voorhees 1984). Organizations' structures and strategies, for example, are often defined in terms of fixed or established patterns of action or decisionmaking. Formal logic, therefore, provides for the identification of things and the reduction or elimination of uncertainty through those identities; something is either "A" or not "A," but not both or something in between (Lebeck and

Table 3-1.   Points of View and Their Axioms.

Formal Logic
- *Axiom of Identity:* A thing is equal to itself; A is A.
- *Axiom of Contradiction:* A thing cannot be itself and something else; A is not and cannot be *not-A*.
- *Axiom of Excluded Middle:* A thing must be one of two mutually exclusive things; A is either A or *not-A*, but not both.

Dialectics
- *Axiom of Transformation (Quantity into Quality):* A change occurs by the gradual increase or decrease within an entity or phenomena to the point where qualitative change occurs.
- *Axiom of Oppositional Struggle:* Every entity or phenomena is a unity of contradictory opposites and change results from their internal struggle.
- *Axiom of Negation of the Negation:* No development can occur without denying its previous form of existence; a change can only advance, it cannot regress.

Trialectics
- *Axiom of Mutation:* Change occurs by a mutation (jump) from one material manifestation point (MMP) to another.
- *Axiom of Circulation:* Inside every MMP is the seed of its apparent opposite; this polarity makes the circulation of energy possible and equilibrium depends on the balanced circulation between these opposites.
- *Axiom of Attraction:* All MMPs are connected by the attraction of energy up or down a hierarchical order.

Sources: D'Andrade & Johnson (1983), Horn (1983a), Voorhees (1985a).

Voorhees 1984). An issue confronting many organization theorists is that acceptable definitions have not been developed, making the process of identification difficult. One example of this is the controversy regarding the concept of organizational effectiveness (e.g., Goodman and Pennings 1977).

Although formal logic is indispensable for consistency in the use of language, it has been criticized for not considering time and thus not providing a convenient and consistent way for considering change (Horn

1983a). Something that is changing is in the process of becoming something different than what it currently is; it is becoming what it was not (Smith 1984). Spouses ("A"), for example, become divorced (not "A"), foes ("A") become friends (not "A"), and friends can sometimes be foes ("A" and not "A"). Change, therefore, involves "A" becoming not "A." But formal logic does not provide for these possibilities and thus does not provide for becoming.

Under formal logic, oppositional tendencies are conceived of as separate and distinctly identifiable entities of the form "A" and not "A." In this way, the duality is framed as an "Either/Or" bipolar dichotomy wherein one pole must be chosen over the other (Bobko 1985; Gharajedaghi 1982). This practice is evidenced in Burrell and Morgan's (1979) position that assumptions about the nature of social science can be framed as objective *or* subjective, and that assumptions about the nature of society can be framed as order *or* conflict. A similar orientation is evidenced in Astley and Van de Ven (1983). Wilden (1980: xxxvi) refers to this as a "persistence in viewing both 'horizontal' relations at a given level, and 'vertical' relations between levels, as single-level relations of (binary) opposition (EITHER 'either/or' OR 'both/and')."

A modification of formal logic weakens the axiom of the excluded middle and considers opposing tendencies as ends of a continua, representing a unidimensional concept of conflict between the tendencies (Gharajedaghi 1982). Although this modification allows for the notion of degree or extent, it still regards opposing tendencies as bipolar (Bobko 1985), requiring a resolution of the confict through some form of compromise. Although the compromise, because it is a mixture of both poles of tension, appears to be a form of integration, it is only superficially so because it does not allow for an outcome that encompasses both poles in their entirety. Like dichotomies, continua are regarded as "Either/Or" relationships (Gharajedaghi 1982).

Dialectics

A second point of view regarding change and identity is dialectics (Voorhees 1986b; Gharajedaghi 1982; Horn 1983a; Lebeck and Voorhees 1984). Where formal logic emphasizes identity, dialectics emphasizes change. As indicated by the three axioms, dialectics views change in terms of gradual increases or decreases in quantity, as inevitably and solely arising out of conflict, and as advancing continuously without limits (Horn 1983a; Lebeck and Voorhees 1984).[6]

Dialectics recognizes two interdependent types of change—quantitative and qualitative. Gradual increases or decreases in quantity are seen as leading to sudden leaps of change in quality, that is, a new form. This interplay is evidenced in Greiner's (1972) discussion of organizational growth phases where gradual increases in size and age bring about periodic qualitative revolutions in management structures and practices. It is also evidenced in Bartunek's (Chapter 4) concept of reframing where she indicates that reframing "is a qualitative, discontinuous, 'second-order' or 'double-loop' shift in understanding of some domain, not an incremental modification of previous understanding." Bartunek suggests that shifts in frames occur after gradual increases in quantities of information and frame possibilities have been "played" with.

Dialectics also recognizes two sources of opposition—internal and external. However, as indicated by the second axiom, change is seen as stemming from the struggle of internal contradictory (i.e., mutually negating) opposites. In this respect, change is seen as self-movement rather than as externally induced. Internal contradictions start small and gradually build up until they can no longer be maintained (D'Andrade and Johnson 1983). This does not mean that external factors cannot add to the gradual build up of contradictions, but that external factors do not themselves constitute the contradiction that brings about the change. Rather, the contradiction is contained within the unity and is only exacerbated or made apparent by external events. In this respect, Wilden (1980: 371) indicates that

> the human organism is quite capable of harboring virulent bacterial strains without succumbing to disease. The emergence of disease involves some triggering factor which we can define provisionally as an 'environmental intrusion.' In other words, only an ecosystem can account for organic diseases. This 'environmental intrusion' can be viewed as a message which, if it is received as information, triggers the 'pre-existing contradictions' in the ecosystem.

This suggests that although external forces may appear to cause the change, it is the interplay of internal contradictions that bring it about. In the absence of internal contradictions, the same external forces would be of little or no consequence. This reasoning is consistent with Forrester's (1971) observation that the known and intended practices of organizations are fully sufficient to create their own difficulties, regardless of what happens in their respective environments. It is also consistent with Greiner's (1972) assertion that management's solution for one set of problems is the basis for their next set of problems, and with research on organizational decline (e.g., Hedberg, Nystrom, and Starbuck 1976). And "since organization is the source of tension in all ecosystems, it is inevitable that any ongoing system will involve contradictions" (Wilden 1980: 367).

Finally, dialectics proposes that once the unity of contradictions can no longer be maintained, they negate each other and a new unity is created. This new unity, the synthesis, is progressive in that it serves as the thesis for latter stages. In this sense, changes are only advances, never regressions.

Under dialectics, contradictory opposites can be characterized as "Both/And" relationships which recognize their mutual interdependence (Gharajedaghi 1982). Unlike the either/or relationships of formal logic, dialectical relationships allow contradictory opposites not only to coexist and interact, but to form something different from either. In this respect, dialectics provides for change through opposition and conflict.

Conceiving of opposing tendencies as dialectical allows for the incorporation of formal logic. As illustrated in Figure 3–2c, movement along the diagonal (from High A to High Not A) is the same as movement along the continuum in Figure 3–2b and adherence to one pole (e.g., High A) or the other (e.g., High Not A) of that diagonal is the same as the dichotomy of Figure 3–2a. The dialectical interactions conception also means that it is possible to reframe continua as dialectical interactions, and convert contradictions to alternatives. For example, treating the tendencies toward stability and change as a unidimensional continua produces a classification of social theories based on their orientation toward one *or* the other poles and leads to a dichotomy of the "sociology of regulation" and the "sociology of radical change" (Burrell and Morgan 1979; Gharajedaghi 1982). If, however, the interaction between these tendencies is considered as dialectical, then four categories are realized: high change/high stability, high change/low stability, low change/low stability, and low change/high stability (Gharajedaghi 1982).

Trialectics

Although dialectics provides an understanding for the basis of change, it has been criticized for its failure to place any limits on change (Horn

Figure 3–2. Oppositional Construals.

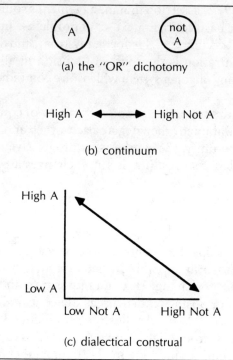

(a) the "OR" dichotomy

(b) continuum

(c) dialectical construal

1983a). Unlimited growth, for example, may not be desirable. It has also been criticized for assuming that conflict is the only generator of change. In response to these criticisms, a third point of view has been offered—trialectics (Horn 1983b).

Trialectics is a system of thought which harnesses the permanence of formal logic and the endless change of dialectics into a logic of cycles and process (Horn 1983a; Lebeck and Voorhees 1984). It does not replace formal logic or dialectics—it supplements them and defines their limits. It recognizes that formal logic is necessary in using language consistently but that it ignores change. It also recognizes that although changes in quantity do produce changes in quality, this is not the only form of change or that these changes need stem from the push of conflict and opposition (Horn 1983b).

Fundamental to trialectics is the notion that all is process; there are no things in the universe other than processes (Horn 1983b). Things, such as people, organizations, rocks, trees, electrons, atoms, planets, and galaxies are names given to abstractions of what is an identifiable and *relatively* constant pattern (Lebeck and Voorhees 1984) from a process of movement and transformation extending over the whole universe (Bohm 1980). What appears as static is, in fact, a dynamic foci of many processes. This notion is consistent with Jantsch's (1975: 5) assertion that "human life is movement. . . . not by and for itself, but within a dynamic world, within movements of a higher order." It is also consistent with Wilber's (1983: 43) notion that it is "hierarchical levels of relational (psychosocial) exchanges that constitute the human compound individual." In the language of trialectics, these relatively constant foci are termed *material manifestation points* (MMPs). They are neutral points of energy retention (i.e., resting points for energy) that neither add to nor subtract from the change process (Horn 1983b). They are what changes.

According to the first axiom of trialectics, all change involves a mutation (jump) from one MMP to another, similar to that of a quantum jump. There is not, as in dialectics, a gradual increase in some quantity necessary before change occurs. Rather, all change is discontinuous. Perceptions of discontinuous jumps, however, are a function of the time scale used (Lebeck and Voorhees 1984). Fine-grained time scales make jumps less perceptible than rough-grained scales.

The significance of time scale differences is illustrated by the debate between gradualists and catastrophists in evolutionary theory (Gould 1980). The Darwinian perspective on evolution holds that changes occur gradually such that ancestor and descendant are "connected by 'infinitely numerous transitional links' forming 'the finest graduated steps' " (Gould 1980: 180). Catastrophists, on the other hand, propose that change can occur suddenly and without intermediate links, such as through punctuated equilibria. Critics of the catastrophe perspective argue that these jumps are more illusory than real because geology is an imperfect record keeper, recording only one step in what must be, based on their assumptions of change, thousands (Gould 1980). The reason catastrophists don't "see" the gradualism that is assumed to exist, therefore, is not because it doesn't occur, but because the time scale of geology is simply too rough-grained. Catastrophists counter that the geological record is accurate; it is the assumption of gradualism that is in doubt (i.e., changes do occur in jumps).

Although the second axiom of trialectics appears to be essentially the same as the second axiom of dialectics, it is significantly different. In dialectics, opposites are antagonistic or contradictory, i.e., mutual negations of the general form A/not A (Goguen and Varela 1979).

According to trialectics, contradictory opposites do not exist in nature; they are projected into nature by dialectical minds, that is, they are constructed. For this reason, the term *apparent opposites* is used.

Apparent opposites are regarded as complementary and interdependent, *not* contradictory. Complementary opposites are those in which the activity of one pole is different from but apparently related to the activity of the other pole (Bateson 1979). They operate by mutual specification (Goguen and Varela 1979). Examples of apparent opposites (complementaries) are day/night, tiger/deer, hate/love, cold/heat (D'Andrade and Johnson 1983), simultaneous/sequential, autonomy/control, holism/reductionism, and environment/system (Goguen and Varela 1979). One cannot conceive of a system if there is no environment from which it is distinguished; and there cannot be an environment if there is no system. Opposition, therefore, does not refer to an antagonistic or contradictory aspect, but to the qualities, characteristics, classes, and relationships between the MMPs in a cycle which serve to define each other.

The construction of an apparent opposite is a function of a frame one uses in that the identification of apparent opposites requires "seeing" the cycle in which they participate (D'Andrade and Johnson 1983). Since, under our assumptions of reality, these cycles are constructed through distinctions, it is possible for one person to "see" an apparent opposite and for another person to not "see" that same opposite. Cell biologists, for example, see different opposites than physiologists, who see still different opposites than population biologists, because of the distinctions they have drawn (Goguen and Varela 1979). This implies that it is through a process of reframing (reconstructing), by moving to a different level or temporal distinction, that apparent opposition and paradox is transcended. It does not mean, however, that movement to this level (reframing) is necessarily gradual, as suggested by dialectics. Rather, it may be very sudden, as suggested by trialectics. In this respect, Oedipus's resolution of the riddle of the sphinx may be viewed as a sudden trialectical jump resulting in a new framing at a different level.

As indicated above, MMPs are relatively stable foci of processes. They are stable because they are in equilibrium. Equilibrium, as treated in trialectics, however, is not a balance of two or more forces pushing on each other. Rather, as indicated in the second axion, it is a dynamically balanced circulation of energy between and within MMPs which unites apparent opposites in an MMP of process.[7] Since nothing exists without polarity and a cycle of movement in which the poles are related,

the circulation of energy requires that some circuit exist. Apparent opposites constitute the polarities that mark the limits of these circuits.
Polarity makes circulation possible; predator and prey could not exist
without each other. This does not mean a thing is itself and its opposite,
but that a thing exists by virtue of its necessary relation to an apparent
opposite (Smith 1984).

Lebeck and Voorhees (1984: 14) provide an example of the second
axiom as it might be applied to a classroom situation:

> The listener and the speaker are apparent opposites. The speaker gives the
> listeners information. They are attempting to follow his line of reasoning
> and assimilate what he is saying. But the listeners are also giving the speaker
> information. He is attending to them and to their level of attention. During
> this time they form a single MMP—the whole room.
>
> But this equilibrium [balanced circulation of energy] can be broken.
> Should one area of this system, one of its polarities [speaker or listeners],
> cease to process and absorb and circulate this energy and information, there
> is a mutation to another state of the system—or two or more systems. Sup-
> pose the speaker presents too much information. Suppose the speaker
> mumbles. The listener cannot assimilate, and stops listening. As a result
> speaker and listener become two separate systems. The listener starts
> whispering to a neighbor—they're in another system. The speaker rushes
> on to the next topic, feeling isolated and unappreciated—decidedly a lower
> state of his system, a lower MMP.

The "mutation to another state of the system" to which Lebeck and
Voorhees refer could be a dialectical struggle between the speaker and
the listeners. Listeners could attempt to disrupt the speaker and assert
their position. The speaker, in turn, could resort to position or coercive authority to gain adherence. Or the mutation could be to formal
logic where listeners take the position that "We are this way and believe
this," and it is clear that "He (the speaker) is that way and believes that."
Or the mutation could be to independent MMPs where the speaker and
listeners do not speak to each other at all (Horn 1983b).

A key distinction, therefore, is that where the motive force of change
in dialectics is the struggle of opposites, in trialectics it is equilibrium,
the balanced circulation of energy. As long as the circulation is balanced,
a given MMP will maintain itself. However, once the balance is disrupted,
alternative MMPs will occur. The energy of water, for example, is always
ready to become gas or solid, but it remains a liquid as long as its
equilibrium is maintained (i.e., no critical change in temperature occurs). Once the equilibrium is lost, however, it will go to gas or to solid.

The third axiom of trialectics indicates that movements from one MMP to another occur because the energy of one MMP is attracted to another higher or lower MMP. Attraction is possible because of the assumption that points of change are pre-established, that is, there are limits to what can occur, and that these points can attract change. "Change, in trialectics, is not assumed to be the occurrence of the new, but the appearance of what has already been established. Negation is not necessary for this kind of change" (D'Andrade and Johnson 1983: 111). Thus, rather than the plant negating the seed, energy is transferred from the seed to the plant. The energy is attracted toward growth into a plant or into recycling through decomposition (D'Andrade and Johnson 1983). Change, therefore, can be ascendant or descendant.

Although trialectics allows for both ascendance and descendance, it has been criticized for its assumption that the points to which MMPs are attracted are preestablished, thereby providing "no room for the emergence of genuine novelty" (Bahm 1984). This criticism, however, may stem from the failure to couch trialectics in a developmental frame, such as that proposed by Wilber (1986). According to developmental theories, there are stages, from higher to lower, through which systems evolve. "Certain classes of behaviors stably emerge only after certain other classes" (Wilber, Engler, and Brown 1986: 9), although there are not necessarily a fixed number of discrete classes. Thus, the "discovery" of new stages between existing stages does not alter the fact that one stage is prior to another. Adding an adolescence stage to the organizational life cycle (e.g., Kimberly and Miles 1980), for example, does not alter the fact that birth (creation) comes prior to maturity. The logic of developmental theories also allows for both forms of morphogenesis (Wilden 1980; cf. Smith 1984): emergence as the system follows a "program" of instruction, and emergence not stemming from this "program." Therefore, if jumps are to preestablished points in a developmental sense—one cannot jump from infant to adult—trialectics is consistent with developmental theories. It is in this sense that we construe such jumps as points along a developmental sequence.

Trialectics has also been criticized for assuming that all movements to these points must occur by jumps, thereby discounting the *possibility* that changing processes involve both continuity and discontinuity (Bahm 1984). As suggested above, however, this criticism may stem from differences in the time frames used.

The different points of view regarding oppositional tendencies have implications for conceptions of the role of paradox in organizational change. Under formal logic, paradoxes are something to be avoided. Rather than embrace the possibility of paradox and develop frameworks or policies (Jantsch 1975) that allow staying in the stream without drowning, the Aristotelian approach develops frameworks that takes one out of the stream by clinging to one bank or the other. The result is, at worst, that one pole is selected over the other; at best, that oscillation occurs between the poles as the situation changes (Jantsch 1975; Van de Ven 1983). This tendency is seen in attempts to deal with the life-in-death paradox (Hampden-Turner 1982). Rather than transcending the paradox, the creation of religious, romantic, heroic, philistine, and artistic "solutions" embraces only the life pole while denying the death pole (e.g., there is life after death). A consequence of this approach is the forcing of rigid models, such as contingency models, onto fluid and dynamic realities.

Adherence to an Aristotelian orientation also leads to a perspective of "change through replacement." Because change is not allowed through the process of becoming, then it must occur through replacement or substitution—replacing "A" with not "A." Consider an organization that is organized on a functional basis ("A"). For a variety of reasons, management feels the functional structure is no longer adequate and decides a product structure (not "A") is needed. Although there is clearly a transition period during which the new product structure is "put in place," the change is not seen so much as a functional structure *becoming* a product structure (i.e., "A" becoming not "A"), as it is a product structure *replacing* a functional structure. In this respect, one structure is viewed as being removed and a new one substituted, just as an old product is taken off the shelf and a new one inserted.

This orientation is evidenced in current paradigm debates (Clark 1986; Lincoln 1986) where it is proposed that a "new" paradigm is emerging as a replacement for the "old." But examination of the characteristics of the two paradigms reveals that the new paradigm is the opposite of the existing paradigm (e.g., simple vs. complex, determinate vs. indeterminate, hierarchic vs. heterarchic). Embracing the "new" paradigm, therefore, is simply embracing the other side of the duality. The operation of Aristotelian logic, therefore, leads to an oscillation between dualities, (e.g., decentralize then centralize then decentralize, etc.).

The dialectical perspective embraces paradox by holding that every object or phenomena is a unity of contradictory oppositional tendencies and that change stems from the struggle of these tendencies. It recognizes, for example, that organizations need to achieve both differentiation and integration, stability and change, collectivity and individuality, etc. In terms of the paradigm debate cited above, systems are seen as simultaneously simple and complex, determinate and indeterminate, hierarchic and heterarchic. The struggle among these opposites is seen as gradually increasing until it suddenly climaxes in the negation of what was, and thereby provides the basis for what will be. Change is thus viewed as being advancement that is *pushed*, not from the replacement of one opposite with the other, but from the synthesis of the two into something which contains the two but yet is different from them (e.g., water contains the gases hydrogen and oxygen but is not itself a gas). The dialectical approach construes organizations as in a constant state of dynamics.

Trialectics also embraces paradox. However, rather than occurring gradually, as suggested by dialectics, all changes are believed to occur in sudden jumps, as in a change in quantum states. These changes result not so much from the push of the conflict of contradictory opposites, but from a disruption in the equilibrium of apparent opposites and the attraction or *pull* to alternative higher or lower possibilities. Dualities, therefore, are not seen simply as different dimensions, but as contained in a circle where the opposites shade into each other much like Uroborus, the self-devouring snake of paradox (Hampden-Turner 1982) or Moribus strips.

Trialectics and dialectics, therefore, give somewhat different perspectives on change. These differences are illustrated in an ecological system over an extended time period (Voorhees 1985b). During this time period, an external observer would see some species become extinct and others emerge. Dialectics would propose that these changes constitute a gradual evolutionary change proceeding via an accumulation of small genetic mutations (Axiom of Transformation) in an environment exerting selective pressures (Axiom of Oppositional Struggle) resulting in a new species arising and supplanting an older one (Axiom of Negation of the Negation). Trialectics, on the other hand, would support the possibility of "punctuated equilibrium" (Axioms of Mutation and Attraction), wherein new species appear suddenly, without apparent predecessors, and that species are not in conflict (e.g., predator and prey), but are complementaries in a unified autopoietic (i.e., self-designing) system maintaining a dissipative structure (Axiom of Circulation).

DEVELOPMENT: TRANSLATIONS, TRANSFORMATIONS, AND TRANSITIONS

Development involves movement to a higher order or level of social complexity (Jantsch 1975; Taylor 1976; Wilber 1983, 1986; Wilber, Engler and Brown 1986) where higher is defined by greater degrees of structuralization, differentiation-integration, and functional capacity, among other variables (Taylor 1976; Wilber 1983). Developmental movement is of a hierarchic nature where each successive level includes, comprehends, or assumes the basic characteristics of the preceding levels, but also adds its own "emergent qualities" not found at those levels (Taylor 1976; Wilber 1983). These qualities are in the form of new technologies, societal structures, and new apperceptions of man-environment relationships (Taylor 1976). It is the fact that junior or lower levels do not include senior or higher levels that makes development hierarchic, and it is the hierarchic movement that distinguishes development from other activity (Jantsch 1975; Wilber 1983).[8]

Wilber (1983) maintains that although higher levels of structure rest on lower levels, they are not caused or constituted by the lower levels. Rather, the higher levels are themselves partially emergent, discontinuous, and revolutionary. The higher levels emerge by "passing through" the lower levels, but do not come from them. A baby chick, for example, comes through the shell but is not made of the shell.

Nevertheless, emergence through lower levels can have significant consequences. Lower levels can incline or predispose higher levels to reproduce distortions (positive or negative). Physical trauma, for example, can lead to emotional disturbances which, in turn, can generate mental disabilities (Wilber 1983). But because distortions at lower levels are only partially passed on, and because of higher levels' emergent freedom, higher levels can redress or overcome the distortions. Growth to a higher level, therefore, does not insure the health of a lower level nor does healing a lower level insure a healthy higher level. Expansion through diversification does not assure the health of existing businesses nor does "getting one's act in order" assure subsequent success.

The metaphor of hierarchical development suggests there are two directions for growth—vertical and horizontal (Taylor 1976; Wilber 1983). Within each hierarchic level, we can construe a horizontal dimension where transactions are within or among systems at the same stage of development (Taylor 1976). Movements within hierarchical levels are horizontal movements and are termed *translations* (Wilber 1983). Using the metaphor of a multi-storied building, Wilber (1983) describes translations as the moving of furniture around on a floor. This is the process we refer to as "jumping around in" (Backoff and Ford 1985) because the organization does not transcend, but remains at one level. As Wilber (1983: 48) indicates, "horizontal or translative growth is a process of transcribing, filling in, or "fleshing out" the surface structures of a given level" with the focus being to integrate, stabilize, and equilibrate its particular level. Translations, therefore, are concerned with morphostasis (Smith 1984; Wilden 1980).

But there are also shifts between levels. Or, as Wilber's (1983) metaphor suggests, movements between floors. Movements from one level to another constitute changes in deep structures and are termed *transformations* (Wilber 1983). Deep structures, which are similar to what Schein (1985) describes as basic assumptions, are "the *rules* of the game, the *patterns* that define the *internal relations* of the various pieces to each other" (Wilber 1983: 45–46, emphasis in the original). Transformations are what we refer to as "jumping through" organizational forms (Backoff and Ford 1985). Transformation is synonymous with transcendence in that each successive level transcends or goes beyond its predecessors. Transformations, therefore, are concerned with morphogenesis (Smith 1984; Wilden 1980).

Regardless of whether growth is translative/morphostatic (movement within a horizontal level) or transformative/morphogenetic (movement between vertical levels), the movement itself is referred to as a *transition*.

One way to illustrate the concepts of translations, transformations, and transitions is through the competing values framework (Quinn and Rohrbaugh 1983). The competing values framework evolved from a study of the underlying cognitive dimensions used in the conceptualization of organizational effectiveness. The results of that study indicate that organizational effectiveness can be construed as an interplay of three sets of apparent opposites: flexibility/stability, internal/external, and means/ends. Each of these is represented by its own dimension, but for sake of illustration, only two dimensions (internal/external [I/E] and flexibility/stability [F/S]) are drawn and are shown in Figure 3–3 as two dimensional "squares" with arrows intersecting in the center and pointing in opposite directions.

Translations are shown in Figure 3–3 as continuous (solid line) and discontinuous (broken) cycles. Cycles are used in keeping with the trialectical notions of opposition and equilibrium.[9] According to the competing values framework, organizations confront the pressures of establishing an equilibrium among the dualities. If they overemphasize one dimension (e.g., internal) while ignoring others (e.g., external), the tension of the duality will increase and the organization will be forced to respond. As a result, organizations can experience different tension cycles (cf. Tichy 1983).

Figure 3-3.   Translations and Transformations.

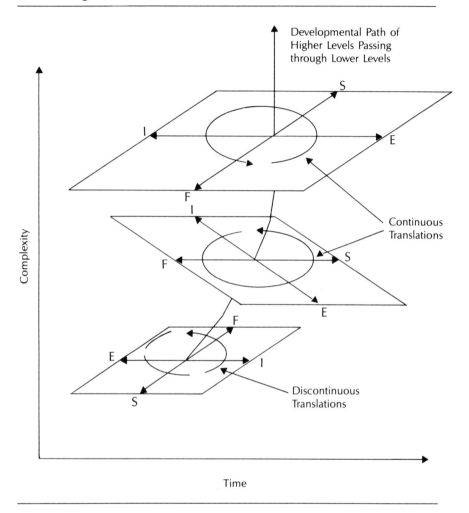

Organizational transformations occur when there are shifts to different developmental levels. These shifts occur when the higher levels emerge from and transcend the lower levels (Taylor 1976; Wilber 1983). These shifts are discontinuous as indicated by the discreteness of each square from the one prior to it (the solid line going from bottom to top shows the direction of development). In the emergence process, the higher levels add their own emergent qualities. This is indicated not only by their location on the complexity dimensions, but also by the differences in their sizes. The movements within and between levels are transitions.

PARADOX IN ORGANIZATIONAL DEVELOPMENT

The process of higher level emergence described by Wilber suggests that paradox is a central factor in organizational development and change. Initially, higher levels are undifferentiated from the lower levels through which they are passing, that is, higher levels are fused and confused with lower levels. If this is the case, the two levels are collapsed, intertwined, and entangled, producing strange loops and tangled hierarchies (Hofstadter 1979). At this point, separable levels are inseparable and undifferentiated, "our sense of direction and foundation seems to falter, and a sense of paradox sets in" (Varela 1984).

Attempts to resolve or accommodate the paradox (Schwartz 1981) bring about change and foster development (movement to higher levels) or dedevelopment (movement to lower levels). Resolution attempts that emphasize one pole over the other (e.g., Aristotelian-based attempts) ignore dualities and the equilibriums they maintain. Such resolution attempts remove organizations from the stream, placing them on one side or the other (Jantsch 1975). This increases stability while reducing resilience (Holling 1976), thereby inhibiting development.

Disruptions of equilibrium result from the dynamic interplay of different levels and force organizations to seek different equilibriums—new MMPs. These levels and their disruptions, however, stem from the distinctions imposed by organizations. Confronted with the apparent pressure of the opposite pole exerting itself—the disruption—organizations attempt to cope through deviation dampening or counteracting processes (Taylor 1976). These counteracting processes are manifested in organizations altering their emphases on different dimensions of performance in an attempt to bring things under control. Decreases in work quality, for example, are corrected by discipline.

But changing the emphasis on performance dimensions does not really change the organization's basic assumptions, its deep structures. It changes the furniture, but not the architecture of the building. In this sense, the use of deviation counteracting processes constitute translations and gives organizations the appearance of jumping around in their structures.

The use of deviation counteracting processes can continue until a point is reached where they can no longer contain or channel the energies that have been generated (Taylor 1976). When this occurs, organizations reach a bifurcation point (Prigogine and Stengers 1984), and can transform to higher or lower levels:

> When the ecosystem is subjected to disturbances that go beyond a certain threshold, the stability of the ecosystem can no longer be maintained within the context of the norms available to it. At this point, the oscillations of the ecosystem can no longer be controlled by the first-order negative feedback which is their source. The ensuing exponential amplification of deviations can be controlled only by second order negative feedback: the destruction of the system or its emergence as a metasystem (Wilden, 375).

To which level a system will move is a function of the attraction of the possibilities. However, embracing the paradox allows for the possibility that the two levels will be differentiated in a new form and development will continue through transcendence to a higher level.

Development in Coevolving Environments

To this point, we have been discussing the developmental movement of a single organization as if it existed in isolation. But, as suggested by the preceding discussions, the movements of individual organizations do not occur by and for themselves. They occur within the movements of higher ordered human systems, e.g., communities, nations, cultures (Jantsch 1975; Taylor 1976). Although human systems, such as organizations, have lives of their own, those lives are embedded in higher order movements which generate and energize the lives of humans and, thereby, the lives of human systems. The life of a human system, therefore, involves "steering a viable course in the flow of a powerful stream" (Jantsch 1975), which is itself changing. Strategic planners, for example, are confronted with the realization that while they are planning, the world for which they are planning is changing.

Organizations, therefore, can be construed as located in coevolving environments. Coevolution "occurs when the direct or indirect interaction of two or more evolving units produces an evolutionary response in each" (Van Valen 1983: 1). When translated into the realm of multileveled systems, coevolution occurs when "the development of structures in what is called microevolution mirrors the development of structures in macroevolution, and vice versa. Macrostructures and microstructures evolve together as a whole" (Briggs and Peat 1984). Thus, "evolving together," suggests more than simply mutualism; rather, it suggests an interpenetration of the systems such that evolutionary patterns are altered. Moreover,

> Coevolution says that changes which take place on the micro scale instantaneously effect changes on the macro scale and the reverse. Neither really "causes" the other in the usual sense. Microevolution doesn't build up in steps to create a macroevolution, nor do great shifts in macro structures cause the micro world to respond. Each level is connected to the other by complex feedback mechanisms. They cause each other simultaneously (Briggs and Peat 1984).

The distinction between "macro" and "micro" is one of scale and perspective. An individual, for example, may be a macro structure for a bacterium, but a micro structure for society. Thus, in the case of social systems, if the microstructure is the individual, the macrostructure is the group; if the microstructure is the group, the macrostructure is the organization; and so on.

In coevolving environments, therefore, as an organization changes, so does everything around it. For example, as a company is changing its products, its competitors also are changing theirs. At the same time, individual employees are changing as is the society within which they and the organization are bound. Coevolution implies that the consequences of organizations' actions inform and are informed by the interplay of all the changes that are being made prior to and during the taking of action by all other micro and macro structures. For this reason, organizations do engage in strategic choice (the choice of action taken) *and* they are subject to natural selection (the consequence of action) —a natural selection that they have themselves helped to create!

If organizations can be construed as processes which are coevolving with other processes, change can be construed as an outcome of the interacting networks of oppositional tendencies and relationships inherent in those coevolving processes (Jantsch 1975; Gharajedaghi 1982). This means that not only do organizations confront "internal" dualities (e.g., differentiation and integration), but that these dualities are nested and play within a network of "external" dualities, (e.g., competition and cooperation) (Axelrod 1984), both of which are in the process of coevolution. These notions of coevolving micro and macro processes within micro and macro processes are depicted in Figure 3–4.

In Figure 3–4 we have construed four MMPs as four human systems— individuals, groups, organizations and populations. Although others

Figure 3-4. Co-Evolution.

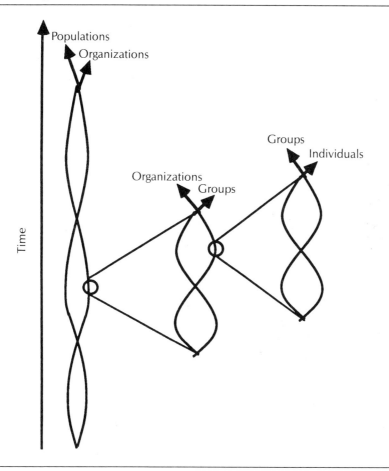

are possible, for example, communities and societies (Jantsch 1975), this construal corresponds with the different human systems frequently studied by organizational theorists (see, for example, Van de Ven and Poole, Chapter 2). To reflect the notion of coevolution, we use the image of the double helix.[10] As indicated in Figure 3–4, individuals are microstructures within groups, which are microstructures within organizations, which are microstructures within populations. Coevolution is represented by the two strands of a single double helix, one strand for the microstructure and the other for the macrostructure.

Conceiving of organizations as embedded in coevolving processes implies that these processes are themselves a source of potential imbalance for the organization. That is, apparently "external" processes are responsible for change. But these processes, as we have presented them, are socially constructed and framed and are not external to, but are the reflections of self-referential organizations. As discussed above, human constructions and organization processes involve the drawing of distinctions which give rise to dualities and apparent opposites, including but not limited to paradox. It is the flow of information or energy within and among these dualities that constitutes organization as an MMP; it is the tension of the dualities created by organization that gives the energy for change. And it is this energy that gives rise to translations and transformations.

CONCLUDING CONSIDERATIONS

Organizational members do not confront environments which are known independent of their frames. Rather, they construct environments through their frames and cannot know an environment other than that which is of their frame.[11] Frames are cognitive structures that form the context and enabling grounds within which construction occurs (Holzner and Marx 1979). They provide the bases for punctuating, bracketing, decomposing, composing, and sorting.

Through the process of training, distinctions and boundaries are drawn. These distinctions, whether construed as contradictory or complementary, are not always immediately evident and may be made manifest only when a higher level of organized complexity is emerging. Hernes (1976) provides an illustration of this in his discussion of the development of numbers (e.g., the creation of negative numbers as the opposite for natural numbers). When apparent opposites are made manifest, a sense of paradox may emerge, challenging existing frames.

The oppositional tendencies of dualities in general and paradoxes in particular, which arise from distinction making, produce tensions. These tensions supply the energy necessary for change (Jantsch 1975). Changes may be stimulated by apparently external factors (an issue of framing), but their seeds are contained within organizations as processes embedded in processes; organizations are self-referential.

These tensions may produce gradual or sudden and abrupt translative (horizontal) changes or transformative (vertical) shifts. Whether transformative shifts will be progressive (to a higher level) or regressive (to a lower level) cannot be known. Nor is it possible to assure progressive transformations through "health enhancing" translative changes. In this sense, *strategic choice is necessary if an organization is to survive, but it is not sufficient.* This means that competently made strategic choices can and do produce organizational failure! Similarly, translative changes are necessary but not sufficient for transformative changes.

How does all this occur within organizations? Organizations, as social constructions, reflect the image of language. Organizations are systems of relations. They do not exist in concrete form as "things" (Briggs and Peat 1984), but as represented in the mutual causality networks of Maruyama (1963) and the interactive modelling of Eden, Jones, and Sims (1983). Organizations are understood (i.e., constructed) through the syntactical semantic framework established through metaphors and metonomies. This implies that changes, both translative and transformative, occur by changing metaphors and metonomies. Altering the metaphor (the "word") or metonomy (the "word" in context) changes the relation and the meaning attached to it. For this reason, the "symbolic" action of management is simultaneously symbolic *and* substantive (cf. Pfeffer 1980).

Organizational members, because of different life experiences and frames, have different metaphors and metonomies. In socially constructed entities, it is in the realm of social interaction that differences in language and metaphors come into proximity and produce oppositional tensions. Some of these tensions may be contradictory and others complementary. And yet, in light of these differences, the terms organization and organization change suggest that some level of coincidental or shared intersubjective meaning or understanding exists (Boulding 1956; Gricar, Bougon and Donnellon 1984; Holzner and Marx 1979). Indeed, unless at least some meanings of the world come to be mutually shared, it would be impossible for people to engage in simple conversation with others, to behave toward one another in an even remotely civil fashion, or simply to make sense out of what goes on around them. In short, without developing some semblance of a shared system of meaning to guide actions, the world would most certainly be a Hobbsian one, "a war of all against all" (Van Maanen 1979: 19). This implies that for change to occur, metaphors and metonomies must be created, altered, or replaced through interaction (Smith 1984).

Interactions involve monologues or dialogues in which assimilation and accommodation result (Reigel 1979). Since demonstration is not possible (Perlman 1982), organizational members must rely on the adherrence obtaining characteristics of their arguments (Dunn 1982).

Through argumentation, organizational members advance, support, modify, and criticize others' constructions in an attempt to reach some coincidental meaning (i.e., an intersubjective reality) that may be institutionalized (Berger and Luckmann 1966). This process is subject to the same considerations discussed above. These interactions may result in gradual or sudden, progressive or regressive, translative or transformative changes in constructions. These, in turn, will produce different organized systems.

Through the process of argumentation, construction and framing occur and distinctions are made. During this process, therefore, paradox can influence organization change. If, as suggested here, realities are constructed, paradox is a function of how construction is accomplished, and the dualities of paradox provide the energy for change, then it is possible to bring about organizational change through the creation of paradox by the management of metaphors and metonomies. (In fact, this is the theory behind the introduction of paradox in psychotherapy.) Such changes are facilitated through the management of monologues and dialogues. Managers, therefore, must become dialogue managers and catalysts.

Management is bound by the distinctions it makes and adheres to, yet free to engage in the making of other distinctions that have been negated or lost through the failure to synthesize. It is the nature of the distinctions drawn that gives rise to such things as status, power, and interests. Management, therefore, is involved not only in the resolution of tensions, but also in their creation and perpetuation. Indeed, as we have suggested here, it is the creation of paradoxical tension which serves as the basis for change, it is through metaphor and metonomy, which provide higher level frames, that the possibility for development, for transformation, exists. For this reason, managers should give greater attention to the processes by which realities are constructed since it is through the alteration of these processes that distinctions are created and the potential for change occurs.

Change, therefore, involves a change in self or identity (Morgan 1986). And, because the distinctions drawn create the identity, management reacts to itself. Organizations, therefore, are not tools which can be applied by someone standing outside the situation. In this respect, Hurst (1986: 26) proposes that:

> The point at which everything starts to go wrong is also the point at which management believes that it can [does] stand outside the system and manipulate the processes for its own benefit. Such actions generate perverse

reactions because management is not outside the system looking in; it is inside the system looking at itself.

Finally, it is to be recognized that environments are not something separate and apart from organizations. Organizations both make and are made by their environments and thus are actors in their own evolutionary history. By changing themselves, they change their environments.

NOTES

1. We recognize that there are numerous different approaches to the study of organizational change. Among these are Goodman 1982; Quinn 1980; and Kimberly and Quinn 1984. Our intent is not to detract from these perspectives, but to examine an alternative perspective on change that has yet to be articulated in the literature of organizations.

2. The use of the term organization as an actor or "thing" throughout this paper creates some difficulty because it reifies and thus may serve to mystify the very processes we are attempting to address. As will become evident, we regard organizations as processes rather than things and that these processes are of human agency. We recognize this difficulty and ask that the reader attempt to keep in mind that the very processes which we are discussing when we use the term organization as a thing or actor also apply and are in reference to organization. In that respect, the discussion is itself self-referential.

3. We recognize that there are many sets of distinctions, among them axiological and action distinctions. In the process of engaging this text, it would be quite natural for the reader to enact these distinctions in interpreting the arguments made in this paper.

4. It should be recognized that different level refers to both those that are "higher" and those that are "lower" in a developmental hierarchy. Development, as will be discussed later in this paper, is moving up the hierarchy, whereas dedevelopment is moving down. Because we are concerned with development, our discussions are in terms of transcendence to higher levels. We recognize, however, that paradox can be dealt with by movement to lower levels.

5. By formal logic, Ichazo is referring to a mode of perception and behavior as characterized, but not limited to, the laws of thought formulated by Aristotle. Dialectics is based on Hegel.

6. We recognize that dialecticians vary in their emphasis on these axioms. We suggest these are prototypical.

7. Dynamically balanced means that the processes stay in the same relationship to one another but are constantly moving (Briggs and Peat, 1984).

8.   The notion of a hierarchy deserves elaboration. Prigogine (as discussed in Briggs and Peat 1984) suggests there is no hierarchy of levels, only different levels. One level does not come "before" or "after" another level because such a system would suggest the universe could be disassembled into simpler and simpler parts with some parts serving as the foundations for other parts. But according to Prigogine, everything is a dynamic interaction, a fluid web of process structures in which all levels are interdependent. This perspective is very much in keeping with the arguments advanced here. But if this is the case, then how does one account for the apparent hierarchies of development? Goguen and Varela (1979) suggest, consistent with the notion of constructed realities, that such hierarchies are constructions brought about by the making of distinctions which establish boundaries and *cognitive points of view* (e.g., frames). One can look at activity in organizations, for example, from the standpoint of individual processes or organizational processes, or any of several other process levels. In this respect, "higher" levels do not depend on "lower" levels for their existence and vice versa. Rather, levels are complementaries. Accordingly, one can think of hierarchies as socially constructed ordered progressions of perspectives imposed by the distinctor.

9.   The cycles shown are illustrative of the paths taken. Cycles themselves may oscillate, producing paths that resemble an "amoeba" form.

10   We are really using a simplified version of the double helix. Our intent is to illustrate the dynamic tensions which exist in a form that is consistent with the notion of cycles. We feel the double helix is one such possible form, although there may be others.

11.   This type of argument has been dismissed by others as being solipistic, i.e., "the view that this world is only in my imagination and the only reality is the imagining 'I' " (Foerster 1984: 59). Foerster (1984), however, argues that the solipism claim becomes problematic if one grants others autonomy. Furthermore, through the process of social construction, shared realities are created.

REFERENCES

Abbott, E. 1983. *Flatland: A Romance of Many Dimensions*. New York: Harper & Row.

Astley, W.G., and A.H. Van de Ven. 1983. "Central Perspectives and Debates in Organization Theory." *Administrative Science Quarterly* 28: 245–73.

Axelrod, R. 1984. *The Evolution of Cooperation*. New York: Basic.

Backoff, R., and J. Ford. 1985. The Developmental Paradox: On Jumping Around In and Through Organizational Forms. Paper presented at the 45th Annual Meeting of the National Academy of Management, San Diego, Calif.

Bahm, A. 1984. Trialectics: Toward a Practical Logic of Unity. Book Review in *Systems Research* 1: 205.

Bales, C. 1977. "Strategic Control: The President's Paradox." *Business Horizons* (August) 17–28.

Bateson, G. 1979. *Mind and Nature*. New York: Bantam.

Berger, P., and T. Luckmann. 1966. *The Social Construction of Reality*. New York: Anchor.

Bobko, P. 1985. "Removing Assumptions of Bipolarity: Towards Variation and Circularity." *Academy of Management Review* 10: 99–108.

Bohm, D. 1980. *Wholeness and the Implicate Order*. London: Ark Paperbacks.

Boulding, K. 1956. *The Image*. Ann Arbor, Mich.: University of Michigan Press.

Braham, M. 1973. "A General Theory of Organization." *General Systems* 23 (13–24).

Briggs, J. and F. Peat. 1984. *Looking Glass Universe: The Emerging Science of Wholeness*. New York: Cornerstone Library.

Burrell, G., and G. Morgan. 1979. *Sociological Paradigms and Organizational Analysis*. London: Heinemann.

Cameron, K. 1986. "Effectiveness as Paradox." *Management Science* 32: 539–53.

Clark, D. 1986. "Emerging Paradigms in Organizational Theory and Research." In *Organizational Theory and Inquiry: The Paradigmatic Revolution,* edited by Y. Lincoln, pp. 43–78. Beverly Hills, CA: Sage.

D'Andrade, P., and D. Johnson. 1983. "Dialectics and Trialectics: A Comparison of Two Analyses of Change." In *Trialectics: Toward a Practical Logic of Unity,* edited by R. Horn. Lexington, Mass.: Information Resources.

Dell, P. 1981. "Paradox Redux." *Journal of Marital and Family Therapy* 7: 127–34.

Duncan, R. 1976. "The Ambidextrous Organization: Designing Dual Structures for Innovation." In *The Management of Organization Design: Strategies and Implementation,* Vol. 1, edited by R. Killman, L. Pond, and D. Slevin. New York: North-Holland.

Dunn, W. 1982. "Reforms as Arguments." *Knowledge: Creation, Diffusion, Utilization* 3: 293–326.

Eden, C.; S. Jones; and D. Sims. 1983. *Messing About in Problems*. New York: Pergamon Press.

Foerster, H., 1984. "On Constructing a Reality." In *The Invented Reality,* edited by P. Watzlawick, pp. 41–61. New York: Norton.

Forrester, J. 1971. "Counterintuitive Behavior of Social Systems." *Technological Review*: 53–68.

Gaines, B., and M. Shaw, 1985. "Three World Views and Systems Philosophy." In *Proceedings of the International Conference on Systems Inquiry.* Los Angeles: Society for General Systems.

Gharajedaghi, J. 1982. "Social Dynamics (Dichotomy or Dialectic)." *General Systems* 27: 251–68.

Giddens, A. 1984. *The Constitution of Society.* Berkeley: University of California Press.

Glasersfeld, E. 1984. An Introduction to Radical Constructivism. In *The Invented Reality,* edited by P. Watzlawick, pp. 17–40. New York: Norton.

Goodman, P., ed. 1982. *Change in Organizations.* San Francisco: Jossey-Bass.

Goodman, P., and J. Pennings, eds. 1977. *New Perspectives on Organizational Effectiveness.* San Francisco: Jossey-Bass.

Goguen, J., and F. Varela. 1979. "Systems and Distinctions; Duality and Complementarity." *International Journal of General Systems* 5: 31–43.

Gould, S. 1980. *The Panda's Thumb.* New York: Norton.

Greiner, L. 1972. "Evolution and Revolution as Organizations Grow." *Harvard Business Review,* July-August.

Gricar, B.; M. Bougon; and A. Donnellon. 1984. "The Construction and Destruction of Coincident Meaning and Collaborative Action." Paper presented at the 44th Annual Meeting of the National Academy of Management, Boston, Massachusetts.

Hampden-Turner, C. 1981. *Maps of the Mind: Charts and Concepts of the Mind and Its Labyrinths.* New York: Collier.

Hedberg, B.L.T.; P. Nystrom; and W. Starbuck. 1976. "Camping on Seesaws: Prescriptions for a Self-Designing Organization." *Administrative Science Quarterly* 21: 41–65.

Hernes, G. 1976. "Structural Change in Social Processes." *American Journal of Sociology* 82: 513–47.

Hofstadter, D. 1979. *Godel, Escher, Bach: An Eternal Golden Braid.* New York: Vintage.

Holling, C. 1976. "Resilience and Stability of Ecosystems." In *Evolution and Consciousness: Human Systems in Transition,* edited by E. Jantsch and C. Waddington. Reading, Mass.: Addison-Wesley.

Holzner, B., and J. Marx. 1979. *Knowledge Application: The Knowledge System in Society.* Boston: Allyn & Bacon.

Horn, R. 1983a. "An Overview of Trialectics Within Applications to Psychology and Public Policy." In *Trialectics: Toward a Practical Logic of Unity,* edited by R. Horn. Lexington, Mass.: Information Resources.

———. 1983b. *Trialectics: Toward a Practical Logic of Unity.* Lexington, Mass.: Information Resources.

Howe, R., and H. Foerster. 1975. "Introductory Comments to Francisco Varela's Calculus for Self-Reference." *International Journal of General Systems* 2: 1–3.

Hrebiniak, L., and W. Joyce. 1985. "Organizational Adaptation: Strategic Choice and Environmental Determinism." *Administrative Science Quarterly* 30: 336–49.

Hurst, D. 1986. "Why Strategic Management is Bankrupt." *Organizational Dynamics* (Autumn): 4–27.

Janstch, E. 1975. *Design for Evolution: Self-Organization and Planning in the Life of Human Systems*. New York: Braziller.

Kimberly, J., and R. Miles. 1980. *The Organizational Life Cycle*. San Francisco, Calif.: Jossey-Bass.

Kimberly, J., and R. Quinn. 1984. *Managing Organizational Transitions*. Homewood, Ill.: Irwin.

Kuhn, T. 1970. *The Structure of Scientific Revolutions,* 2d ed. Chicago: University of Chicago Press.

Lebeck, M., and B. Voorhees. 1984. *Laws of Thought*. Lexington Institute Monograph No. 84-101, Lexington Institute, Lexington, Mass.

Lincoln, Y. 1986. "Introduction." In *Organizational Theory and Inquiry: The Paradigmatic Revolution,* edited by Y. Lincoln. Beverly Hills: Sage.

Martin, J.; M. Feldman; M. Hatch; and S. Sitkin. 1983. "The Uniqueness Paradox in Organizational Stories." *Administrative Science Quarterly* 28: 438–53.

Maruyama, M. 1963. "The Second Cybernetics: Deviation-Amplifying Mutual Causal Processes." *American Scientist* 51: 164–79.

Masuch, M. 1985. "Vicious Circles in Organizations." *Administrative Science Quarterly* 30: 14–33.

Morgan, G. 1986. *Images of Organization*. Beverly Hills, Calif.: Sage.

Perlman, C. 1982. *The Realm of Rhetoric*. Notre Dame, In.: University of Notre Dame Press.

Peters, T., and R. Waterman. 1982. *In Search of Excellence*. New York: Harper & Row.

Pfeffer, J. 1978. *Organizational Design*. Arlington Heights, Ill.: AHM Publishing.

————. 1980. "Management as Symbolic Action." In *Research in Organizational Behavior,* Vol. 3, edited by B. Staw and L. Cummings, pp. 1–52. Greenwich, Conn.: JAI.

Prigogine, I., and I. Stengers. 1984. *Order Out of Chaos*. New York: Bantam.

Quinn, J. 1980. *Strategies for Change*. Homewood, Ill.: Irwin.

Quinn, R. and J. Kimberly. 1984. "Paradox, Planning, and Perseverance: Guidelines for Managerial Practice." In *Managing Organizational Transitions,* edited by J. Kimberly and R. Quinn. Homewood, Ill.: Irwin.

Quinn, R. and J. Rohrbaugh. 1983. "A Spatial Model of Effectiveness Criteria: Toward a Competing Values Approach to Organizational Analysis." *Management Science* 29: 362–77.

Reigel, K. 1979. *Foundations of Dialectical Psychology*. New York: Academic Press.

Schein, E. 1985. *Organizational Culture and Leadership*. San Francisco: Jossey-Bass.

Schön, D. 1983. *The Reflective Practitioner.* New York: Basic.

Schwartz, D. 1981. "Isomorphisms of Spencer-Brown's Law of Form and Varela's Calculus for Self-Reference." *International Journal of General Systems* 6: 239–55.

Seltzer, L. 1986. *Paradoxical Strategies in Psychotherapy.* New York: Wiley.

Smith, K. 1984. "Philosophical Problems in Thinking about Organizational Change." In *Change in Organizations,* edited by P. Goodman. San Francisco: Jossey-Bass.

Taylor, A. 1976. "Process and Structure in Sociocultural Systems." In *Evolution and Consciousness: Human Systems in Transition,* edited by E. Jantsch and C. Waddington. Reading, Mass.: Addison-Wesley.

Thompson, J. 1967. *Organizations in Action.* New York: McGraw-Hill.

Tichy, N. 1983. *Managing Strategic Change.* New York: Wiley.

Torbert, W.R. 1985. "On-Line Reframing: An Integrative Approach to Organizational Management." *Organizational Dynamics* 14(1): 60–79.

Troncale, L. 1985. Duality/Complementarity as a General Systems Isomorphy." In *Proceedings of the Interntional Conference on Systems Inquiry.* Los Angeles: Society for General Systems Research.

Van Maanen, J. 1979. "On the Understanding of Interpersonal Relations." In *Essays in Interpersonal Dynamics,* edited by W. Bennis; J. Van Maanen; and F. Stelle. Homewood, Ill.: Dorsey.

Van Valen, L. 1983. "How Pervasive is Coevolution?" in *Coevolution,* edited by M. Nitecki. Chicago, Ill.: University of Chicago Press.

Van de Ven, A. 1983. In Search of Excellence: Lessons from America's Best-Run Companies. By T. Peters & R. Waterman. New York: Harper & Row, 1982. *Administrative Science Quarterly* 28: 621–24.

Varela, F. 1975. "A Calculus for Self-Reference." *International Journal of General Systems* 2: 5–24.

———. 1984. "The Creative Circle: Sketches on the Natural History of Circularity." In *The Invented Reality,* edited by P. Watzlawick, pp. 309–23. New York: Norton.

Voorhees, B. 1985a. "Neither Being Nor Not-Being." In *Proceedings of the International Conference on Systems Inquiry.* Los Angeles: Society for General Systems Research.

———. 1985b. "Philosophical Issues in Trialectical Logic." In *Proceedings of the International Conference on Systems Inquiry.* Los Angeles: Society for General Systems Research.

———. 1986a. "Toward Duality Theory." *General Systems Bulletin* 16(2): 58–61.

———. 1986b. "Trialectical Critique of Constructivist Epistemology." In *Proceedings of the International Conference on Mental Images, Values, and Reality.* Philadelphia, Pa.: Society for General Systems Research.

Watzlawick, P. 1984. "Foreword." In *The Invented Reality,* edited by P. Watzlawick, pp. 9–11. New York: Norton.

Watzlawick, P.; J. Bavelas; and D. Jackson. 1967. *Pragmatics of Human Communication.* New York: Norton.

Weick, K. 1979. *The Social Psychology of Organizing,* 2d ed. Reading, Mass.: Addison-Wesley.

Wilber, K. 1983. *A Sociable God: Toward a New Understanding of Religion.* Boulder, Colo.: New Science Library.

———. 1986. "The Spectrum of Development." In *Transformations of Consciousness: Conventional and Contemplative Perspectives on Development,* edited by K. Wilber, J. Engler and D. Brown. Boston, Mass.: Shambala.

Wilber, K.; J. Engler; and D. Brown, eds. 1986. *Transformations of Consciousness: Conventional and Contemplative Perspectives on Development.* Boston, Mass.: Shambala.

Wilden, A. 1980. *Systems and Structure: Essays in Communication and Exchange.* New York: Tavistock Publications.

BEING, THOUGHT, AND ACTION

Michael P. Thompson

Jeffrey Ford and Robert Backoff have encompassed an imposing literature and offer some important insights. Their work is difficult and they introduce us to some sources not widely known or readily accessible. I thus feel a responsibility not only to react to a few dimensions of their work, but to summarize what I think are their most central points.

I feel anxious in this attempt, because we are, all of us who are authors and discussants in this book, asking for indulgence. Our editors have attempted to synthesize some usually disparate fields and literatures, and most of the authors have approached their tasks from very high altitude. This book, even as theoretical discussions go, is high on the abstraction ladder. We should not assume that the implications for fruitful research or better management are self-evident here. However, having waded through these chapters, I find myself approaching my own projects, both scholarly and managerial, with some deeper questions and heightened sensitivities.

When Ford and Backoff talk about "logic" they are not using it to mean the study of the principles of inference and demonstration. They, and the authors whose work they draw from, are using "logics" to mean the fundamental frames or assumptions we bring into our perceptions of ourselves and the world. Logic, in an informal sense, is a term we use for the intellectual activities we engage in when we are thinking, not privately, but when we are trying to convince one another. However, the discussion here is not about public methods of persuasion and demonstration, but about how we frame problems, how we see the world, how we define and describe situations. Lebeck and Voorhees (1984) use the term "metaprogrammatic" to describe our efforts to see how our individual and collective minds are programmed or disposed to view the world.

Virtually all of the writers whose works Ford and Backoff refer to seem to share the belief that these cognitive and emotional schema or points of view can be changed—that the software of the heart and mind is pliable.

We encounter in this discussion three "logics" or points of view that are labeled with the shorthand terms "practical logic," "dialectics," and "trialectics." But these are really just labels, and we should not assume that philosophers such as Oscar Ichazo (1982) intend to mean any particular school, or period of time, or any one philosophical system, in using them. There are dialectical patterns of thought in Aristotle, and Hegel was not the inventor of dialectical thinking. Nor does Ichazo claim to be the first person to engage in what he himself calls trialectical thinking.

Ichazo claims there is a better, more effective, and more appropriate way of dealing with certain kinds of problems and situations. Ford and Backoff make a modest claim in their discussion of trialectics that it might be helpful in viewing change and in managing transitions. However, the authors they derive their material from drive a much harder bargain. Lebeck and Voorhees (1984: 3) allude several times to Einstein's statement, "We shall require a substantially new manner of thinking if mankind is to survive," to imply that trialectics represents, at least in embryo, that new manner of thinking. In virtually every assertion Ichazo (1982) makes about the applications of trialectics he presents this mode of thought and perception as one equally significant to dialectics or formal logic.

So Ford and Backoff introduce us, not to a line of thought presenting itself as a new approach to management practice or organizational theory, but to a new, or recently distilled, method and attitude with which to view the world. But this method does not apply in all situations, as some of Ichazo's more cautious disciples have pointed out. For example, Lebeck and Voorhees (1984: 9) point out:

> Often trialectics doesn't tell us anything about a situation that we need to know. We don't need quantum mechanics to catch a train. Formal logic will do for many of the situations that face us. And dialectics can handle a

significant number of those remaining. It is only in ill defined and complex areas—interpersonal relations and international relations, for example—that we require trialectics. (Lebeck and Voorhees 1984: 9)

Ford and Backoff begin with one of the most dominant themes of contemporary thought in virtually every field dealing with human cognition or behavior: the assertion that we construct what we call reality, and that this construction is carried out through language. Ford and Backoff talk about how we construct reality and make sense of events and things, particularly as these efforts relate to organizational change and the management of transitions in organizations. A summary of their discussion of organizational change includes these points:

1. Reality is socially constructed, primarily through the symbol creating and using capacities of human language. Members of an organization construe their situation, individually or collectively, through some kind of frame, vantage point, image or organizing principle. This vantage point is linguistically constructed. It is rooted in the sum total of a group or individual's experience, but is expressed and mediated through language.

2. The process of doing organizational work, of building units and assigning tasks, of organizing people and evaluating and rewarding performance, requires us to make *distinctions* and assign labels that define, identify and evaluate things and people.

3. These distinctions and labels lead to *dualities;* the inevitable rubbing of these dualities against each other creates a sense of paradox or tension. Organization itself is a source of tension.

4. The discomfort arising from these paradoxes creates a felt need for change. People feel the need to challenge the existing frame. Ford and Backoff make the important point that the tensions arising from apparent paradoxes create much of the energy necessary for growth and change. The additional energy comes from the higher order multiple systems in which the organization is embedded.

5. Change may be stimulated by factors external to the organization, but the seeds of change are contained within the organization; the locus of control is internal.

6. Change is manifest as a new frame or paradigm—a different way of construing the world.

7. That new frame is established through language, specifically through argument—dialogue and monologue—and is rooted in

the actual metaphors and metonomies that members of the organization invent. Argument is the engine of organizational change.

The core challenge thus facing all human systems is to steer a safe course through the "tension field" created by the dualities we ourselves invent. Ford and Backoff's discussion is a metatheoretical guide to avoiding some common traps of traditional thinking, particularly as it applies to the study and management of change.

Ford and Backoff are primarily discussing what they see as the three fundamental ways in which "oppositional tendencies" or dualities in organizations and, in fact, all systems, can be both conceived and handled. These three approaches or vantage points are: formal logic, dialectics, and trialectics. The authors' choice for the most effective and valid approach is trialectics.

With the basic assertion that reality is a social construction, Ford and Backoff also hold with those who argue that organizations themselves are fundamentally processes, not things. In fact, they argue that all objects and collectivities we apprehend are processes, "dynamic foci of processes," or "neutral points of energy retention." The formal term in trialectic parlance for these focal points is "material manifestation points" (MMPs). These MMPs "neither add to nor subtract from the change process, but are that which changes."

For the sake of economy, I will not discuss the forms of paradox presented by the authors, but repeat their working definition of a paradox as a "thing constructed by individuals when oppositional tendencies are brought into recognizable proximity or interaction."

Ford and Backoff say they want to help managers "facilitate the process of organizational transformation," but I think theirs is primarily a philosophical discussion about how to view change in human and physical systems. We get off on the wrong track, they say, from the very point of perception in viewing change, or managing or studying change, because we fall into one of several perceptual traps.

Drawing directly on Ichazo's framework, Ford and Backoff describe "formal logic" and dialectics as perceptual traps, or at least as approaches to making sense of the world that are less encompassing, and less valid than the approach they favor, trialectics. They also say their undertaking is worth the labor because we usually don't examine our assumptions about how we are looking at something, how we are making sense of it.

First, we must examine the ways in which we apprehend "identity," or the status of an object or event or system. Next we must expose the assumptions and methods we apply in observing change in objects, events or systems. Everything thus revolves around how we view identity and change.

Formal logic as a tool in both the observation and description of change is weak because it sets up polarities, mutually exclusive categories of either/or: "This unit is either in charge of marketing or not;" "The defendant in this hearing is either mentally fit to manage his own affairs or not." Even with the benefit of viewing these polarities on a continuum, and introducing the notion of degree or extent, formal logic "still regards opposing tendencies as bipolar, requiring a resolution of the conflict through some form of compromise." The poles on the continuum are still regarded as either/or relationships.

Dialectics, on the other hand, emphasizes not identity but change. Formal logic is equipped to deal with being, dialectics with becoming. Dialectics, as espoused in the literature Ford and Backoff cite, "views change in terms of *gradual* increases or decreases in *quantity* as solely arising out of conflict, and as advancing *continuously* without limits" (emphasis added). There are six key concepts in their treatment of dialectics:

1. Change is gradual.
2. The gradient that moves incrementally is quantity.
3. The gradual change in quantity results in sudden leaps in quality.
4. The locus of qualitative change is internal to the system or organization. External factors may exacerbate the felt need, but paradoxes or dualities that ultimately trigger change are those internal to the system.
5. The new unity or synthesis that emerges becomes *inevitably* the "thesis" upon which the forces of change will in time converge. Change thus advances, but never regresses. A dialectical view of the world sees all change as moving forward, but never regressing.
6. A dialectical view of change is thus rooted in opposition and conflict.

Again, by dialectics Ford and Backoff mean a point of view that is biased toward seeing change as arising only out of conflict and ignoring the desirability, or even the possibility, of limitations or boundaries. This would describe the point of view or disposition of a culture that sees unlimited growth as the desirable outcome for the future. Further, it would describe an organization that tends to resort to force as the only reliable method for bringing about change. Why? At the root of this version of dialectics is the belief that change can emerge only from conflict. Ergo, to introduce change, introduce conflict in the system to cause change. The two major weaknesses they cite in dialectical methods of thought and action are that they recognize no limits, and they are rooted in conflict.

They then present a conceptual approach, from which they draw heavily from Horn (1983) and Lebeck and Voorhees (1984). This approach is trialectics. Ford and Backoff argue that trialectics can supplement formal logic and dialectics. Given the inability of formal logic to deal with change and process, however, the real issue is between dialectics and trialectics.

Our authors are arguing for the two added benefits trialectics offers: first, freedom from the notion that the only form of change is through quantitative increases or decreases; second, freedom from the notion that all change stems from opposition.

Implicit in this whole discussion is the notion that we encompass all the circumstances we observe and come to grips with them through language. We invent metaphors and other analogies for events and people that help us make sense of them, or convince others that we see things as they really are. Without language we could not symbolize our environment. Without language there is only sensation. Cultures themselves, according to S.A. Tyler, "are not material phenomena; they are cognitive organizations of material phenomena" (Gardner 1985: 347).

Ford and Backoff would agree with those structural anthropologists such as Claude Levi-Strauss that our constructions of reality are reflective of our language. For example, Ford and Backoff refer to Robert Horn's argument that contradictory opposites do not really exist in nature, but that we project them onto nature with our dialectical minds. We thus construct opposition where it does not really exist.

I think it's vital not to beg the question of whether dualities actually exist in nature. I have read the sources our authors draw upon, and remain at least partially unconvinced that the dualities are purely human constructions. The energy generated by opposition is real. The tension between the tiger seeking his dinner and the deer fleeing for her life is real. It can be argued, as Ford and Backoff do argue, that in a larger scheme the tiger/deer dichotomy is really a continuous complementarity of a larger ecological system, a system in equilibrium. True, but in a real and immediate context there is opposition, and immense energy and conflict radiating from that opposition.

But again, what about this duality? We know from structural analysis of human languages that the notion of opposition and duality is part of the deep structure of those languages (Hawkes 1977: 87–95). But a crucial and perhaps unanswerable question is: does that duality exist in our language because we have built it in through our observations of what we see around us, or is it the case that language contains those structured dualities because of some innate structure, or because we, in trying to encompass and shape a reality, have a need for order and economy in expression? Have we, in the process of making sense of our world, imposed the structure of our language on the world as we see it, even though the structure is a distortion? The villian/hero, good/evil, hunter/hunted dichotomies are, according to Ichazo and his disciples, linguistic distinctions, not natural, phenomenal ones. They are polar ends of the same manifestation point (Horn 1983: 21). The question is ultimately unanswerable, because we would have to put our language aside for a while to answer it.

Trialectics is the term Ichazo uses for a new mode of thinking. This mode is probably most directly rooted in the new physics, the work of Bohr, Planck and Einstein. Central to trialectics is the notion that change is not gradual, as it is in dialectics, but occurs in leaps. Max Planck's image of "quanta," packets of energy popping from black bodies, comes to mind in Ford and Backoff's discussion of change. They describe it as sudden, though sometimes inconspicuous leaps. In addition to the idea that change occurs in leaps is the notion that energy, in its movement, comes to rest on predetermined or fixed shelves or levels. These are the material manifestation points Ford and Backoff cover where changes occur. The example Ichazo uses is the temperature level at which water turns to vapor. Water as it is heated remains a liquid until it reaches a certain temperature. It then undergoes, within a very narrow increment, a qualitative change.

This is an intriguing concept whose frustration is caused by the examples Ford and Backoff draw upon, and the examples given in the primary sources they use. Because the examples are taken from the physical sciences, one must extrapolate the implications to human behavior. Ichazo himself refers to the importance of his MMP's in understanding human cognitive and emotional development. "There are points where change occurs," he says, "in childhood, adolescence and maturity" (Ichazo 1982: 62). The implication is that if we look carefully we can somehow observe or even predict where in human development these resting places or plateaus of energys are, and understand human development better.

But is the human psyche like a crystal that breaks at a particular moment when the stress factor reaches a specific, predetermined point? And do we walk into certain, fixed levels of development as we mature individually and collectively? This is what Ichazo is implying. He also sees trialectics as the next stage or level of human cognition into which we must move if we are to survive. His claims for the significance of his insights are virtually unlimited.

Related to the concept of MMPs is the notion of change occurring at the margin. The last few calories of heat added to water change it to vapor; the final straw breaks the camel's back. Every straw contributed to the fracture, but the final added increment triggered the damage. An instinct for when people and systems are on the margin is one of the greatest gifts a manager or leader or spouse can have. Who can address change without noting when a system is on the margin? Jude Wanniski reminds us that while very few people think on the margin, we all act on the margin" (Wanniski 1978: 43).

> Individuals who can think on the margin always have an advantage over those who cannot. In suffering less illusion they have greater control over their lives. . . . Mother sees father, for what appears to be very little reason, yelling at the children. If she does think on the margin, she will probe to find out what is bothering him, thereby removing from his back not the 10,001st straw, but several down in the rest of the bundle. . . . The same is true of managers, politicians, economists. The most successful are not necessarily those with the greatest raw intelligence, but those with the widest life experience feeding an ability to think on the margin. (Wanniski 1978: 43–44)

At what point do increases in taxes result in a decrease in revenue? At what point do attention and affection in a human relationship become stifling and limiting? At what point is direction and support from a supervisor seen as a vote of no-confidence or mistrust? How can we at home, at school and in the workplace help ourselves and others to think on the margin, read the symptoms of impending fracture in others, and react appropriately? These are questions worth pondering as we think about change and transformation. If Ichazo is right—that change occurs at points predetermined by the structure of the system, and that one cannot force some patterns of behavior into the wrong shelves or resting points of energy—we should rethink the modes of influence we apply in everything from childrearing to on-the-job training.

I want to go back to the basic notion of paradox. Cameron and Quinn, in their introductory discussion, point out that paradox is a situation, or the perception of a situation, in which contradictory elements are simultaneously present, but about which we do not have to choose, as is the case with a dilemma. This is significant for leadership and management, because it is usually our own discomfort with paradox that urges us to eradicate it and opt for the replacement model of formal logic.

The simplicity of this point is deceptive. For several years now, I have watched the leaders of a large public institution send its members on one fruitless reorganization mission after another. The bias of replacement and the trap of thinking that a unit or a bureau must be uniquely one thing or another are alluring pitfalls indeed. And the irony of these particular traps is that the changes leaders make are often politically oriented, and ego centered. In our efforts to distance ourselves from the failure of the previous regime, we are sometimes met at the back door with the same problem we had just chased out the front door. The swings between decentralization and centralization and coercive control and no accountability are part of the history of many institutions. But Ford and Backoff give good advice when they caution against being too eager to avoid the discomfort of paradox by replacing the sources of pain, or choosing the opposite of what we think is the problem.

The word *paradox* comes from the Greek "paradoxos," from "para," meaning against or over, and "doxos," meaning contrary to the received wisdom or common sense. We use the word paradox in everyday life when we are puzzled by what is going on around us. We also use it for instances in which we thought something was wrong or invalid, and certainly contradictory, but which turned out to be right, or effective, or appropriate.

This is exactly what the Apostle Paul said to the early Christians in Corinth who were impoverished and persecuted. Paul was trying to get them to see their circumstance, and his own as well, in a different way. He wanted them to embrace the paradox and be transformed to a new level of existence and perception:

> But in all things approving ourselves as the ministers of God, in much patience, in afflictions, in necessities, in distresses.
>
> As unknown, and yet well known, as dying, and behold we live; as chastened and not killed;
>
> As sorrowful yet always rejoicing; as poor yet making many rich; as having nothing, and yet possessing all things (2d Corinthians 6: 4, 9–10)

This is a sublime way of saying, "Things are not what they seem." E.F. Schumacher expresses in modern language a similar thought in a preface to a book about voluntary poverty. Schumacher looks on the dark side of the same point Paul made to the Corinthians. Paul said, this current evil, this present agony, is in truth a source of limitless joy. Things are not what they now seem. Schumacher says (VandenBroeck 1978: iii) this current distraction, this prosperity, this pursuit of the "good life" will eventually bend back on itself and fracture before us. He also said that if we are not prudent we will become what we most hate. Things are not now what they seem:

> But *life,* disconcertingly and reassuringly, is bigger than straight-line logic; it conforms with a kind of *curved* logic which turns things around and often, before you become aware of it, turns them into their opposites.
>   Pacifists become militants.
>   Freedom fighters become tyrants.
>   Blessings become curses.
>   Labor saving devices become intolerable burdens.
>   Help becomes hindrance.
>   More becomes less. (VandenBroeck 1978: xiii)

Schumacher has his finger on perhaps the ultimate paradox, that unbridled efforts can cause what we are tyring to prevent. A parent demands respect and in so demanding inspires his child's rebellion; an insecure supervisor imposes too many controls, and triggers the unlimited capacity of her fellow employees to sabotage her every effort to track and audit their performance. A tyrant ultimately has to face the backlash of revolt. The laws of cause and effect are not as straightforward as we might suppose. The curved logic of E.F. Schumacher that takes into account the passions and needs of real people, and the inevitable recoil of systems on the margin, is a more reliable guide to the way the system really behaves.

When we perceive tension or crisis in our personal lives or our organizations, we have two choices. We can attempt to alter the situation (Lazarus calls this instrumental coping) (Goleman 1985: 51), or we can act on our own *feelings* toward the problem, (emotion focused coping). My impression is that because we live in an increasingly symbolic world, and increasingly dense environments, we tend to use emotion focused methods of dealing with the world rather than the instrumental ones. The irony is that we often come to believe we have changed something out there when, in fact, we have only dealt with our feelings about it. Or, in an intermediate step between emotional and instrumental coping, we have changed the way we describe or talk about or define something, but we have not really changed it at all. This delusion is not always bad, but it is important to know that it occurs. We invent metaphors and images and arguments to justify our choices, or cope with a state of affairs, and then forget that the word is not the thing; that our discourse about something does not necessarily change it. Our justification for the federal deficit doesn't pull us out of debt.

The emergence in modern times of an increasingly symbolic environment is important to any discussion of change. We are, at times, in the same situation as the man in the joke who, wanting to catch a pesty mouse and being out of real cheese, put a picture of a piece of cheese in his mousetrap and caught a picture of a mouse. In an age of information, as we call it, we deal more and more, not with the "concrete apprehension" of one person by another (Levi-Strauss 1963: 365) but through indirect reconstructions. These reconstructions are mediated by written documents, electronic media, and other people who are layered between us in an organizational hierarchy.

Even the practical nuts and bolts of daily life are mediated through countless symbol systems. The economy, for example, often thought to be bedrock platform onto which most human activity settles, is perhaps more symbolic and tenuous than most things we experience. The "real" economy of goods and services is perhaps less concrete and influential than the "symbolic" economy of money and credit. In a culture that has so rapidly moved from an agricultural to a manufacturing to a service economy in which people's personalities are their major capital, and in which the products they provide are so intangible, our symbol systems are playing an ever greater role in our lives.

The major point of difference between trialectics and dialectics, according to Ford and Backoff, is that in trialectics there is no real opposition or rather, no contradiction in nature, but only complementarity or interdependence. Where a dialectical thinker will see two forces locked in opposition and conflict, a trialectical thinker will see a larger system in which *apparent* opposites are framed in a cycle of circulating energy. The equilibrium of the cycle is broken when the balance is disrupted and change to another MMP occurs. This is much easier to accept when one thinks of a relatively benign ecological system like a coast line or a tundra. It is harder to not see "opposites" or contrary forces when one thinks of Hitler's methodical deception of peaceful emissaries from countries all over Europe, while he engineered a massive military build-up that was suddenly unleashed on the world. I'm not sure how Ichazo would describe such conflict, though obviously he believes his framework of trialectics would also encompass such behavior.

In Ford and Backoff's discussion we have an academic synthesis of some important intellectual concepts. I think the devotees of Oscar Ichazo are correct in arguing that there is a kind of higher order thinking we can describe as a "trialectic," and that thinkers such as Bateson, Maruyama, Boulding, Churchman and others have provided some models of that thinking.

But one final point. I have said that an "epistemological transition," as Horn calls it (Horn 1983: iv), is necessary. How is this to come about? How does Ichazo propose to make us more holistic or trialectic in our habits of thought and modes of action? Ichazo believes that the best mode of influence is that of rational argument. He is not talking about a moral revolution but a cognitive one, or at least, he says that the effort to bring about change must focus on the mind. Ichazo says we must understand:

> If there is going to be unity among human beings, it will occur because we have achieved that unity by means of reason, by means of science and not by means of good will. Although good will is a strong and positive quality, it is not enough, as human history has proved ad nauseum. We must agree about our spiritual reality, and about what our psyche is. (Horn 1983: iii)

I think human history has also proved that rational appeals alone are seldom sufficient to move a culture in any direction. That was certainly one of the lessons of the enlightenment in Western Europe. And how exactly does Ichazo propose to help us agree about our spiritual reality, a topic even more contentious and ego-driven than sports and politics? But what is the real persuasive power of Ichazo's ideas? I submit it is found in Ichazo himself. The real devotees of his method are those who have lived and worked with him, and who have joined him not only in discussion, but in the mediation and spiritual exercises so central to his philosophy. Oscar Ichazo is presenting not a way of thinking, but a way of being and acting. I would further argue that discussions of how to think are most effective when a person has already committed to a prescribed way of behaving; that we can act ourselves into a better mode of thinking more readily than we can think ourselves into a better mode of acting. And the most powerful sources of influence are relationships, not arguments, or reasons, or methods. This point should, I think, be central to any attempt to understand or implement change.

REFERENCES

Gardner, Howard. 1985. *The Mind's New Science*. New York: Basic Books.

Goleman, Daniel. 1985. *Vital Lies and Simple Truths: The Psychology of Self-Deception*. New York: Simon and Schuster.

Hawkes, Terrence. 1977. *Structuralism and Semiotics*. Berkeley: University of California Press.

Horn, Robert E. 1983. *Trialectics: Toward a Practical Logic of Unity*. Lexington, Mass.: Lexington Institute.

Ichazo, Oscar. 1982. *Between Metaphysics and Protoanalysis*. New York: Arica.

Lebeck, Michael, and Burton Voorhees. 1984. "Laws of Thought." Lexington Institute Monograph no. 84-101. Lexington, Mass.: Lexington Institute.

Levi-Strauss, Claude. 1963. *Structural Anthropology*. New York: Basic Books.

VandenBroeck, Goldian, ed. 1978. *Less Is More: The Art of Voluntary Poverty*. New York: Harper & Row.

Wanniski, Jude. 1978. *The Way the World Works*. New York: Simon and Schuster.

4 THE DYNAMICS OF PERSONAL AND ORGANIZATIONAL REFRAMING

Jean M. Bartunek

Organizational transformation necessarily involves reframing. For example, virtually all definitions of transformational leadership in organizations view one of its integral components as the development in organizational members of a qualitatively different and more encompassing vision of what the organization might be (Bass 1985; Roberts 1985; Tichy and Ulrich 1984). Descriptions of other types of transformation, such as one resulting from a bank merger (Buono, Bowditch, and Lewis 1985), also focus on the qualitatively different understandings that organization members develop. Such reframing is frequently achieved through paradoxical processes.

Superficial shadows of transformation also occur. On these occasions, organizational members learn to pay lip service to new perspectives without really owning or, perhaps, understanding them. On these occasions, in other words, reframing does not take place. Because apparently similar, but actually dissimilar, change occurs in both transformation and its shadow, an important issue for understanding transformation is determining whether reframing has really occurred. That issue is the first focus of this chapter.

The literature addressing organizational transformation sometimes gives the impression that it is both desirable and relatively easy for a

I am grateful for the helpful comments of Teresa Amabile, Kim Cameron, David Donovan, Michael Harrison, John Kimberly, Meryl Louis, Marilyn McMorrow, Robert Quinn, and William Torbert.

leader to change organizational members' understandings to frames that correspond closely to those the leader wants (e.g., Akin and Hopelain 1986; Allen 1985). This view is implicit in the understanding that a normal component of managers' jobs is the management of subordinates' "meaning" (Pfeffer 1981; Smircich and Morgan 1982). It is also consistent with the expectation that organizations can socialize new members in such a way that they fully adopt the organization's perspective on different issues. However, processes of significant transformation in understanding are much more complex than is sometimes assumed. Thus, the second focus of this chapter is the development of a model which more adequately describes the reframing process.

Reframing has been discussed on both individual and organizational levels, occasionally with some overlap between the two. Many approaches to reframing (e.g., Bartunek, Gordon, and Weathersby 1983; Ball-Rokeach, Rokeach, and Grube 1984) deal with changes in individuals' understandings. Other approaches (e.g., Bartunek 1984; Gray, Bougon, and Donnellon 1985; Kilmann, Saxton, and Serpa 1985) deal more with ways organizations, or subgroups within them, change their understandings. This chapter addresses reframing processes in both individuals and organizations.

DEFINITION OF TERMS

The term "frame" is similar to many other terms developed recently to describe ways people make sense of situations. The most commonly used of these terms is probably "schema." A frame, or schema, is best understood as a generalized cognitive structure, framework, or template people use to impose structure on, and impart meaning to, some particular domain. Schemata include several components, including general knowledge about the domain, specifications of its attributes and the relationships among them, and specific instances, or examples, of the domain (Bartunek and Moch 1987; Crocker, Fiske, and Taylor 1984; Fiske and Taylor 1984; Gioia 1986; Lord and Foti 1986; Markus and Zajonc 1985; Neisser 1976; Weick 1979). Although schemata do not include affective and behavioral components, they cue and are cued by affect and behavior (Fiske and Taylor 1984).

Based on this description, reframing primarily refers to the imposition of a qualitatively new framework or template on some particular domain, a new "lens" for seeing and understanding it. Reframing is a qualitative, discontinuous, "second-order" or "double-loop" shift in the understanding of some domain (Argyris and Schön 1974; Bartunek and Moch 1987; Ford and Backoff, Chapter 3; Watzlawick, Weakland, and Fisch 1974), not an incremental modification of previous understanding. That is, reframing does not occur if a person holds an opinion more or less strongly than before, or if there is a slight nuance in understanding that was not present before. It does occur if a person adopts a qualitatively different opinion than previously.

Assumptions Underlying the Approach

Several assumptions underlie this paper. The first is that any particular experience can be understood in multiple ways (Ferrier 1986; Gergen 1982; Goffman 1974; Steier and Smith 1985; Woodruff and Engle 1985). In most situations there is not one objective "correct" understanding, although some understandings (including paradoxical ones) take more components of a situation into account than others do (Crocker, Fiske, and Taylor 1984).

The second assumption, following Torbert (1985, 1987), is that it is possible to describe two qualitatively different types of frames. In reality, these represent two ends of a continuum of centrality to a person. At one end are perspectives on a particular situation that derive at least partially from factors that are not part of a person's central identity. For example, a caddy and a golfer interpret a golf game in very different ways, simply because of their different roles (Goffman 1974). At the other end of the spectrum are overall world views, integrated and consistent sets of beliefs, values, assumptions and understandings (e.g., Kegan 1982; Loevinger 1976). These are much more central. While the process of reframing of both situationally based perspectives and world views is similar, it is much more difficult to reframe world views, because of their greater centrality.

A third assumption is that reframing occurs when a person already has a perspective on a situation and that perspective changes. There are some situations when, perhaps because of lack of experience, a person has no particular perspective on the situation at all. The process of initial development of a frame differs considerably from the process accompanying a change in perspective.

Finally, the fourth assumption is that there is a substantial difference between "true" reframing, which involves a change in root understanding, and paying lip service to, or "mouthing" a new perspective. This difference is similar to the difference between theories in use and espoused theories (Argyris and Schön 1974).

THE REFRAMING PROCESS

The beginnings of reframing are fairly well agreed upon (Ball-Rokeach, Rokeach, and Grube 1984; Bartunek 1984; Crocker, Fiske, and Taylor 1984; Kegan 1982; Osiek 1986). Every reframing process starts with some particular trigger or instigator, a statement, person, or an important event that, in Lewin's (1947) terms, "unfreezes" a particular way of understanding a situation, that is, indicates that this understanding is inadequate or wrong. The instigator may also (explicitly or implicitly) indicate a way of understanding that is qualitatively different than the one currently used. The challenge to the present understanding usually has to be very strong; once particular frames are developed, they tend to endure (Nystrom and Starbuck 1984; Wicker 1985).

What happens after the original message is communicated to the person or organization? What is the process through which reframing takes place?

These questions have not often been asked. Crocker, Fiske, and Taylor (1984), and Markus and Zajonc (1985), for example, suggest that much less is known about processes of change in frames than about their structure. These questions form the basis for the discussion that will follow.

While processes of reframing have not been discussed very much, there have been dynamic models developed in other areas. One which is particularly pertinent is creativity. As will be shown below, true reframing, when changes occur in the root understanding of some phenomenon, has characteristics that are similar to creative activity. I will use a model of the creative process as a basis for developing a similar model of processes of reframing. I will apply this model to the reframing process in both individuals and organizations.

CREATIVITY AS A MODEL FOR REFRAMING

Amabile (1983: 33) defines a creative act as follows: "a product or response will be judged as creative to the extent that (a) it is both a novel and appropriate, useful, correct or valuable response to the task at hand,

and (b) the task is heuristic rather than algorithmic." The two "hallmark characteristics" of a creative act, according to Amabile, are its novelty and appropriateness. The fact that the task is heuristic means that there are not already developed algorithms for solving it; the process is to be "discovered" (cf. Getzels and Csikszentmihalyi 1976).

This definition suggests why creativity may be used as a basis for understanding reframing. When reframing occurs the frame developed is, almost by definition, "novel" for the individual or organization developing it. Moreover, since the instigation for reframing is a challenge to the appropriateness of the original frame, the new frame developed is likely to be experienced as more fitting. Finally, there is unlikely to be an algorithm developed for achieving a discontinuous shift in perspectives. Already developed algorithms only work within predefined frameworks.

If reframing can be considered as creative, then it is reasonable to explore the creative process as a basis for understanding reframing. The popular view of this process is that the creative product simply springs full blown from the head of the creative person, just as Athena emerged full blown from the head of Zeus (cf. Rothenberg 1979). But the process is not quite so simple.

The Creative Process

In 1926 Wallas gave an informal description of four stages of creative thinking that is still widely used. He labeled these stages preparation, incubation, illumination, and verification. Amabile (1983: 78–81) built on this description to develop a more detailed five-stage framework of the creative process. Her framework will be presented here, and then modified to apply to reframing. It is summarized in Figure 4–1.

The initial step in the creative process is the presentation of a task to be engaged in or problem to be solved. Individuals may present the problem to themselves or the task may be presented by someone else.

The second stage in the process is a preparation stage for problem solving. At this point the individual builds up or reactivates information relevant to the problem or task, including knowledge of response algorithms for working problems in the domain in question. This stage will take very little or a considerable amount of time in inverse proportion to the amount of information already available.

In the third stage the individual generates response possibilities to the task by searching through the available information and exploring

Figure 4–1.   Stages of the Creative Process.

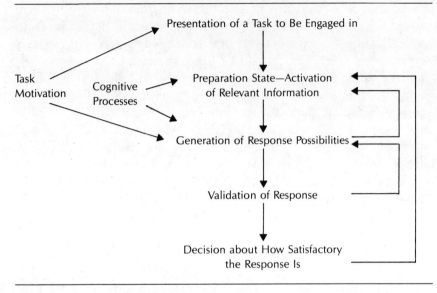

Source: Based on Amabile (1983).

relevant environmental features. The more possibilities explored, the greater the number of response possibilities generated, and the more the person "plays" with the information generated (i.e., takes risks and attends to environmental aspects not obviously relevant to attainment of a solution), the more likely the eventual product is to be novel (the first hallmark characteristic of creativity).

In the fourth stage one or more of the responses is validated. That is, the person tests a particular response for appropriateness against relevant criteria, and determines if the response is appropriate, correct, useful, and valuable (the second hallmark characteristic of creativity). This testing can take place mentally and/or behaviorally.

Finally, the fifth stage is a decisionmaking stage. Here the person decides how satisfactory the outcome is. If there is satisfaction, the process terminates. If there is partial satisfaction, a sense of "getting warmer," the process returns to the first stage and begins again.

This model indicates that creativity has cyclical trial and error characteristics. The outcome of one round of creative work often begins another. In addition, cycles continually take place within the creative process. For example, if the outcome of response generation is not adequate, the person may return to information gathering.

Factors Affecting the Creativity of the Outcome

I have already suggested some factors, built into Amabile's (1983) model, which will affect the creativity of a particular outcome. These include the number of response possibilities produced and the degree to which the person plays with the information developed. Other factors affecting the creativity of a particular outcome have been identified, including various personality characteristics and conceptual and environmental blocks (Adams 1979; Amabile 1983; Getzels and Csikszentmihalyi 1976; McCaskey 1982). Two factors which are particularly relevant to reframing include the type of information generated during the preparation and response generation stages (Rothenberg 1979; 1986) and the constraints on a person to achieve a particular outcome. In the creativity literature, the constraint most frequently discussed is the task motivation of the person engaged in the task (Deci 1972). Information generation and the constraints exemplified by extrinsic motivation are discussed below.

Information Generation. A considerable amount of research (for example, Koestler 1964; Mednick 1962; Rothenberg 1979, 1986) suggests that not only the quantity of information generated during the preparation and response generation stages, but also the type of information generated and the way the information is perceived, are crucial to creativity. This research has focused on the fact that creativity necessarily involves paradoxical elements, that is, the simultaneous presence of contradictory components. Koestler (1964), for example, proposed that creativity depends on perceiving a situation in two self-consistent, but habitually incompatible frames of reference. Recently, Rothenberg (1979) has developed a detailed theory of types of paradox that might be present. He has suggested that information might be combined in either of two ways, which he has labelled "Janusian" and "homospatial" thinking. Janusian thinking involves "actively conceiving two or more opposite or antithetical ideas, images, and concepts simultaneously" (Rothenberg 1979: 55). Homospatial thinking occurs when someone actively conceives "two or more discrete entities occupying the same space" (Rothenberg 1986: 379). Wolfgang Pauli's notion of the necessity in physics for a synthesis of rational understanding and the mystical experience of unity (cf. Wilber 1984) illustrates Janusian thinking. The imposition in the mind of concrete objects such as rivers, discrete sensations such as "rough," and sound patterns and written words are illustrations of homospatial thinking. According to Rothenberg, processes such as Janusian and homospatial thinking are necessary for the creation of novel images.

Task Motivation. Task motivation also affects creativity. Amabile and her coworkers (e.g., Amabile 1983, 1985; Amabile, Hennessey, and Grossman 1986) have conducted several studies whose results indicate that the degree to which a person is intrinsically motivated to perform a task, that is, interested in it for its own sake rather than because of external factors such as potential rewards or sanctions, has a substantial impact on creativity. Intrinsic motivation affects creativity at two stages of the creative process. It affects it at the very beginning: the more intrinsically motivated a person is to develop a new understanding, the more willing the person will be to become engaged in the process. It also affects the response generation stage. The more intrinsically motivated people are, the more likely they are to play with information to form multiple, novel, responses.

Both the type of information generation that takes place and the types of constraints experienced by those engaged in reframing should affect its outcome. The ways these factors affect reframing will be incorporated into the discussion of the reframing process.

Additional Factors Relevant to Reframing

Research in creativity can help us understand reframing, but it needs to be supplemented. Affect, which is an integral component of reframing, has been addressed only minimally in studies of creativity. Affective components of reframing are discussed below.

The outcome measures considered for creativity are often thought of somewhat differently than those considered for reframing. The major outcome variable in assessments of creativity is the extent to which the product is creative, defined as novel and appropriate. This is also an important outcome of reframing, but it is not always the one at least implicitly desired by people who instigate reframing processes. The desirable outcome for such people is often that others come to understand some phenomenon in some specific way, not a "creative" one.

I propose that the way new frames are really developed is through a process similar to the creative one. If a manager or someone else strongly pressures a person to understand some phenomenon in such a way that the outcome of the reframing process is constrained, the person is less likely to begin the process, but, instead, simply to pay lip service to the new perspective. In this case, unless something happens that allows the person to struggle with the new and old perspectives, the perspective eventually adopted is less likely to be understood or to endure. When the person does have the opportunity to experience the interplay of perspectives, the frame the person adopts may or may not be exactly that desired by the other person.

THE PROCESS OF INDIVIDUAL REFRAMING

In the following pages I present a model of individual reframing adapted from the above description of the creative process. A summary of the stages of reframing is shown in Figure 4–2. These stages are conceptually distinct, but may overlap in practice. After presentation of the model and of factors affecting the reframing process, I give an example of this process.

As suggested above, reframing commences with an event that signals that the present framework for understanding no longer works. This challenge to the present frame, if sufficiently strong, "unfreezes" the

Figure 4–2.   Stages of Individual and Organizational Reframing.

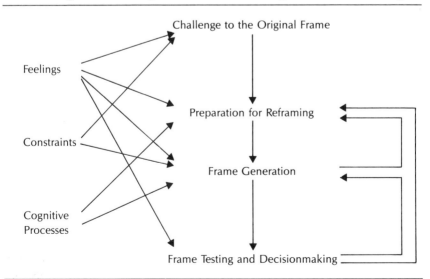

present understanding and initiates the process of developing a more adequate one. The challenge may come from internal or external sources. That is, individuals themselves may experience particular frames as inadequate for understanding. Conversely, they may be convinced by others that their frame is inadequate.

The second stage is followed by a "preparation for reframing" in which the person builds up information that will be used to develop new understandings. This new information might emerge from external suggestions and/or internal cognitive processes. It is likely that it takes place subconsciously. At its beginning, at least, the person is unlikely to be aware that information relevant to new frames is developing. The primary awareness is likely to be of the loss of the old frame (e.g., Kegan 1982).

During the preparation stage, the individual may accumulate a few or several, similar, discrepant, or totally contradictory pieces of information relevant to potential new frames. The discrepant information, if held jointly with other information and/or with the original perspective, has the potential for generating janusian or homospatial thinking.

In the third stage, frame generation, the individual more or less consciously searches through the information that has been accumulating, and develops possible new understandings from it. The new frames may be more or less novel, depending on factors such as the amount and diversity of information accumulated and whether the person's thinking and playing processes enable janusian or homospatial combinations. As suggested above, there is likely to be considerable cycling back and forth between this and the second stage.

In the fourth stage, testing, a particular frame is more or less consciously tried out (either mentally or behaviorally) to determine its appropriateness. In this stage, for example, a person might start to act out of a particular new frame or think about what acting out of it might mean. If the frame feels comfortable and right it is adopted; if not, the process of frame generation cycles back to an earlier stage or begins again. This process results eventually in a new understanding of a particular situation.

Affective Aspects of Reframing

Affect is a component of reframing at several stages of the process. Showers and Cantor (1985), for example, indicate that some moods, such as chronic depression, tend to be associated with narrow, inflexible cognitive processes. When these moods are present, the process is unlikely to begin: any major change in understanding is less likely to occur.

Even when such moods are not present, the awareness of discrepant information that initiates reframing typically includes negative feelings. There is bound to be some tension associated with the breakdown of the original frame (e.g., Lofland and Stark 1965), and this tension may be accompanied by anger (Osiek 1986). Initial stages of the process, at least when the frame concerns an issue that is important to a person, may include a strong sense of loss (e.g., Kegan 1982; Tannenbaum and Hanna 1985).

Early in the preparation stage it is normal to experience an impasse, when it is clear that former understandings are inadequate, but no new adequate ones have consciously evolved (cf. Fitzgerald 1984). This experience is sometimes accompanied by anxiety or hopelessness that an adequate understanding can be reached.

When new ways of understanding do begin to become conscious, there may be a sense of a plethora of possibilities with no clear criteria for choice. This experience may generate a sense of anxiety or panic. There may also be positive feelings at this point if the person is playing with possible ideas or frames. There may be at least occasional enjoyment of the playing.

For successful reframing to occur, it is necessary for the person to allow the various negative and positive feelings to occur, to move through them rather than avoid them. The achievement of the new understanding, when it happens, is likely to be accompanied by a sense of clarity, as well as satisfaction.

Factors Affecting Reframing

As is the case with creativity, capacities for combining discrepant information should affect the reframing process. The more people can allow discrepant pieces of information to exist simultaneously with each other, the more likely the frames they develop should be novel ones, truly different from their original perspective. This capacity will depend in part on individuals' cognitive complexity, the extent to which they already have the capability for viewing phenomena from multiple perspectives (Bartunek, Gordon, and Weathersby 1983).

External constraints on the acceptable outcome of reframing should affect the reframing process during two stages. They should affect whether the process is begun at all and the novelty of the frames developed.

In particular, external constraints on the outcomes of reframing should affect the beginnings of reframing. If people feel they have no choice in the acceptable manner of understanding, but are strongly pressured to adopt a particular perspective, it is unlikely that they will pass through all the steps of reframing. Instead, they are more likely either to reject the new perspective or to pay lip service to it, without making it their own. The new perspective will not be fully understood, and in times of meaningful challenge is unlikely to endure.

When the reframing process is begun, the types of constraints present should affect the range of alternate understandings generated. Strong external pressures to adopt a particular perspective should decrease the playfulness of frame generation, thus decreasing the paradoxical possibilities presented by discrepant information. Consequently, new frames developed should be less creative than they might otherwise be.

An Illustration of Individual Reframing

The reframing process for individuals can be illustrated with an example derived from discussion about the facilitation of quality circles in Quality of Working Life programs. Some concern has been expressed in unions that facilitating quality circles causes union members to take the perspective of management (e.g., Parker, 1985). Based on the reframing model presented above, I will suggest ways this or other outcomes may occur.

The first issue to be considered is whether the reframing process will begin at all. One factor which has an effect here is whether the challenge to the union perspective is strong enough; if not, no reframing will take place. Another is the type of external constraints the individual experiences. If pressure to adopt a managerial perspective is strong enough, the person might not begin the reframing process, but, instead, either refuse the facilitator position out of hand or espouse the management perspective without thinking about it. If the process does begin, the route through which the union representative will arrive at a particular perspective will be similar to the reframing model presented above.

In the first stage of the process, union facilitators may have their union perspective challenged. The challenge may come, for example, if the training for the facilitator role focuses on "learning to think the company way." This type of challenge generates a considerable amount of tension.

In the preparation stage, the strongest experience may be one of impasse. Perhaps the union perspective no longer seems adequate, but thinking the company way isn't right either. Consequently, the person is likely to feel somewhat at a loss. During this stage, information pertinent to new possible understandings of the union member's role should develop, although the person may not be aware that this is happening. The information will be based on learning the company perspective, while simultaneously being a member of the union. The different pieces of information are likely to be somewhat contradictory; thus, they have the potential for fostering janusian thinking. The person's cognitive complexity will affect the extent to which he or she is able to hold the different pieces of discrepant information simultaneously, for example to perceive the "company" and "union" perspective at the same time.

In the third stage, the person will combine the discrepant information in ways that result in several different possible understandings that might be applied to the new role. These might include, for example: "I am a union member who can also appreciate the company"; "The company isn't as bad as I thought"; or "The company is out to control the union even more than I thought."

Eventually, the union facilitator will more or less consciously try out one of the understandings developed previously, perhaps by expressing opinions in terms of it and determining the reaction to them. When a particular understanding feels "comfortable," it will be adopted.

Implications for Management

As suggested at the beginning of this paper, much literature dealing with the way managers "manage" subordinates' understanding implies that a manager can have substantial influence on subordinates' frames (cf. Smircich and Morgan 1982; Wilkins and Patterson 1985). However, as Thomas's (in press) recent work suggests, managers' true influence capacities may be somewhat limited. It seems likely that what many managers do is put pressure on subordinates to adopt some particular perspective, thus inducing them to pay lip service to particular viewpoints rather than beginning the reframing process (cf. Davis 1985; Smircich and Morgan 1982). It is a fair guess that one reason many business fads *are* fads is that many organizational members never develop their own understanding of and responses to particular organizational problem solutions; they are simply told to adopt some particular perspective and they do it ("Business Fads . . ." 1986).

While managers cannot totally control reframing, they can affect it in two ways: by presenting an initial stimulus for reframing, and by establishing conditions that enable janusian and/or homospatial thinking. These factors are discussed below.

First, a manager can have a considerable impact on the initiation of reframing by making subordinates aware of limitations of the perspectives they hold and by suggesting alternative perspectives. There are several methods that may be used to achieve this effect. For example, Torbert (1985: 68) describes an occasion in which he used role reversal to initiate the process. He asked participants in a consultation, a president and vice president of a company, simply to take each other's roles for a time, so they could understand each other's perspectives. Bartunek, Gordon, and Weathersby (1983) and Weathersby, Bartunek, and Gordon (1982) suggest that reframing can be initiated if people are helped to set aside their habitual mode of understanding and "get into the head" of people who take a different perspective. This step is accomplished more easily if people who typically take the alternative perspective help the other learn it. Thus, for example, members of an accounting department might help members of a human resources department to understand organizational functioning from the perspective of accountants. A third approach is simply to "relabel" particular actions, to suggest different meanings or implications that can be attached to them. This is common in some approaches to psychotherapy (e.g., Bandler and Grinder 1982). The purpose of all of these strategies is to initiate the reframing process; if reframing is to occur, the remaining stages of the process will have to take place as well.

Two conditions are important. The first is supporting the reframing process, appreciating its difficulty but encouraging people to pass through its various stages. The second, complementary, condition is refraining from constraining the outcome of the process. That is, although the manager may introduce a particular alternative perspective, the manager does not control or demand adoption of that perspective.

The above recommendations have janusian characteristics. They suggest that managers set the change process in motion in a specific direction, but do not constrain its outcomes. Managers should be simultaneously encouraging and neutral (Ferrier 1986), both taking control and fostering autonomy. This dual, janusian focus should increase the discrepant information that individuals experience. Those who have the cognitive capacity for dealing with such discrepant information should be more likely to develop creative new understandings; that is, they should be more likely to develop understandings that go beyond their own or their manager's original perspective.

ORGANIZATIONAL REFRAMING

Organizations (and groups within them) also have frames. Organizational frames, sometimes referred to as organizational schemata, interpretive schemes, or culture (cf. Bartunek 1984; Jelinek, Smircich, and Hirsch 1983), are shared meanings or frames of reference in the organization as a whole or particular subgroup in it (e.g., Bartunek and Moch 1987; Gioia 1986; Gray, Bougon, and Donnellon 1985; Ouchi and Wilkins 1985; Smircich 1983; Shrivastava and Schneider 1984). Organizational frames are often sustained and communicated through organizational myths, stories, and dominant metaphors (Martin 1982; Martin, Feldman, Hatch, and Simkin 1983). They are unlikely to serve all organizational members' interests equally (Giddens 1979; Gray, Bougon, and Donnellon 1985). Those whose interests are slighted are unlikely to have the same perspectives as those whose interests are being adequately looked after.

Reframing in individuals refers to a discontinuous change in a person's understanding. Reframing in organizations refers to a discontinuous change in the organization's (or group's) shared meaning, or culture.

Processes of Organizational Reframing

Processes of organizational reframing have been discussed by several authors (e.g., Bartunek 1984; Gray, Bougon, and Donnellon 1985; Gemmill and Smith 1985; Smith 1986). The discussion in those papers is consistent with the proposition that organizational reframing proceeds through stages similar to those associated with reframing processes for individuals. However, the process in organizations or organizational subgroups is more complex than the process for individuals, simply because it is likely to include interaction among different groups who hold different perspectives. A description of the reframing process for organizations is presented below.

Organizational reframing usually begins with a crisis that indicates that present shared understandings are no longer adequate (e.g., Bartunek 1984; Fiol and Lyles 1985; Gemmill and Smith 1985; Gray, Bougon, and Donnellon 1985; Tushman and Romanelli 1985). Several types of crisis may occur: performance may be poor, managerial succession may occur, some powerful subgroups' interests may no longer be served by the present frame, management practices may no longer be successful, or there may be a major environmental shift (Bartunek 1984; Gray, Bougon, and Donnellon 1985; Hedberg 1981). To initiate reframing, the experience of crisis must be strong enough to unfreeze dominant organizational members' present understanding (Lewin 1947) by presenting a major challenge to their validity.

For individuals, the second stage of the reframing process, preparation, is the more or less conscious development of new information. A similar, though more complex, process occurs for organizations. Gemmill and Smith (1985) suggest, for example, that after unfreezing takes place there occurs a period of "experimentation" when new information is generated. In individuals this information is generated within the person. In organizations it is likely that different information will be developed in different subgroups, who are more or less aware of each others' understandings.

In individuals, the extent to which the person had the cognitive capacity to hold discrepant pieces of information at this stage was important. Because different organizational information is likely to be generated by different subgroups, the extent to which organizational leaders can hold the discrepant and often contradictory information generated by different groups is crucial to the process.

In the third stage, frame generation, new possible frames are generated from the information developed earlier. This stage is also affected by the existence of multiple subgroups; during it the different subgroups are likely to develop different frames. As the frames are developed and presented, they, and the groups holding them, are likely to interact with each other in some manner. The forms of the interaction may vary: particular perspectives may be presented as dominant or the potential value of several different perspectives may be acknowledged. Organizational leaders will have a strong impact on the form this interaction takes. The extent to which leaders enable different perspectives to be heard simultaneously and accepted will affect how novel the frames that emerge at this stage are.

The processes that take place during the third stage will eventually result, in the fourth stage, in one or more new understandings that incorporate conflicting perspectives to a greater or lesser extent. If conflicting perspectives have been heard and considered simultaneously, the syntheses will not be simply the imposition of one position or compromises between different positions (cf. Cameron 1986). Rather, they will be creative new understandings that are simultaneously novel and appropriate for the organization.

During this fourth stage, organizational members will more or less consciously think or act out of newly developed perspectives. When one is comfortable, they will adopt and "refreeze" a particular shared understanding (Lewin 1947). If no particular understanding is adequate, the process will cycle back to an earlier stage or begin again.

Affective Aspects of the Process.   As is the case with individual reframing, organizational reframing is not affect-free. Rather, there are likely to be strong feelings throughout the process. For example, Hedberg (1981) suggests that the process is often paralyzing and disorienting, and experienced as a sequence of deaths and rebirths. During the initial stages, in addition to the experience of crisis, the primary feeling is likely to be of shock, defensiveness, a strong sense of loss of the formerly shared frame, or anger at it (Deal 1985; Tannenbaum and Hanna 1985; Fink, Beak, and Taddeo 1971; Osiek 1986; Tunstall 1985).

There are likely to be other feelings throughout the transformation process. During the preparation stage, ambiguity and confusion will be experienced, both when it is unclear that any satisfactory new understanding is developing and when multiple conflicting pieces of information begin to develop (e.g., Hoffman 1981). During both this stage and the next one there is likely to be considerable tension and conflict between groups that hold different new perspectives (Bartunek 1984). The final stage, when a new understanding is acceptable, is likely to be accompanied by a sense of "rightness" and satisfaction, at least by members whose perspectives have been incorporated.

Factors Affecting Reframing.   Cognitive processes and constraints both affect the organizational reframing process. As has been noted above, the extent to which different perspectives can simultaneously exist and thus present the potential for paradoxical processes will depend considerably on the ability of leaders to "hold" the different and conflicting perspectives. This includes their ability to appreciate competing perspectives even if they disagree with them as well as not to reject groups which hold deviant ideas out of hand. The more leaders have this capability, the more appropriate and novel the eventual new understanding should be.

External constraints play a role in organizational frame change as well as in individual frame change. Meyer and Rowan (1977), for example, have described ways organizations sometimes develop structural features whose primary purpose is not to reflect deep-seated convictions, but to signal to an external environment that the organization is acceptable. The more reframing comes about because of an experienced need on the part of the organization, rather than simply in response to constraints, the more the organization will pass through the reframing process in such a way that the understandings (and accompanying structural features) it develops are appropriate for itself, rather than simply for the external environment.

An Illustration of Organizational Reframing.   The organizational reframing process can be illustrated with an example (adapted from Bartunek 1984) of a religious order that qualitatively changed its understanding of its educational mission. The order administers several schools, and had, until the 1960s, understood its educational mission to be virtually synonymous with activities in the schools. A challenge to that shared understanding emerged in the late 1960s, when several order members expressed dissatisfaction with working in the order's schools and said that order members should be doing work oriented more explicitly towards social justice. This challenge initiated the reframing process.

During the second stage of the process, new information was developed through the experiences of order members who began doing social justice work and through the development of new organizational arrangemenets for the order's schools. These activities resulted in conflict in the order that was experienced by many as work for justice vs. work in the order's schools.

During the late 1960s and early 1970s, various meetings were held in which the educational mission of the order was discussed. Over the course of the meetings, the third reframing stage took place, in that various definitions of the order's educational mission evolved. For instance, the definition of the mission was first expanded to include teaching in public schools in addition to those of the order, and then came to include justice-oriented work and education as two "options" order members were to choose.

After several years, a new way of understanding the educational mission was reached. The order's leaders began to think of the educational mission in such a way that they no longer considered education to be equivalent with the order's schools, but saw it, instead, as "inseparable from work for justice." The order's leaders experienced this synthesis as asserting the validity of both the school and justice perspectives, but understanding each in a way that extended beyond its original formulation. The synthesis incorporated the conflicting perspectives in a new way—not at the level of specific jobs, either in schools or in social justice-oriented work—but at a deeper level that allowed their simultaneous existence. The fact that the order's leaders allowed both perspectives to exist during the intermediate stages of reframing made a synthesis developed out of both of them possible later.

Implications for Managers

I suggested above that managers concerned about individuals' reframing should focus their attention on setting the process of change in motion and fostering conditions that facilitate freedom in and support the reframing process. These two functions, along with managerial capacity to allow the existence of conflicting perspectives, are important for organizational reframing as well. How can they be carried out in organizational settings?

First, it may not be the manager who creates the initial challenge to the shared understanding; that challenge may come from lower level participants, an external source, or, perhaps, a formally designated change agent (Bartunek 1984; Bartunek and Moch 1987). When the challenge comes from another source, the manager need not initiate change, but may have to respond to it. Often, however, it is the manager who initiates the change process.

Various methods might be used to initiate such processes, most of which have been discussed from the perspective of change agents. Those who describe these methods tend to concur that, while it is possible to initiate reframing, it is not possible to control the overall process. Steier and Smith (1985: 64) comment, for example, "Our actions may be viewed as perturbations. . . . That is, organizations are never changed by the actions of the intervener. The most we can do is catalyze conditions under which change may occur."

What are some processes that may be used to initiate change? One that Bartunek and Moch (1987) suggest for change agents is to advocate strongly a particular frame that differs from the present one. The expectation is not that this new frame will be the one eventually adopted, but that advocating the new frame will cause a "perturbation" in the system that will initiate change.

A second suggestion derived from family therapy (e.g., Siporin and Gummer, Chapter 6; Woodruff and Engle 1985) is to relabel current shared frameworks, perhaps by suggesting a different type of intent than the current one. This might happen, for example, if a manager labels a particular understanding of the organization's mission as detrimental to adaptation rather than helpful to it or says a particular organizational story or symbol no longer describes the reality of the organization. Charles Brown, the chairman of AT&T, illustrated this type of action during its divestiture. He "laid the ancient 'Ma Bell' sobriquet to rest, calling it inadequate to a high technology business" (Tunstall 1985: 51).

During the transformation process it is important to encourage the existence of varying perspectives, in part by supporting different groups. Using planning processes that consciously foster interaction between different perspectives is one way of doing this. For example, Mason and Mitroff (1981) have developed a dialectical inquiry process in which groups that take different perspectives on a particular problem are encouraged to debate each other about underlying assumptions. This process can be used to foster the development of multiple novel frames.

The effects of managerial constraints on the outcomes of organizational reframing are likely to be similar to their effects on individual reframing. The more managers or other change agents place strong pressure on organizational members to adopt a particular understanding, the more likely the organization or group is either to reject the new understanding or simply to pay lip service to it, perhaps by developing structures that signal surface compliance but that do not endure.

Thus, effective managerial action on an organizational reframing also has janusian characteristics. It again includes simultaneous foci on encouragement and neutrality, or on control and autonomy: instigating and encouraging change, but leaving freedom about the content of the outcome. Effective action on this level includes an additional component: acceptance of the simultaneous validity of the perspectives of differing groups. The more effective the manager's controlling and facilitating actions, the more creative, novel, and appropriate the eventual understanding will be.

SUMMARY AND CONCLUSION

The material discussed in this chapter may be summarized as follows. I have proposed that reframing, in both individuals and organizations, follows a course that is similar to creative processes. Reframing begins with a crisis or challenge: to develop a more adequate understanding of some phenomenon than the present understanding. It proceeds to include information gathering, the generation of alternate possible frames, and then trying out and eventually adopting a particular frame. The process has cyclic, trial-and-error components built into it. When particular frames are not acceptable, the process reverts to an earlier stage or begins again.

The course of reframing is affected by the ways discrepant components are considered. The more the simultaneous validity of discrepant elements is accepted, the greater the potential for creative new understandings to develop.

The reframing process includes considerable affect throughout. It begins in tension, is likely to include a sense of loss, hopelessness and confusion, may have some element of playfulness, and eventually results in clarity and satisfaction. While the eventual outcome of the process is likely to be experienced positively, the bulk of it will be affectively difficult.

The process is affected by two important elements: the cognitive capacities of the people involved and constraints imposed by external factors. The more people have the capacity to "hold" two or more differing pieces of information, and the fewer the constraints on them to develop some particular new understanding, the more likely it is that they will develop novel, appropriate understandings.

Finally, effective managerial action during reframing processes is itself "paradoxical," including considerable control over the initiation of reframing or presentation of an alternative perspective, but autonomy and some degree of neutrality with respect to the eventual outcome of reframing. These janusian processes are not easily implemented. Moreover, they increase the likelihood that the outcome of reframing does not correspond fully to the manager's original perspective.

Because of its effects on the outcomes of reframing, this dual focus increases the likelihood that a manager's own perspective can be affected and changed through the manager's fostering of others' reframing. Thus, individuals' and organizations' reframing processes can work in tandem with those of the organization's managers to foster the ongoing development of understanding.

REFERENCES

Adams, J.L. 1979. *Conceptual Blockbusting,* 2d ed. New York: Norton.

Akin, G., and D. Hopelain. 1986. "Finding the Culture of Productivity." *Organizational Dynamics* 14, no. 3: 19–32.

Allen, R.F. 1985. "Four Phases for Bringing about Cultural Change." In *Gaining Control of the Corporate Culture,* edited by R.H. Kilmann, M.J. Saxton, and R. Serpa, pp. 332–50. San Francisco: Jossey-Bass.

Amabile, T.M. 1983. *The Social Psychology of Creativity.* New York: Springer-Verlag.

———. 1985. "Motivation and Creativity: Effects of Motivational Orientation on Creative Writers." *Journal of Personality and Social Psychology* 48: 393–99.

Amabile, T.M., B.A. Hennessey; and B.S. Grossman. 1986. "Social Influences on Creativity: the Effects of Contracted-for Reward." *Journal of Personality and Social Psychology* 50: 14–23.

Argyris, C., D.A. Schön. 1974. *Theory in Practice: Increasing Professional Effectiveness.* San Francisco: Jossey-Bass.

Ball-Rokeach, S.J.; M. Rokeach; and J.W. Grube. 1984. *The Great American Values Test: Influencing Behavior and Belief through Television.* New York: The Free Press.

Bandler, R., and J. Grinder. 1982. *Reframing.* Moab, Utah: Real People Press.

Bartunek, J.M. 1984. "Changing Interpretive Schemes and Organizational Restructuring: The Example of a Religious Order." *Administrative Science Quarterly* 29: 355–72.

Bartunek, J.M.; J.R. Gordon; and R.P. Weathersby. 1983. "Developing 'Complicated' Understanding in Administrators." *Academy of Management Review* 8: 273–84.

Bartunek, J.M., and M.K. Moch. 1987. "First, Second, and Third Order Organization Development Interventions: a Cognitive Approach." *Journal of Applied Behavioral Science* 23: 483–500.

Bass, B.M. 1985. *Leadership and Performance Beyond Expectations.* New York: Free Press.

"Business Fads: What's in—and out." 1986. *Business Week* (January 20): 52–61.

Buono, A.F.; J.L. Bowditch; and J.W. Lewis III. 1985. "When Cultures Collide: the Anatomy of a Merger." *Human Relations* 38: 477–500.

Cameron, K.S. 1986. "Effectiveness as Paradox: Consensus and Conflict in Conceptions of Organizational Effectiveness." *Management Science* 32: 539–53.

Crocker, J.; S.T. Fiske; and S.E. Taylor. 1984. "Schematic Bases of Belief Change." In *Attitudinal Judgment,* edited by J.R. Eiser, pp. 197–226. New York: Springer Verlag.

Davis, T.R.V. 1985. "Managing Culture at the Bottom." In *Gaining Control of the Corporate Culture,* edited by R.H. Kilmann, M.J. Saxton, and R. Serpa, pp. 163–83. San Francisco: Jossey-Bass.

Deal, T.E. 1985. "Cultural Change: Opportunity, Silent Killer, or Metamorphosis." In *Gaining Control of the Corporate Culture,* edited by R.H. Kilmann, M.J. Saxton, and R. Serpa, pp. 292–331. San Francisco: Jossey-Bass.

Deci, E. 1972. "The Effects of Contingent and Noncontingent Rewards and Controls on Intrinsic Motivation." *Organizational Behavior and Human Performance* 8: 217–29.

Ferrier, M. 1986. "Testing the Limits in Milan System Therapy: Working with an Individual." In *Journeys,* edited by D. Effron, pp. 200–21. New York: Brunner/Mazel.

Fink, S.L., J. Beak, and K. Taddeo. 1971. "Organizational Crisis and Change." *Journal of Applied Behavioral Science* 7: 15–37.

Fiol, C.M., and M.A. Lyles. 1985. "Organizational Learning." *Academy of Management Review* 10: 803–13.

Fiske, S.T., and S.E. Taylor. 1984. *Social Cognition.* Reading, Mass.: Addison Wesley.

Fitzgerald, C. 1984. "Impasse and Dark Night." In *Living with Apocalypse,* edited by T.H. Edwards, pp. 93–116. New York: Harper and Row.

Gemmill, G., and C. Smith. 1985. "A Dissipative Structure Model of Organization Transformation." *Human Relations* 38: 751–66.

Gergen, K.J. 1982. *Toward Transformation in Social Knowledge.* New York: Springer-Verlag.

Getzels, J.W., and M. Csikszentmihalyi. 1976. *The Creative Vision.* New York: Wiley.

Giddens, A. 1979. *Central Problems in Social Theory.* Berkeley, Calif.: University of California Press.

Gioia, D.A. 1986. "Symbols, Scripts, and Sensemaking." In *The Thinking Organization,* edited by H.P. Sims and D.A. Gioia, pp. 49–74. San Francisco: Jossey-Bass.

Goffman, E. 1974. *Frame Analysis.* New York: Harper.

Gray, B.; M.G. Bougon; and A. Donnellon. 1985. "Organizations as Constructions and Destructions of Meaning." *Journal of Management* 11: 83–95.

Hedberg, B. 1981. "How Organizations Learn and Unlearn." In *Handbook of Organization Design,* edited by P.C. Nystrom and W.H. Starbuck, vol. 1, pp. 3–27. Oxford: Oxford University Press.

Hoffman, L. 1981. *Foundations of Family Therapy.* New York: Basic Books.

Jelinek, M.; L. Smircich; and P. Hirsch. 1983. "Introduction: A Code of Many Colors." *Administrative Science Quarterly* 28: 331–38.

Kegan, R. 1982. *The Evolving Self.* Cambridge, Mass.: Harvard University Press.

Kilmann, R.H.; M.J. Saxton; and R. Serpa. 1985. *Gaining Control of the Corporate Culture.* San Francisco: Jossey-Bass.

Koestler, A. 1964. *The Act of Creation.* New York: Macmillan.

Lewin, K. 1947. "Frontiers in Group Dynamics." *Human Relations* 1: 1–41.

Loevinger, J. 1976. *Ego Development.* San Francisco: Jossey-Bass.

Lofland, J., and R. Stark. 1965. "Becoming a World-saver: A Theory of Conversion to a Deviant Perspective." *American Sociological Review* 30: 862–75.

Lord, R.G., and R.J. Foti. 1986. "Schema Theories, Information Processing, and Organizational Behavior." In *The Thinking Organization,* edited by H.P. Sims and D.A. Gioia, pp. 20–48. San Francisco: Jossey-Bass.

McCaskey, M.B. 1982. *The Executive Challenge: Managing Change and Ambiguity.* Boston: Pitman.

Markus, H., and R. Zajonc. 1985. "The Cognitive Perspective in Social Psychology." In *The Handbook of Social Psychology,* edited by G. Lindzey and E. Aronson, vol. 1, pp. 137–230. New York: Random House.

Martin, J. 1982. "Stories and Scripts in Organizational Settings." In *Cognitive Social Psychology,* edited by A. Hastorf and A. Isen, pp. 255–305. New York: North Holland.

Martin, J.; M.S. Feldman; M.J. Hatch; and S. Simkin. 1983. "The Uniqueness Paradox in Organizational Stories." *Administrative Science Quarterly* 28: 438–53.

Mason, R.O., and I.I. Mitroff. 1981. *Challenging Strategic Planning Assumptions.* New York: Wiley.

Mednick, S. 1962. "The Associative Basis of the Creative Process." *Psychological Review* 69: 220–32.

Meyer, J.M., and B. Rowan. 1977. "Institutionalized Organizations: Formal Structure as Myth and Ceremony." *American Journal of Sociology* 83: 340–63.

Neisser, U. 1976. *Cognition and Reality.* San Francisco: Freeman.

Nystrom, P., and W.H. Starbuck. 1984. "To Avoid Organizational Crises, Unlearn." *Organizational Dynamics* 12, no. 4: 53–65.

Osiek, C. 1986. *Beyond Anger.* Boston: Paulist Press.

Ouchi, W.G., and A.L. Wilkins. 1985. "Organizational Culture." *Annual Review of Sociology* 11: 457–83.

Parker, M. 1985. *Inside the Circle: a Union Guide to QWL*. Boston: South End Press.

Pfeffer, J. 1981. "Management as Symbolic Action: The Creation and Maintenance of Organizational Paradigms." In *Research in Organizational Behavior*, edited by L.L. Cummings and B.M. Staw, vol. 3, pp. 1–51. Greenwich, Conn.: JAI Press.

Roberts, N.C. 1985. "Transforming Leadership: a Process of Collective Action." *Human Relations* 38: 1023–46.

Rothenberg, A. 1979. *The Emerging Goddess*. Chicago: University of Chicago Press.

———. 1986. "Artistic Creation as Stimulated by Superimposed Versus Combined-composite Visual Images." *Journal of Personality and Social Psychology* 50: 370–81.

Showers, C., and N. Cantor. 1985. "Social Cognition: A Look at Motivated Strategies." *Annual Review of Psychology* 36: 275–305.

Shrivastava, P., and S. Schneider. 1984. "Organizational Frames of Reference." *Human Relations* 37: 795–807.

Smircich, L. 1983. "Organizations as Shared Meaning." In *Organizational Symbolism*, edited by L.R. Pondy, P. Frost, G. Morgan, and T. Dandridge, pp. 55–65. Greenwich, Conn.: JAI Press.

Smircich, L., and G. Morgan. 1982. "Leadership: the Management of Meaning." *Journal of Applied Behavioral Science* 18: 257–73.

Smith, C. 1986. "A Process Model of Whole-System Change in Organizations." Paper presented at meeting of the Academy of Management, Chicago, Illinois, August 13–16.

Steier, F., and K.K. Smith. 1985. "Organizations and Second Order Cybernetics." *Journal of Strategic and Systemic Therapies* 4, no. 4: 53–65.

Tannenbaum, R., and R.W. Hanna. 1985. "Holding On, Letting Go, and Moving On: Understanding a Neglected Perspective on Change." In *Human Systems Development*, edited by R. Tannenbaum, N. Margulies, and F. Massasrik, pp. 95–121. San Francisco: Jossey-Bass.

Thomas, R.J. In press. "Participation and Control: A Shopfloor Perspective on Employee Participation." In *Perspectives in Organizational Sociology: Theory and Research*, edited by S. Bacharach and R. Magjuka. Greenwich, Conn.: JAI Press.

Tichy, N., and D. Ulrich. 1984. "Revitalizing Organizations: The Leadership Role." In *Managing Organizational Transitions*, edited by J.R. Kimberly and R.E. Quinn, pp. 240–66. Homewood, Ill.: Irwin.

Torbert, W.R. 1985. "On-line Reframing: An Integrative Approach to Organizational Management." *Organizational Dynamics*, 14, no. 1: 60–79.

———. 1987. *Managing the Corporate Dream*. Homewood, Ill.: Dow Jones Irwin.

Tunstall, W.B. 1985. "Break-up of the Bell System: A Case Study in Cultural Transformation." In *Gaining Control of the Corporate Culture*, edited by

R.H. Kilmann, M.J. Saxton, and R. Serpa, pp. 44–65. San Francisco: Jossey-Bass.

Tushman, M.L., and E. Romanelli. 1985. "Organizational Evolution: a Metamorphosis Model of Convergence and Reorientation." In *Research in Organizational Behavior,* edited by L.L. Cummings and B.M. Staw, vol. 7, pp. 171–222. Greenwich, Conn.: JAI Press.

Wallas, G. 1926. *The Art of Thought.* New York: Harcourt, Brace.

Watzlawick, P.; J.H. Weakland; and R. Fisch. 1974. *Change: Principles of Problem Formation and Problem Resolution.* New York: Norton.

Weathersby, R.P.; J.M. Bartunek; and J.R. Gordon. 1982. "Teaching for 'Complicated' Understanding." *Exchange: the Organizational Behavior Teaching Journal* 7, no. 4: 7–15.

Weick, K.E. 1979. *The Social Psychology of Organizing.* Reading, Mass.: Addison-Wesley.

Wicker, A.W. 1985. "Getting Out of Our Conceptual Ruts." *American Psychologist* 40: 1094–1103.

Wilber, K., ed. 1984. *Quantum Questions: Mystical Writings of the World's Great Physicists.* Boulder, Colo.: Shambala Publications.

Wilkins, A.L., and K.J. Patterson. 1985. "You Can't Get There From Here: What Will Make Culture-change Projects Fail." In *Gaining Control of the Corporate Culture,* edited by R.H. Kilmann, M.J. Saxton, and R. Serpa, pp. 262–91. San Francisco: Jossey-Bass.

Woodruff, A.F., and T. Engle. 1985. "Strategic Therapy and Agency Development: Using Circular Thinking to Turn the Corner." *Journal of Strategic and Systemic Therapies* 4, no. 4: 25–29.

REFRAMING AND THE PROBLEM OF ORGANIZATIONAL CHANGE

John R. Kimberly

The editors of this book have granted considerable license to commentators on the various chapters. Having read an earlier version of Bartunek's chapter and having provided comments to the author previously, I will make just a few comments on the chapter *per se* and will use this as an opportunity to reflect more broadly on two themes that the chapter has stimulated me to consider, the problem of organizational change and the interplay between organizational biographies and organizational transitions.

In my view, the basic contribution of Bartunek's chapter is that it provides new language for discussing what is really a very old problem, the problem of introducing and managing change in human systems. It is almost always useful to go outside existing explanatory frameworks and perspectives on a given problem to generate new insights into the problem. Bartunek does this well. By exploring the literature on creative processes, and introducing the concept of reframing into the analysis of organizational transformation, Bartunek challenges the reader to think more deeply about existing frameworks for understanding the change and transformation process. Although I do not believe that she has succeeded in reframing the problem of organizational change, I do think that the introduction of the conceptual apparatus is worthwhile in and of itself.

Two further comments might help stimulate critical reflection on the applicability of the framework Bartunek proposes. First, I wonder about

163

the appropriateness of the stage approach to the analysis of the creative process. There is no question that creative processes unfold, but I have my doubts about how linear these processes are. The stage approach implies linearity, even with feedback loops built in. Somewhat more important, however, is the assumption which appears to underline the description of the creative process presented in Figure 4–1. The first stage in this process is called "Presentation of a task to be engaged in." My own reading of the literature on creativity suggests strongly that perhaps the most fundamental part of the process is the act of seeing a problem or a task where no one else has seen it before. To see an old problem in a new way, or to see a problem or opportunity in an area where no one has previously seen it is central to creativity. It is the rare case where a task is presented in the fashion implied in the model and that this presentation itself engages the creative process. The engagement is stimulated by a concatenation of events which is difficult at best to orchestrate or to manage. To the extent that Bartunek wishes to draw analogies between the creative process and the process of individual and/or organizational reframing, the nonlinear "messy" nature of stimuli to creativity is problematic.

A second issue which deserves further reflection in my view is that of "adoption" of a new "frame." Bartunek's argument is that old frames or ways of thinking are challenged by a variety of data, often conflicting and contradictory, that these conflicts and contradictions are somehow reconciled, and that the understructure of the reconciliation provides the basis for the new frame or understanding. Bartunek argues "If the frame feels comfortable and right it is adopted; if not, the process of frame generation cycles back to an earlier stage or begins again." The problem, of course, is one of possible tautology. How do we know if a frame is adopted? If it feels comfortable. How do we know if it feels comfortable? If it is adopted. There is both a binary quality to the "outcome" (adopted or not adopted) and an implicit "ending" of the cycle that I find to be troublesome. I do not believe that new understandings replace old understandings in the same way that a new rug replaces an old rug. In the later case, you can describe and measure and point to the old rug, you can do the same for the new rug, and the one replaces the other in a temporally obvious way. Not so with understandings. Understandings, in my view, do not have clearly demarcated beginnings and endings. They are characterized much more by flows than they are by sequences. And, as I will argue below, I believe that organizational life is captured much more usefully and fully by models, theories, perspectives, or frames which emphasize flows rather than discrete events, sequences, or stages.

THE PROBLEM OF ORGANIZATIONAL CHANGE

As I read Bartunek's chapter, reframing is more about the problem of organizational change than it is about paradox. Paradox may be embedded in the organizational change process and reframing may therefore provoke or stem from paradox, but the central phenomenon that Bartunek describes is the phenomenon of change or transformation. In many ways, the themes that emerge in Bartunek's analysis of change and transformation are reminiscent of work on organizational change produced in the mid-1960s to mid-1970s. That work saw the problem of organizational change as complex, but as subject to managerial control through careful application of certain techniques of "planned change." Central to the ideology of planned change was the notion that "real" change was only likely if the people who were supposed to do the changing "owned" or "bought into" the process and the outcome. This meant that those affected by the change had to understand it and to see the benefits of it for themselves before they could be expected to embrace it. This idea, of course, is as old as Greek philosophy. That it has endured for so long is testimony to the simple truth that it represents.

One reads in Bartunek's thinking about reframing many of the same fundamental ideas about the forces that lead people and organizations to change. It interests me to note how widespread the acknowledgment of the simple truth is and yet how widespread behavioral ignorance of the simple truth is at the same time. Is this not paradoxical?

INERTIA AND TRANSITION

Bartunek's discussion of the reframing process suggests that the process starts with some event that acts as a "trigger." She states further "The challenge to the present understanding usually has to be very strong; once particular frames are developed they tend to endure." This observation is one which has been made by other people who have been interested in the problem of organizational change as well. "Resistance to change" seems to be the rule rather than the exception. People resist, frames endure, change efforts become sidetracked, powerful forces tend to reinforce the *status quo.*

What accounts for what many experience or describe as organizational inertia? Or, phrased differently, why are organizational transitions —major changes in organizational strategy, structure and/or process (Kimberly and Quinn 1984)—relatively infrequent? Some recent work that several colleagues and I have done on the creation of new organizations is beginning to provide some answers, I believe, to these questions (Kimberly 1979; Kimberly, Norling, and Weiss 1983; Kimberly 1987; Kimberly and Rottman 1987). The concept of organizational "biography" and serious exploration of its implications reveal the understructure of the forces for stability.

In some respects, organizations are like individual people. Every human being shares certain attributes as a consequence of being a person. He or she also has a unique genetic makeup and a unique set of life experiences. No effort to understand individual behavior would be complete without taking both the unique and the common into account.

Organizations are like individual people in that they are both unique in some ways and share some common attributes. They are like individual people in another important respect as well; yesterday's events shape today's behavior and constrain tomorrow's options. Just as it is helpful to know certain things about an individual person's past in understanding and predicting his or her behavior today (different theories, of course, suggest very different dimensions of a person's past as relevant), so it would be helpful to know certain things about an organization's past to understand and predict its current behavior. The concept of biography is intended to focus attention on both the idiographic and the nomethetic aspects of organizational life. It is also intended to move thinking beyond the concept of organizational life cycles, a concept whose limitations are well-known.

Our work in new organizations suggests that, just as for individual people, early experiences and decisions are powerful shapers of later behavior and options. These decisions, we hypothesize, set the organization on a course from which it is difficult, though not impossible, to diverge. Myriad forces reinforce chosen courses, and major transitions are generally infrequent. Change occurs, but is typically incremental rather than revolutionary. Thus, there is the outward appearance of stability, even rigidity. An organization characterized by multiple transitions in a relatively short period of time is exceptional and its behavior would merit special attention.

The framework for understanding organizational biographies that we are developing highlights the importance of four kinds of choices in shaping the developmental trajectory that an organization follows. These are decisions about governance, about domain, about core values (often embedded in expertise), and design. Initial decisions about these four factors together define the basic conditions of the early life experience of every organization and together shape the cognitive and affective environments of individuals in the organization. External forces play a major role in influencing these decisions. No matter how these choices get made, however, they strongly influence the future course of the organization by limiting the range of feasible alternatives, by shaping the internal culture, and by defining the organization's identity. In a rough way, decisions about core values and governance shape culture, and decisions about domain and design define identity. And all four determine how the organization is connected to its environment. The governance structure defines both the set of major stakeholders and potential sources of legitimation and support; domain defines both market niches and clientele; the early hires define a network of contacts with other people in the organization as well as core values; and design reflects how the organization chooses to define its interdependence with its task environment. None of these factors is immutable. However, the magnitude of the effort required to change how an organization thinks of itself and the world around it (and vice versa) should not be underestimated.

The biographical perspective suggests strongly that the problem of organizational inertia is more than a problem of individual "resistance to change," and involves more than the process of unfreezing and refreezing frames at the individual level. There is a set of organization-level issues which derive from the consequences of decisions made early in an organization's life. To change the organizational frame, one needs really to change the fundamental content of at least one, and more likely all of the categories of decisions that we have been discussing. Such change is not impossible, but the magnitude of the task strongly suggests why it is not frequent. The fundamental problem, and in a sense, the paradox, is that the energy and the perspective needed to transform in any one of these four arenas can only come from outside those arenas.

Those who have become a part of the culture and the identity of the organization are those least able to precipitate major changes. For what Bartunek calls organizational reframing to occur, and for what I would call an organizational transition to occur, I would expect substantial external induction and involvement to be required. This, of course, is really an hypothesis about change that needs to be subjected to empirical scrutiny, rather than simply an assertion to be accepted uncritically. Continued serious work on paradox and transformation may well provide the empirical test.

REFERENCES

Kimberly, John R. 1979. "Issues in the Creation of Organizations: Initiation, Innovation, and Institutionalization." *Academy of Management Journal* 22: 437–57.

——— . 1987. "The study of Organization: Toward a Biographical Perspective." In *Handbook of Organizational Behavior,* edited by Jay W. Lorsch, pp. 223–37. Englewood Cliffs, N.J.: Prentice-Hall.

Kimberly, John R.; Frederick Norling; and Janet A. Weiss. 1983. "Pondering the Performance Puzzle: Effectiveness in Interorganizational Settings." In *Organizational Theory and Public Policy,* edited by Richard W. Hall and Robert E. Quinn. Beverly Hills, Calif.: Sage.

Kimberly, John R., and Robert E. Quinn, eds. 1984. *Managing Organizational Transitions.* Homewood, Ill.: Richard D. Irwin.

Kimberly, John R. and David B. Rottman. 1987. "Environment, Structure and Performance: A Biographical View." *Journal of Management Studies* 24: 595–622.

5 PARADOXICAL DEMANDS AND THE CREATION OF EXCELLENCE
The Case of Just-in-Time Manufacturing

Kathleen M. Eisenhardt and Brian J. Westcott

In the past few years, the popular press as well as academic writers have been heralding major changes in manufacturing (e.g., "America's Best-Managed Factories" 1984). We are told "Why Japanese Factories Work" (Hayes 1981) and how to obtain "The Incline of Quality" (Leonard and Sasser 1982). The life cycle metaphor is used to describe how products and processes evolve together, and how factories should change over time (Hayes and Wheelwright 1979). Product strategies for technological, market, and cost leadership are being mapped onto appropriate manufacturing organizations and processes. We are reminded of the strategy and manufacturing fit (Jelinek and Goldhar 1984). Concerns, which go beyond traditional emphasis on costs, are also apparent. Quality is a major concern. So is inventory. There is an avalanche of ideas as U.S. manufacturers are pushed into change by global competition and pulled into change by advances in manufacturing technology such as robotics, flexible manufacturing systems, and computer-integrated manufacturing.

Amid this avalanche, there is an emergent set of ideas which is crystallizing around the notions of just-in-time (JIT) manufacturing. At one level, JIT is an approach to inventory control in which raw material, work-in-process, and finished goods inventory are all minimized or pushed to zero. In other words, inventory is available "just-in-time" for use. However, at a more philosophical level, just-in-time is an approach

169

to organizational change that is based on a continuous process of paradox resolution. Paradox is confronted directly or even created. Innovation occurs through the new vision that is created by that confrontation.

The term "paradox" comes from the Greek word, "paradoxos," which means contrary to expectation. It refers to a condition which is seemingly contradictory or opposed to common sense and yet is perhaps possible, or to a condition which possesses seemingly contradictory qualities (Van de Ven and Poole, Chapter 2). As noted in earlier chapters (e.g., Ford and Backoff, Chapter 3), the contribution of paradox to management thinking is the recognition of its power to generate creative insight and change. The resolution of paradox involves critical evaluation of assumptions, which then leads to the qualitative and discontinuous reframing of a problem, which Bartunek (Chapter 4) describes. This reframing fosters creative insights leading to organizational innovation and improvement. Managers in any environment continuously face the paradox of short- versus long-run considerations, forces for change versus those for stability, tight versus loose control, and conflicting constituencies. Thus, successful performance in most organizational settings requires coping with or even creating paradox (Cameron and Quinn, Chapter 1).

The purpose of this chapter is to explore the role of paradox in creating innovations and ultimately excellence through the example of just-in-time manufacturing. Just-in-time manufacturing illustrates in a concrete way how paradoxical demands generate organizational innovation and ultimately superior performance. This chapter begins with a discussion of the themes of paradox that underlie the just-in-time philosophy. The just-in-time philosophy then is illustrated by juxtaposing just-in-time manufacturing decisions with the more traditional decisionmaking in U.S. manufacturing. The paper concludes with a discussion of the organizational implications of paradoxical demands as illustrated by the just-in-time example.

BACKGROUND

Just-in-time manufacturing has its genesis in the manufacturing plants of post–World War II Japan. Toyota, with its Kanban system, is probably the most widely recognized pioneer and practitioner of the JIT techniques (Schonberger 1982a). The Toyota manufacturing system is highly regarded for its efficient production of high-quality cars. One of the first introductions of just-in-time in the United States was by Kawasaki in its mid-Western motorcycle plant in 1980 (Schonberger 1982b). Just-in-time techniques have since been adopted by a variety of U.S. manufacturers including FMC, Harley-Davidson, General Motors, Hewlett-Packard, and Apple Computer. Although implementation of JIT techniques varies widely, a striking feature of even rudimentary and partial implementations of the just-in-time ideas is the impressive gains achieved in manufacturing performance.

One example is Hewlett-Packard's workstation printer plant in Vancouver, Washington. After an initial investment of $50,000 to restructure the plant layout for JIT, there were impressive results. These include a 20 percent increase in shipments, 40 percent reduction in floor space, 30 percent reduction in scrap and rework, 50 percent increase in labor efficiency, and an 82 percent cut in work-in-process inventory ("JIT: On the Move and Out of the Aisles" 1984).

Another example is Black and Decker. JIT was implemented at one of its Maryland plants. Subsequently, over a three-year period, throughput increased 300 percent, inventories were cut by 50 percent, inventory turns went from 3.6 to 40 per year, and manufacturing lead times were cut in half ("Annual Conference Report" 1986). A General Electric appliance plant improved quality by 53 percent, reduced the manufacturing cycle time from five to six days to eighteen hours, and improved throughput by more than 20 percent in 40 percent less floor space. All of this occurred in the first eighteen months of just-in-time operation ("Annual Conference Report" 1986).

These kinds of dramatic cost, quality, and throughput gains are not unusual in just-in-time applications. In fact, it is these and other impressive gains in practical settings that suggest the importance of the themes of paradox underlying just-in-time ideas for advances in theories of organizational change and innovation. Moreover, less quantitative, but equally important, gains have occurred in manufacturing service and the job content of direct labor employees. In sum, the practical successes of just-in-time point to potential advances in theories of innovation and change.

WESTERN AND EASTERN PHILOSOPHIES

To understand what is unique about just-in-time, it is helpful to recognize several basic differences between Western and Eastern thought.

Western thinking is characterized by linear thought processes (Van de Ven 1983). Outcomes have causes. There are beginnings and ends. There is planning and then execution. Western thought is also characterized by the notion of tradeoffs. The popular saying, "You can't have your cake and eat it too," is characteristic of the frequent understanding of reality in terms of tradeoffs by many Westerners. Tradeoffs between cost and quality, quality and speed, short-run and long-run, profits and sales, family and job, teaching and research, and so on, capture the way in which many Westerners often think about personal, group, and organizational issues. Only infrequently do many of us stop to consider the assumptions underlying the validity of these tradeoffs.

In contrast with Western thought, Eastern thinking emphasizes the timeless, eternal qualities of life and the attainment of perfection (Hiriyanna 1985). Life is flow and motion and constant change. There is no finality, only ceaseless becoming of something else and never-ending change. In Eastern thinking, the concept of tradeoffs is not present. One does not think in terms of opposites, but rather in terms of harmony of the whole. Mutually exclusive alternatives are not really opposing. Rather, we simply do not yet understand their interrelationship (Humphreys 1985). In a world of harmony, all things are absolutely and intrinsically linked. For example, God, man, and nature are not really distinct entities, but rather are extensions of one another in the thinking of Eastern religions.

In Eastern thinking there are few assumptions. For example, in Buddhism, the religion which binds together the various Eastern cultures of India, China, Japan and Southeast Asia (Humphreys 1985), there are no assumptions or dogmas. For example, no assumptions are made about God or about one's soul. This is quite different from Western Christianity which contains many articles of faith. There is also no concept of fate in Eastern thinking. Similarly, there are no causes and effects, merely different facets of the same phenomenon. If there appear to be causes and effects, it is only because of an illusion of time. The Eastern world truly is composed of "chicken and egg" phenomena.

Ultimate ideals are important as well in Eastern thought. For example, Zen Buddhism revolves around the pursuit of perfection (Suzuki 1973). The Forbidden City of Beijing contains numerous buildings with names such as the Palace of Eternal Harmony and the Palace of Supreme Tranquility. Although eternal harmony, supreme tranquility, and the like are impossible to achieve from the Western viewpoint, nonetheless these ultimate goals provide the impetus for continual improvement and pursuit of perfection, characteristics of Eastern philosophy. For example, in Buddhist thought, pursuit of perfection in this life means a better situation in one's next life such that, in successive lives, people can approach perfection (e.g., Hiriyanna 1985).

In sum, Eastern thought is characterized by harmony of competing values, timelessness, and the pursuit of perfection. These same characteristics appear in the themes of paradoxical demand that underlie just-in-time manufacturing.

UNDERLYING THEMES

Three themes form the basis of the just-in-time philosophy (Figure 5–1). One is constant pressure to resolve the paradox of multiple, seemingly conflicting goals. In the manufacturing context, the most widely discussed of these goals is quality. However, low cost and service are important as well. The traditional Western view of these goals is expressed in terms of tradeoffs of mutually exclusive options. For example, increased quality means greater costs, and decreased inventory may lengthen service time. To pursue these as multiple goals is, therefore, traditionally regarded as poor management because conflicting goals confuse and frustrate subordinates. In contrast, the pursuit of multiple conflicting goals is an important, underlying theme of JIT.

Multiple conflicting goals create paradox as mutually exclusive demands are forced to exist side-by-side (Van de Ven and Poole, Chapter 2). Paradoxical demands create tension between opposing forces. However, such tension also creates the unfreezing which is necessary for innovation and change (Schein 1961). The unfreezing process stimulates individuals to reframe their understanding of a phenomenon in a qualitatively different and discontinuous way (Bartunek, Chapter 4). As Bartunek notes, this reframing process is crucial to innovation and genuine change. Thus, the major effect of creating paradoxical demands is creativity. People are forced to look beyond the obvious and to reexamine the basic assumptions which underlie the paradox presented by conflicting goals. Creative reframing occurs as people resolve the paradox through new insights into the linkages between apparently conflicting demands. Consistent with Eastern thinking, the underlying harmony of competing values is sought. For example, the traditional way to obtain the proper inventory level is to balance set-up or ordering costs with carrying costs (i.e., EOQ economic order quantity). These

Figure 5–1. A Process Model Linking Paradoxical Demands with Innovation and Performance.

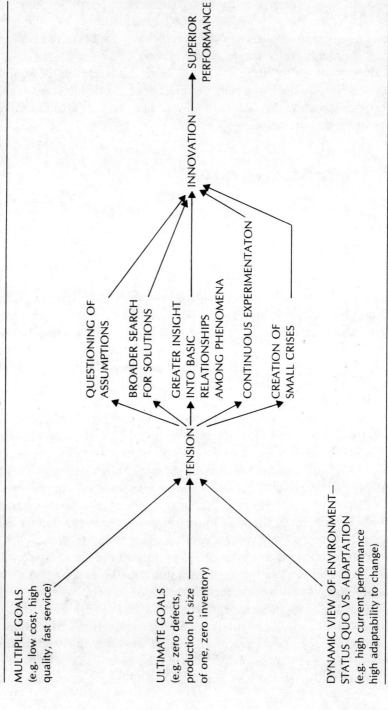

costs are assumed to be predetermined and fixed, and demands for high quality conflict with those for efficiency. In contrast, both cost and quality objectives are pursued in just-in-time. This leads to examination of fixed cost assumptions, and ultimately, to more creative ways to perform set-ups and to interact with suppliers. The result is a new and broader conceptualization or gestalt of the relationships among inventory, cost, and quality issues.

The second key theme is the creation of paradox through pursuit of ultimate goals. Paradox is created by the pursuit of perfection, which seemingly contradicts common sense. In the manufacturing context, examples of such ultimate demands include zero defects, optimal production lot size of one, zero inventory, and zero equipment set-up times. Obviously, it is impossible to run a physical process with no defects or with no downtime. Perfection is not possible. Yet, consistent with Eastern thinking, in just-in-time, people are continually asked to strive for perfection. In contrast, in traditional manufacturing plants, quality, production and inventory goals are set in terms of achievable standards such as so many defects per thousand, production units per hour, and inventory turns per year, respectively. An ultimate goal such as zero inventory is regarded, at best, as foolish and, more likely, as demoralizing to the workforce because of the inability to achieve it. But, the paradox of pursuing ultimate goals is an important theme of JIT.

Ultimate goals create paradox because they contradict common sense and yet are treated as possible and achievable outcomes. Paradox is created by juxtaposition of the limitations of the physical manufacturing system with ultimate goals for perfection. The major effect of the paradox of ultimate goals is creativity. Ultimate goals create tension for continual learning and improvement (e.g., less scrap than last year, better quality than last month, shorter set-up times), rather than for maintenance of the status quo by meeting predetermined standards. Clear, ultimate goals (e.g., zero defects, zero set-up time, optimal lot size of one) are unlikely ever to be achieved, but they provide continual motivation against complacency. People are forced not only to look beyond the obvious once, but also to keep on doing it day after day. Continual reframing occurs as people try to resolve the paradox through new insights that can further improve the process. For example, the traditional way to manage a manufacturing plant is to ramp up production to a stable level of throughput and quality. The manufacturing process is then buffered from the external environment to preclude change. In contrast, continual improvement in performance is pursued in just-in-time. This leads to continual reconceptualization of the process using experimentation—pushing the process to its limits by tactics such as reducing buffer stock, eliminating a work station or changing set-up procedures. This experimentation is captured in the just-in-time analogy of smoothing the flow of the river by removing the rocks. The result is continual change of the process such that manufacturing management resembles fluid and adaptive motion, rather than execution of a fixed set of routines.

The third theme is a dynamic view of the environment. Technology is expected to change. Customer demands are expected to change. Competitors are expected to introduce new products, alter advertising approaches, open new plants, and so on. Consistent with Eastern thinking, constant flow and motion and change are the norm. In contrast, in the traditional Western approach, manufacturers attempt to buffer their plants from changes in the outside world. Long, uninterrupted production runs are the ideal. Responsiveness is just too difficult given a fixed plant and a specialized workforce. In contrast, coping with an inherently dynamic environment is an important theme of JIT.

A dynamic view of the environment creates paradox by forcing individuals to be be focused enough to respond to the current situation as well as flexible enough to respond if it changes. The major effect is the creation of tension through the heightened awareness of changes in external stimuli. People are thus more sensitive to change and to ways in which they can take advantage of it. For example, in traditional manufacturing, investment is made in relatively fixed capital equipment and a specialized labor force. This type of investment creates highly efficient production, if the environment does not change. In contrast, adaptation to change as well as highly efficient production are demanded in true JIT implementations. This leads to cross-training of the workforce and more versatile capital equipment. The result, again, is a more fluid, adaptive management. The implication is that the manufacturing process should be managed with adaptation in mind. This means maintaining low inventory levels, developing a flexible work force, and using inexpensive and/or versatile capital equipment.

In summary, the underlying philosophy of just-in-time manufacturing rests on the resolution of the paradoxical demands posed by pursuit of multiple, conflicting goals, and ultimate goals in a dynamic environment. These ideas have led to important changes in the conceptualization of manufacturing management—that is, renewed concern for quality, just-in-time production which is responsive to the marketplace, integration of the work force into the planning and problem-solving aspects of production, and an emphasis on seeking solutions by challenging assumptions. Moreover, for many firms, just-in-time manufacturing has led to impressive improvements in manufacturing performance.

CHANGES IN OPERATING DECISIONS

Just-in-time ideas can be demonstrated by examining how the operating decisions in a just-in-time environment differ from those in a traditional environment. In the following sections, we consider four major types of operating decisions for which manufacturing is typically responsible in U.S. firms: quality control; production planning; inventory; and capital equipment. The differences between traditional and just-in-time manufacturing are illustrated by the differences in these decision areas. We have culled our examples from the trade press and from our own observations and conversations in the United States and overseas.[1] The static, assumption-oriented perspective of traditional manufacturing contrasts with that of just-in-time. In particular, the pursuit of paradoxical demands in conjunction with a dynamic view of the external environment creates a continual rethinking of the manufacturing process and continual transformation of manufacturing practice in just-in-time settings.

Quality Control

In many U.S. manufacturing plants, quality products are achieved by "inspecting quality in." For example, incoming raw materials are inspected for suitable levels of quality. If these materials fail the quality inspection, they are either reworked or sent back to the supplier. Similarly, quality is achieved within the production process by inspection of parts and product at various stages of the manufacturing process. This inspection is frequently conducted by quality control inspectors, not the direct labor workforce. Defects are then taken off-line for rework or possibly scrap. Usually, a separate work force is responsible for rework. While process improvements do occur, once an acceptable defect level is reached, interest in improvement often wanes (Table 5–1).

In this traditional scenario, the route to greater quality is through more inspections, better raw materials, more rework, more expensive equipment, more skilled workforce, and so on. In other words, higher

Table 5-1. Traditional vs. Just-in-Time Quality.

	Traditional	Just-in-Time
Key ideas	Inspect quality	Build quality in
	Quality must be balanced with other goals, especially cost	Quality is dominant goal
Material and incoming parts		
Inspection	Statistical acceptance inspection of each incoming lot	None, once vendor reliability is established
Acceptable levels of defects	Parts per hundred	None
In process		
Inspection	Inspect quality in series of separate checks by QC inspecters during process	Employees inspect own work
Acceptable level of defects	Parts per hundred	None
Final test	Statistical acceptance sampling	All units inspected

quality is associated with greater cost. Low cost and high quality are seen as paradoxical demands—demands that are mutually exclusive.

But what happens if both low cost and high quality are demanded and thus treated, not as mutually exclusive tradeoffs, but rather as equally valued and expected outcomes? As noted in several earlier chapters, (e.g., Ford and Backoff, Chapter 3; Bartunek, Chapter 4) the key value of paradox is the creative insight which follows from confrontation with it. In the case of JIT, confrontation with the cost/quality paradox forces manufacturing people to move beyond the simple solution of "add more inspection" to a more complete understanding of the underlying inter-relationship between cost and quality.

The JIT approach typically challenges the assumption of a fixed manufacturing process. Process change is seen as not only possible, but also desirable (Schonberger 1982b). The JIT approach also challenges the assumption that the process is necessarily flawed and thus that rework is inevitable. The rework issue is particularly important because of its major and often hidden cost implications. Finally, the JIT approach challenges the assumption that direct labor employees are best managed with minimal responsibilities. Overall, the JIT emphasis is on "building quality in," which means making the product right the first time (Schonberger 1982b). To "build quality in" is to reframe the issue of manufacturing quality in a way which both breaks with the traditional emphasis on inspection and recognizes the underlying interrelationship and harmony between cost and quality. Quality is improved while costs are lowered through the reduction of rework and scrap, and reduction of quality control inspections.

Resolution of the cost/quality paradox has led not only to an overall reframing of the quality/cost relationship, but also to important innovations. One is supplier relations. For example, JIT suppliers are frequently responsible for their own quality, and very little inspection, if any, is done on incoming parts. Often, there is no acceptable level of defects and vendor certification is important. Vendor certification often involves visits to supplier plants and the exchange of process quality information on a regular basis. In exchange, the purchasing firm often supplies product design information, and sometimes, process improvement procedures. Overall, the relationship is a much more intensive one than in the traditional scenario.

A peripherals plant of a major computer vendor provides a good example. This firm formerly performed acceptance sampling of incoming shipments. Rejected lots were returned to the supplier—adding time, costing shipping charges, and increasing inventory. Moreover, suppliers sometimes simply shipped back the rejected lot with the hope that it might pass the next inspection. Now the firm contracts only with suppliers who guarantee defect-free shipments. At times, this has meant contracting with a higher cost supplier. However, the firm saves inspection time, inventory holding costs, and rework such that overall cost is actually lower.[2]

A consumer power tools plant, located in the Southeast, provides an additional example of the enhanced relationship between using and supplying firms. ("Richardson-Vicks, Inc." 1984). The plant strengthened its ties with key suppliers by reducing the number of suppliers by 40 percent in less than a year, and increasing its volume to the remaining suppliers and establishing a minimum level of purchase. The plant has begun vendor certification and has eliminated incoming lot inspection for suppliers who ship ten "no problem" lots in a row. Also, only two parts are purchased from suppliers that are more than two hours away.

Resolution of the cost/quality paradox through "building quality in" has also often meant innovations in the jobs of direct labor employees. In the JIT approach, the employees are frequently responsible for quality control, and have input into the improvement of the production process as well as the product. This represents a major departure from traditional practices. Inspections by quality control personnel are generally eliminated until final test. Rather, direct labor employees are expected to track quality and solve problems at their own work stations and to flag problems originating at work stations prior to their own. They are often expected to participate in problem-solving groups as well. The result has been elimination of much of the fragmented responsibility for quality among the direct labor, rework and quality control personnel, as well as enhanced job latitude for direct labor employees.

The JIT approach was recently used by a Bay Area computer manufacturer in a final assembly line.[3] In the highly competitive small computer industry, quality and cost are both important. The quality checks were built directly into the design of each work station on the line. Direct labor employees became responsible directly for their own quality. There are now fewer quality control inspectors than in the past, while the overall level of quality has increased. The direct labor employees perform quality checks and do their own rework. These changes enhance efficiency because direct labor employees receive less pay than their quality control and rework colleagues, and because problems are flagged much sooner in the process. Quality also improved because now the assembly, inspection, and rework functions are all done by the people who understand the manufacturing process. It is no longer fragmented across three separate workforces. In another example, equipment operators at a major truck engine plant kept scatter diagrams of the location of porosity and hard spots in order to track down the casting quality problems of supplying foundries. Major changes in the production process were made as a result of these efforts ("Detroit Diesel Allison" 1984).

The quality control practices of JIT manufacturers illustrate the power of paradoxical demands to generate innovation and improvement. Basically, the confrontation of the cost/quality paradox leads employees to move beyond the simple solution of increased quality control inspection.

Pushing for just cost or just quality is less likely to produce innovation. Pushing for both goals triggers a reconceptualization of the underlying relationship between cost and quality, and to subsequent innovations and performance improvements in areas such as supplier relations and job content of direct labor employees.

Production Planning

Traditional production planning is a complicated process. Demand for various products is forecasted over a specified time horizon. This information is then utilized to prepare a master production schedule. A material requirements planning (MRP) or similar system then explodes material requirements into parts and subassembly requirements. This determines the factory schedule to produce these parts and the order schedule for suppliers. In effect, demand is "pushed" through the plant. Ideally, the factory is loaded to full capacity and production moves continuously. When errors occur in the process, they are placed to the side for rework or allowed to continue processing. The plant emphasis is on maximum capacity utilization, long production runs, and high volume production. Production lot sizes reflect a balance between set-up and inventory costs, often using a mathematical calculation. These costs are assumed to be static (Table 5–2).

In this scenario, the route to lower costs is longer and longer production runs because equipment set-up times are fixed and the process itself is relatively immutable. But, such runs come at the expense of greater finished goods inventory, and decreased product mix flexibility in the face of changing circumstances. Again, the various manufacturing goals are treated as paradoxical.

What happens if high product mix, low inventory, and throughput are each goals, as in the JIT philosophy? The problem takes on a new character in which the throughput/product mix/inventory paradox forces key assumptions to be identified and examined. The resulting JIT approach challenges the assumptions of fixed set-up times and fixed process by pressing for continuous lot size reduction. The ultimate goals are a lot size of one and zero set-up time. These goals are pursued through changes in supplier relations, set-ups and production scheduling, and workforce specialization. These changes represent novel approaches to these issues which are triggered by the resolution of the paradox.

Table 5–2.   Traditional vs. Just-in-Time Production Planning.

	Traditional	Just-in-Time
Key ideas	Build what you think that you will need and prepare for something to go wrong	Build what you need as simply as you can
	High capacity utilization and long efficient runs are the prime goals	Building to actual demand is the prime goal
Supplier lot sizes	Order number based on an optimal order policy equation + some error	Exact number needed for time between deliveries
Production lot sizes	Based on an optimal order policy model that considers balance between set-up and carrying costs	Constantly attempt to reduce economic size to one by lowering set-up costs
Scheduling	Centralized Push system—master schedule is created based on forecasted demand. A Materials Requirement Planning (MRP) system that calculates when necessary parts should be made	Decentralized Pull system—orders pulled through the system
Forecasting	Needed for MRP—used extensively	Less dependant on forecasting. More on day-to-day-output and quick response
Capacity utilization	A major goal—factory loaded to maximum output whenever possible	Factory not loaded to capacity to allow for correction of errors and experimentation with process

The changes in supplier relations often revolve around lot size reduction. The key idea is to reduce delivery time to a minimum so that many small shipments of the exact number of parts needed can be made. Ideally, the delivered lot size is one, but in reality, most firms are simply trying to reduce lot sizes and lead times. For example, General Motors used to keep a ten-day supply of seats and other parts made by Lear Siegler ("Business Gets a Grip on Inventories" 1984). Now, GM sends in orders at four to eight hour intervals and expects immediate shipment.

Many firms are also reducing production lot sizes to resolve the throughput/product mix/inventory paradox. The key to decreasing production lot sizes is continuous pressure to reduce set-up times which are regarded as fixed in traditional plants. At times, the results are dramatic. For example, a Midwestern heavy equipment manufacturer has reduced some set-ups from six hours to twenty minutes ("Detroit Diesel Allison" 1984). A California computer manufacturer reduced some set-ups from ninety minutes to three. A military equipment supplier now uses a simple jig to reduce machining set-ups dramatically.[4]

A related change is scheduling using a "pull" system such as Kanban. "Pull" scheduling means that the manufacturing schedule is initiated from actual demand, not forecasted demand. This substantially different approach to plant scheduling comes about when plant managers are forced to achieve the multiple goals of high throughput, high product mix flexibility, and low inventory. Thus, needed parts are produced upon request and not in anticipation of demand. When a part request is received, the part is made and sent to the requested area. Thus, forecasting of demand is not used extensively, and changes in demand are accommodated through the efficiency and adaptability of the plant. Although true "pull" scheduling represents a distant goal for most firms, a few are using it. For example, a major electronics manufacturer has a plant that can produce 120 types of printed circuit boards.[5] The production level for each board type is scheduled daily, not weekly or monthly as in the past. Obviously, this has required a dramatic reduction in efficient lot size through reduced set-up times, and a highly skilled and adaptable workforce, in what is still largely a manual process. A final change is a de-emphasis of full capacity operation as an objective. This permits correction of errors on the spot and continuous experimentation with the production process in order to highlight and solve weaknesses.

The JIT practices regarding production planning illustrate several of the themes that underlie JIT. One is the paradoxical demand of multiple,

PARADOX AND TRANSFORMATION

seemingly conflicting goals. The pressure to achieve throughput and efficient small batch production forces employees to question the basic assumptions of the importance of long production runs, fixed process and set-ups, and large lot sizes. Much of the traditional wisdom of production planning rests on these ideas and the importance of full capacity operation. The pressures to produce a broad product mix with small batch size and to be efficient as well require fundamental changes and innovations in thinking.

The other key point is the use of ultimate goals to continue the pressure for improvement. Obviously, the pursuit of perfection in terms of goals such as zero set-up time and optimal lot size of one (as well as zero defects, from the prior section) are unachievable in most situations. However, they create a paradox by treating an unachievable outcome as attainable. This paradox requires constant resolution and creates continual pressure for improvement. On the one hand, there is positive reinforcement for past improvements, while at the same time a clear, ultimate goal provides pressure for future performance. Thus, there is continuing pressure to locate ways to improve.

Inventory

In traditional manufacturing, inventory is costly because it ties up working capital, occupies floor space, and may become obsolete. However, it is traditionally regarded as important to buffer the production process from uncertainties in order to permit long, uninterrupted runs. These uncertainties can be in delivery times for incoming parts and material, production problems, and product demand. Thus, firms use inventory stocks of raw material, work in process, and finished goods. Appropriate levels of inventory are determined analytically by balancing set-up or ordering costs with carrying and shortage costs for a given level of plant reliability. The changing demand for the end product is used to determine the appropriate amount of finished goods inventory. Overall, the traditional approach to inventory is to have enough "just in case." In this scenario, increasing the service level and/or throughput means creating inventory. But this obviously, in turn, raises costs. Thus, in traditional manufacturing, a paradox exists between reliable service and the cost of inventory (Table 5–3). The route to more reliable service (and shorter lead times) is clearly through greater inventory and thus greater cost.

Table 5-3. Traditional vs. Just-in-Time Inventory.

	Traditional	Just-in-Time
Key ideas	Just in case	Just in time
	Balance low inventory against demand uncertainty and unanticipated problems	Minimal inventory is a prime goal
Supplier parts and material	An amount calculated from an EOQ type equation and to cover other areas of uncertainty, such as strikes, hold-up of delivery	Use Just-in-Time (JIT) to minimize delivery times—constantly work to reduce time. Inventory minimized to that needed between deliveries
Work in process buffer stock	Calculate statistically acceptable levels to cover unexpected delays and problems	Try to reduce to zero—improve process to make this possible
Finished goods	Produce to meet forecast demand. Use EOQ models to produce correct quantity	Try to minimize. Goal is to have a mixed model line and match production to demand

The "just-in-case" philosophy of traditional manufacturing relies upon several assumptions: fixed process and fixed set-ups, which create a service/inventory/cost paradox. As in the case of quality and production, the key to resolving the paradox is first challenging the underlying assumptions, which then leads to a reconceptualization of the manufacturing issue at hand. In particular, examination of these assumptions has led most just-in-time practitioners to a new understanding of inventory. Inventory is not simply a buffer, but rather the "root of all evil" (Schonberger 1982b). Inventory wastes space, ties up working capital, and hides problems. Therefore, the goal is often minimal inventory. The approach is to have enough inventory "just in time." Minimal inventory not only reduces carrying costs, but also improves both productivity and quality by highlighting problems. The reason is simple. JIT creates many small crises because minimal inventory requires a smooth production process and high product/process quality. These small crises are catalysts to improve the production process. For example, a division of a Fortune 500 computer maker had a four-year problem with a supplier that was hidden by bringing in material from the supplier very early and stockpiling it. The switch to JIT highlighted this supplier problem, which employees then fixed.[6]

The results of JIT inventory have been dramatic in some firms. For example, a major auto manufacturer has increased production throughput 50 percent due to space reduction caused by decreased inventory ("JIT: On the Move and Out of the Aisles" 1984). A valve manufacturer reduced inventories 80 percent ("Kanban, American Style" 1984). A medical products plant has increased inventory turns almost three-fold, dropping finished goods inventory by 42 percent, and total inventory by 39 percent ("Richardson-Vicks, Inc." 1984). All were accomplished with no stockouts. However, what is more interesting than simply inventory reduction is the relationship of the reduction to improved productivity and quality. Quality improves because minimal inventory exposes product and process problems. They cannot be hidden by excess stock. Rather, they have to be fixed. Productivity improves because improved quality means a more reliable process that reduces scrap and rework, and because inventory space becomes available for manufacturing or other uses. A good example of this synergy is Harley-Davidson, a major U.S. motorcycle manufacturer. Since the firm switched to JIT, work-in-process inventory has been cut 65 to 70 percent, dealer reported defects dropped 24 percent, and price increases have been held to 3 percent in three years ("How Just-In-Time Inventories Combat Foreign Competition" 1984). Thus, the paradox of multiple, seemingly conflicting demands forces a new conceptualization in which the underlying harmony of competing values is revealed.

The other aspect of the just-in-time approach to inventory is the use of a zero inventory goal. This type of ultimate goal creates pressure for continuous improvement. Thus, some JIT manufacturers continuously and deliberately cut the buffer stock between stages of production in order to expose problems. They then solve the resulting problems and thereby reduce inventory and often improve quality without sacrificing throughput. This cycle is then repeated and the firm is able to approach zero inventory.

In sum, the just-in-time approach to inventory decisions once again illustrates the use of paradoxical demands in the form of multiple goals to generate innovations and ultimate goals to continue the process of innovation. However, most importantly, the approach to inventory illustrates the holistic view of an organization that occurs when paradox is confronted. The interrelationship and even harmony between apparently conflicting elements of cost, quality, service, and throughput are revealed.

Capital Equipment

The capital investment decision traditionally involves looking at the economic value of discrete projects using net present value calculations or, possibly, payback. Presumably, capital equipment should ultimately improve ROI through efficiency improvements. However, the risk is that the equipment will become obsolete. Thus, capital equipment may promote efficiency, but it is also expensive and potentially obsolete (Table 5–4).

The just-in-time view of capital equipment is to regard it as important for improving quality and/or safety, decreasing set-up times, and raising productivity. The ultimate decision criterion is not a hurdle rate for ROI, but rather whether the equipment is necessary to compete in the marketplace. This implies different, less quantitative and more holistic procedures for capital budgeting. For example, a well-known computer maker has altered its capital budgeting process to include effects on the overall production process, product quality, speed in getting new products into production, and product flexibility.[7] Firm managers concede that the process is more subjective than net present value calculations based on well-defined costs and benefits. However, they argue that they improve their competitive position by accepting capital projects that make sense strategically.

Another difference is in the type of capital equipment. The experience of many U.S. manufacturers with flexible manufacturing systems (FMS) highlights the traditional approach. These manufacturers typically purchase very large and complex turn-key systems from machine tool vendors (Jaikumar 1984). The implementation is carried out by a team of experts, usually provided by the vendor. For most, FMS has not lived up to expectations. On average, these firms produce two or three parts per system.

In contrast, in just-in-time, process adaptability is important. For example, in one plant that we visited, most of the production equipment is on wheels.[8] The remainder of the equipment is on movable

Table 5–4.   Traditional vs. Just-in-Time Capital Equipment.

	Traditional	Just-in-Time
Key ideas	Increased capitalization is used to lower costs	Increased capitalization is used to improve quality
Amount	Large amount per employee—highly capitalized	Large amount per employee—highly capitalized
Type	Large, multifunction machines and complex systems	Many smaller, specialized machines; some developed in-house
Maintenance	Scheduled in at intervals—usually done by people in separate departments	Machine operator responsible for own machine. Checks every day and may do repairs
Layout	Machines are grouped by function. Layout is difficult to reconfigure	Machines are grouped by product. Layout can be easily reconfigured

standards. Nothing is permanently attached to the floor, walls, or ceiling. The plant can be re-configured on a weekend. The flexible approach to capital equipment means the firm can be more responsive to the changing environment. In sum, the approach to capital equipment used by JIT manufacturers is based on the underlying theme of a dynamic environment of constant change.

ORGANIZATIONAL IMPLICATIONS

In the prior sections, we described how the themes underlying just-in-time manufacturing (i.e., multiple goals, ultimate goals, dynamic view of the environment) have changed the way that manufacturers approach basic decisions concerning quality control, production planning, inventory planning, and capital equipment configuration. The paradoxical demands which are the underlying themes of just-in-time have created major innovations in the conceptualization of basic issues in manufacturing, and frequently superior manufacturing performance on multiple performance dimensions. In this section, we look at how these same paradoxical themes have changed organizational relationships and work content in just-in-time situations.

Just-in-time manufacturing illustrates some of the organizing implications of paradox management. The most general implication is that paradox management encourages closer linkages between various organizational segments. Consistent with Eastern thought, there is a much greater sense of the holistic and harmonious interrelationships among people inside and outside of the organization. For example, traditional manufacturing attempts to decouple the manufacturing process from the supplier through the use of inventory. The responsibility of the supplier is to deliver the product as specified at the agreed price. The relationship between the suppliers and the company is not well developed. Because the selection of suppliers depends largely on cost, there is often a large number of suppliers. In just-in-time, the emphasis is on development of a long-term and wide-ranging relationship with suppliers, with relatively fewer suppliers. The goal of this relationship is a "just-in-time" supply of high quality parts and material.

Relationships within the organization vary between traditional and JIT scenarios. The organization structure in the traditional firm emphasizes specialization and compartmentalization. Quality control, accounting, and manufacturing engineering are among the strong support staff groups in many plants. There is typically also a clear separation between product design and manufacturing. Finally, the first line supervisor or foreman has an important position as the representative of management to the direct labor work force. In contrast, managing by paradox in the just-in-time environment forces the reduction of these barriers because continual improvement on multiple performance dimensions in an environment of change is simply too broad a mission to be solved within a specialized and compartmentalized organization.

There are three specific trends that highlight the move to a holistic organization. One is the change of traditional staff department personnel to a coaching role. Foremen and direct labor employees are given much greater responsibility for quality, maintenance, analysis of information, and improvements. These staff departments now have a more advisory role, and in many cases, the number of employees in these departments has dropped. A second trend is that the job of the foreman has changed from "parts expediter" and "disciplinarian" to manager. Often, these people are now involved in leading quality and other problem-solving teams, reviewing process performance data, and enhancing the manufacturing process. A third trend is the increased integration of manufacturing with other parts of the firm, especially product design. The new assumption is that poor product quality is as much a function of poor product design as it is a manufacturing problem. For example, one major computer manufacturer is attacking the traditional separation of manufacturing and product design by forming design teams of manufacturing and product engineers early in the product development process.[9] This same manufacturer is experimenting with career paths for engineers that include manufacturing experience.

The final organizational implication of the just-in-time style of paradox management concerns the work of direct labor employees. The traditional approach is to view the work force as a variable cost. The size of this resource can be adjusted as the need arises by temporary layoffs and rehiring when needed. These people normally are allowed to do only a very restricted number of tasks. The job design is relatively fixed and the employee is not expected to be particularly responsible for or involved in factory operations.

In the just-in-time scenario, employees are expected to do more. There is likely to be more variety and responsibility in the work. While this is similar to quality of working life (QWL), the motivation is different. QWL has humanistic objectives, whereas JIT is very much oriented toward (and often achieves) superior manufacturing performance along multiple performance dimensions. There is also likely to be more change in the work content because a just-in-time process is always changing. Thus, sometimes employees will have a job with wide skill variety and autonomy; at other times, they will be asked to perform a very regimented and repetitive job.

SUMMARY

The purpose of this chapter is to explore the role of paradox in creating innovation and ultimately superior performance through the example of just-in-time manufacturing. As Cameron and Quinn state in Chapter 1, superior performance or effectiveness frequently forces management of paradox. Successful managers in any type of organization constantly face the tension of long-run versus short-run concerns, forces for change versus those for stability, tight versus loose control, and conflicting constituencies. In other words, superior performance in organizational settings means continual achievement on multiple and at least partially conflicting goals in a dynamic environment. The hoped-for contributions of this chapter are both to reiterate the need to manage paradoxes, and to extend thinking about what it means to manage paradox.

Explicit creation of paradox in the form of multiple and ultimate goals in a dynamic context creates organizational innovation and, ultimately, superior performance. This is the central idea of this chapter. Paradoxical goals such as these create the kind of unfreezing tensions crucial to change in social systems. Specifically, paradoxical goals encourage people to widen their field of vision and to look beyond the obvious for solutions. They encourage people to examine critically the validity of basic assumptions upon which paradoxes frequently rest, and to try to understand the underlying interrelationships among apparently conflicting objectives. Paradoxical goals encourage people to experiment and to accept the failures inherent in the pursuit of improvement.

However, do paradoxical goals lead to better performance? Recent work by Bourgeois and Eisenhardt (1988) on top management teams in high-speed environments suggests that teams that pursue both fast and high-quality decision processes are more successful. Cameron's (1986) study of the management of colleges and universities also points to the linkage between managing paradoxes and effectiveness. But, more specific to this chapter, in the manufacturing setting, the evidence is compelling that Japanese manufacturers, by and large, are superior to U.S. manufacturers on many dimensions of manufacturing performance (e.g., Garvin 1983). It is also true that most Japanese manufacturers manage using the themes of just-in-time. Additionally, U.S. manufacturers, who have adopted just-in-time, frequently report substantial improvements in quality, throughput, lead times, and the like. Dramatic examples such as the valve manufacturer ("Kanban, American-Style" 1984) that cut lead times from twenty-four weeks to six, increased labor productivity by 50 percent, cut inventory 80 percent, reduced cycle time from two months to three days and returned to competitiveness, are not uncommon. Some of these manufacturers have simply mimicked the just-in-time practices by focusing their improvements on a few obvious JIT practices (for example, reduction of set-up times, tighter vendor certification, reduced inventory). While even this kind of mimicry of the practices generated by just-in-time is often successful, manufacturers who adopt the paradox philosophy which produced these practices probably have greater and more continuous success. Thus, the evidence is beginning to build that management of paradox is important to understanding innovation and superior performance in social settings.

NOTES

1. There is no systematic organizational research, of which we are aware, regarding just-in-time. Therefore, our examples are necessarily anecdotal and draw from both our own observations and experience as well as from trade publications. Just-in-time is a case in which practitioner advances are clearly ahead of formal research.
2. This information is based on extensive conversations with a key manager of a Rocky Mountain peripherals plant of a major computer vendor by the lead author.
3. This information is based on a supervised student consulting project by the lead author with a major Bay Area small computer vendor in which the referenced assembly line was designed and implemented.
4. These examples are the result of an informal survey, including discussions with plant personnel and personal observation, of major users of JIT techniques in the Bay Area.
5. This information is based on a supervised student consulting project by a colleague with a major Bay Area electronics manufacturer.
6. See note 4.
7. See note 4.
8. See note 4.
9. See note 2.

REFERENCES

"America's Best-Managed Factories." 1984. *Fortune* (May 28): 16–24.

"Annual Conference Report." 1986. *Target* (Spring): 7–9.

"Black and Decker." 1984. *JIT Technical Development Newsletter,* 4 (June): 17–18.

Bourgeois, L. Jay, and Kathleen M. Eisenhardt. 1988. "Strategic Decision Processes in High Velocity Environments: Four Cases in the Microcomputer Industry." *Management Science.*

"Business Gets a Grip on Inventories." 1984. *Business Week* (May 14): 38–39.

Cameron, Kim S., 1986. "Effectiveness as Paradox." *Management Science* (May): 539–53.

"Detroit Diesel Allison." 1984. *JIT Technical Development Newsletter* 3 (March): 2–3.

Garvin, David. 1983. "Quality on the Line." *Harvard Business Review* (September-October): 65–75.

Hayes, Robert H. 1981. "Why Japanese Factories Work." *Harvard Business Review* (July-August): 57–66.

Hayes, Robert H., and Steven C. Wheelwright. 1979. "The Dynamics of Process-Product Life Cycles." *Harvard Business Review* (March-April): 127–36.

Hiriyanna, M. 1985. *Essentials of Indian Philosophy.* London: George Allen and Unwin Publishers.

"How Just-In-Time Inventories Combat Foreign Competition." 1984. *Business Week* (May 14): 176–79.

Humphreys, Christmas. 1985. *Buddhism.* Harmondsworth, England: Penguin Books.

Jaikumar, Ramchandran. 1984. "Flexible Manufacturing Systems: A Managerial Perspective." Discussion Draft. Harvard Business School.

Jelinek, Maryann, and Joel D. Goldhar. 1984. "The Strategic Implications of the Factory of the Future." *Sloan Management Review* (January-February): 29–38.

"JIT: On the Move and Out of the Aisles." 1984. *Manufacturing Engineering.*

"Kanban, American-Style." 1984. *Forbes* (October 8): 66–70.

Leonard, Frank S., and W. Earl Sasser. 1982. "The Incline of Quality." *Harvard Business Review* (September-October): 163–71.

"Richardson-Vicks, Inc." 1984. *JIT Technical Development Newsletter* 4 (June): 2–3.

Schonberger, Richard J. 1982a. "The Transfer of Japanese Manufacturing Approaches to U.S. Industry." *Academy of Management Review* 7, no. 3: 479–87.

———. 1982b. *Japanese Manufacturing Techniques.* New York.

Suzuki, D.T. 1973. *Zen and Japanese Culture.* Princeton, N.J.: Princeton University Press.

Van de Ven, Andrew H. 1983. "Review of *In Search of Excellence.*" *Administrative Science Quarterly* 28: 621–24.

THE PUZZLE OF PARADOX IN JUST-IN-TIME MANUFACTURING

Victoria Buenger and Richard L. Daft

The chapter by Eisenhardt and Westcott takes on the double challenge of making lucid a philosophy of just-in-time manufacturing whose roots are in a foreign culture and identifying a diverse set of practical applications of the philosophy. The authors give a clear account of the themes that underlie the just-in-time philosophy and of the numerous applications of these principles in manufacturing. The chapter, which is well-organized and well-argued, certainly fulfills its stated purpose to explore the role of paradox in creating innovation and excellence through the example of just-in-time manufacturing. Furthermore, the chapter's use of examples helps convince the reader that the JIT approach is resulting in impressive improvements in manufacturing performance.

The chapter begins by introducing and comparing Eastern philosophy with Western philosophy: Westerners think in terms of opposites and tradeoffs, while Easterners think in terms of the harmony of the whole. The Eastern ideals of harmony of competing values, timelessness, and the pursuit of perfection underlie the themes of just-in-time manufacturing. The chapter goes on to argue that Eastern thinking provides a grounding for problem solving in organizations. Basically, paradoxical demands such as the pursuit of multiple goals, the pursuit of ultimate goals, and a dynamic view of the environment create a tension within workers and within the organization. Eisenhardt and Westcott credit several innovation-inducing behaviors to the presence of this tension.

The chapter argues that tension leads to a questioning of assumptions, a broader search for solutions, a greater insight into basic relationships among phenomena, a tendency toward continuous experimentation, and finally, the creation of small crises. These behaviors occur because of the new vision that is created by the confrontation of paradox. Once a worker is thinking and questioning, creativity, innovation, and ultimately superior performance follow.

The chapter then examines the differences between just-in-time management and traditional management in several areas of manufacturing operations. Quality control, production planning, inventory, and capital equipment are the four types of operating decisions considered; in each, the static perspective of traditional manufacturing contrasts with and falls short of just-in-time. Thus we find that in the area of quality control traditional manufacturers "inspect quality in" while JIT manufacturers "build quality in." We discover that JIT reduces traditional costs of production and inventory, while coming closer to matching demand. And we learn that organizations can purchase capital equipment to improve competitive position rather than to reduce costs.

Each of these applications of the just-in-time philosophy has direct implications for organizations, and the chapter explores two of them. The first and most general is that JIT and paradox management encourage closer linkages between various organizational segments. Boundaries between departments will likely blur, and the organization will be more like one entity. The other implication concerns the role of direct labor employees in the JIT organization. In the new scenario, employees are expected to take on more responsibility, and it is likely that their jobs will have more variety and be more stimulating. A third implication, which Eisenhardt and Westcott do not address specifically, but which permeates the chapter, is the optimist flavor of JIT. The authors seem convinced that American manufacturers can re-assert their dominance in world markets by using just-in-time manufacturing processes to emphasize quality and to keep costs under control. We believe this element of hope for American business is a major contribution of this chapter.

WHAT IS PARADOX?

While we recognize many distinctive contributions of Eisenhardt and Westcott's chapter, we have some criticisms to make. The most basic revolves around the definition and use of paradox to support their arguments. We believe that the just-in-time philosophy and the manufacturing practices associated with it can claim a number of positive achievements in the United States, but creating, confronting, and resolving paradox are not among them. The arguments put forth in the chapter make intuitive sense in explaining why JIT practices might improve performance and effectiveness. Nonetheless, to say that positive results are attributable to a built-in system of paradox management is to misunderstand paradox. Just because multiple goals are being pursued does not mean that paradox is created, nor does achieving those goals necessarily resolve the supposed paradox. Important to the definition of paradox is the simultaneous presence and attainment of seemingly mutually exclusive ends. When the chapter refers to the presence of multiple, even conflicting goals, the pursuit of absolute goals, and a dynamic view of the environment, it has not identified paradoxical states. More accurately, the chapter identifies a set of conditions that nurtures an atmosphere of creative thinking and promotes the questioning of assumptions. It is that characteristic of the just-in-time manufacturing philosophy, rather than any innate ability to deal with paradox, that leads to the observed improvements in performance and the creation of excellence.

As most contributors to this book have admitted, paradox is a slippery concept. Because it is a matter of perception or point of view, authors frequently disagree about what constitutes paradox. In our understanding two elements must be present before a paradox exists: simultaneously occurring mutually exclusive states; and a lack of understanding or knowledge of how such a condition can be explained. The Eisenhardt and Westcott chapter adopts a much looser definition of paradox that emphasizes the presence of conflict on a number of levels. Basically, three underlying themes of the just-in-time philosophy—the pressure to achieve multiple, seemingly conflicting goals; the pursuit of ultimate or absolute goals; and the adoption of a dynamic view of the environment—supposedly create paradoxical demands. Finding new and better ways to do business resolves the paradox, improves performance, and sets the stage for further paradox creation where the cycle can then be repeated. We believe this is an oversimplification, both of what paradox really is and of why just-in-time manufacturing has produced such notable successes.

DOES JIT RESOLVE A PARADOX?

First of all, paradox ceases to exist when contradictory states do not exist simultaneously, when states are not, in fact, contradictory, or when they can be explained. Except in the most extreme cases of just-in-time manufacturing, paradox does not exist. What the chapter overlooks is that contradictory states don't need to exist for JIT to succeed. The presence or absence of paradox is secondary to the ultimate contribution of just-in-time manufacturing—the creation of an awareness of ways of thinking that are different from the traditional manufacturing perspective. The ability to stimulate such an awareness is not unique to JIT. Quinn and Rohrbough's (1983) competing values model and subsequent studies which link that model to organizational effectiveness and the life cycle (Quinn and Cameron 1983) promote the same kind of thinking without ever mentioning paradox. The decisionmaking literature and writings on innovation also report that where performance gaps emerge, individuals and organizations are challenged to find better methods for operating. Thus our criticism of Eisenhardt and Westcott's chapter is not their defense of the just-in-time manufacturing system, but is their repeated admonitions that it is the constant presence of paradox that makes it all possible. In truth, we feel the chapter has gone out of its way to point out paradox where none exists in situations where paradox is neither a necessary nor sufficient condition for the pursuit of creative problem solving.

The overemphasis on paradox is perhaps most noticeable in the discussion of JIT's constant pressure to achieve multiple, seemingly conflicting goals. Multiple goals, the chapter claims, "create paradox as mutually exclusive demands are forced to exist side by side. We would agree that *maximizing* multiple, *mutually exclusive* goals simultaneously would be paradoxical. However, *pursuing* multiple, *sometimes* conflicting goals at the same time is not paradoxical at all and is, in fact, characteristic of all organizations and systems. Sports teams, business firms, and biological systems are among the entities that achieve success by taking a holistic approach. This does not imply that all goals take on equal value, but that for the system to function properly it cannot pursue one goal to the exclusion of all others. For example, a study by Hall (1980) pointed to the necessity of pursuing multiple goals, even in a stressed environment faced by firms in declining industries. Hall recommended that businesses in declining industries can avoid being dragged down in the decline by adopting multiple goals. He suggested that such a company should either follow a low-cost strategy which maintained an acceptable level of quality, or a high-quality strategy which kept costs fairly low. In both cases, the seemingly contradictory goals of low cost and high quality are pursued.

According to the chapter, traditional management eschews the pursuit of multiple goals, and thus it takes the creation of a paradox to force people to look beyond the obvious and to reexamine basic assumptions. Frankly, we don't agree and we don't see the paradox. Companies have always had to balance different goals and subgoals within the organization. Just-in-time management just offers a fresh way of framing those problems.

Another point the chapter does not consider is that multiple goals may not be in conflict at all. Increasing product quality does not necessarily increase costs if a new technology or new techniques are adopted. Technological progress often advances both goals, so there is no conflict. Choose almost any industry, and history will bear this out. Many automobile manufacturers thought Henry Ford was crazy when in 1913 he doubled his line workers' daily pay rate to $5, shortened work hours, and instituted a relentless parade of price cuts. But it was only paradoxical to observers who did not comprehend the economics of Ford's newly perfected moving assembly line, which cut the number of manhours required to assemble the Model T from 12 to 1.5 (Lacey 1986). Similarly, railroad operators in the early years thought they had to make tradeoffs between the distance a train line could run and the level of safety they could guarantee. Over long distances, coordination among various lines was considered impossible. Two factors, one managerial, the other technical, released the railroads from that dilemma. First, railroads adopted the Army's line and staff structure which created a network of management that could be spread over greater distances while coordination and efficiency were maintained. Coupling this new organization structure with the laying of telegraph lines ensured more reliable communication and guaranteed that trains could move across expanses without the hazard of collisions (Chandler 1977).

The tobacco industry also used technology to attain multiple goals. Throughout much of the nineteenth century, industry leaders thought tobacco was being processed and packaged as efficiently as possible. Companies like R.J. Reynolds placed cigarette papers inside each pouch of tobacco in response to the growing popularity of cigarette smoking. Efforts weren't made to manufacture cigarettes because it was incredibly expensive to produce a cigarette of acceptable quality. Perhaps if the world were static, cigarettes would never have been commercially produced, but changes in demand and developments in machine technology led to experimentation. The earliest available record of R.J. Reynolds' desire to manufacture cigarettes is dated 4 March 1912. By the end of

1924 cigarette manufacturing at R.J. Reynolds was virtually automatic from start to finish. Those twelve years witnessed astonishing gains in the quality of cigarettes and packages and in the effort to make the product cheaply (Tilley 1985). What the Eisenhardt and Westcott chapter would call paradox—a seeming impasse between cost and quality which delayed the production of cigarettes for decades—disappeared not because of just-in-time management practices or creative problem solving, but because the goals were no longer in conflict. Technology moved the industry to an entirely new plateau.

Although the pressure to achieve multiple goals seems to be the chapter's primary focus, it also points to the pursuit of ultimate goals and the adoption of a dynamic view of the environment as paradox-creating conditions. These, even more than the pressure to achieve multiple goals, must be taken to their logical extremes before paradox can emerge. Thus, achieving the "impossible" goal and being simultaneously flexible and rigid create the paradox that leads to improved performance and gains in production. While we agree that achieving the impossible or simultaneously being rigid and flexible is paradoxical, we would hasten to add that those conditions can never actually exist. The pursuit of the impossible and its attainment are two distinct things. Working toward ultimate goals does not imply paradox; it means having aspirations. If ultimate goals are reached and sustained, then the problem is transcended, and participants enter nirvana. As to maintaining a dynamic view of the environment, we hardly believe that the suggestion that an organization be responsive and adaptive is new or paradox creating. The product/market life cycle curve predicts that all (or most) industries are subject to rapid, often turbulent, change during the growth and shakeout stages, and only those participants able to cope with an inherently dynamic environment will survive. Management's concern with environmental scanning and information processing is another indication that firms outside the circle of JIT disciples are aware of the need to view the environment dynamically and prepare to respond to change.

Eisenhardt and Westcott claim some remarkable things for JIT manufacturing, and most are probably true. The key is that they would still be true if paradox were never mentioned. Often it takes radical ideas to shake individuals out of their old habits, and to get managers to abandon such traditional management practices as EOQ or inspecting for quality. The just-in-time philosophy does foster a new and creative way of approaching management, and it highlights problems frequently ignored under more traditional approaches. That is good management. There is no reason to suggest that the secret is the creation and resolution of paradox.

AN EMERGING PARADOX AND
SUGGESTED RESEARCH

The puzzling thing about just-in-time manufacturing in the United States is not that it confronts paradox on a daily basis, but that in the long term a large, perhaps unsolvable paradox does emerge. Eisenhardt and Westcott skirted this issue in their discussion of the basic differences between Western and Eastern thought. They did not ask "what happens in the long run?" Americans are distinctive in their devotion to the ideals of democracy, equality, and liberty. Intimately tied to those beliefs and flowing from them is a disdain for special privilege and a commitment to the competitive spirit. What happens when employees are asked to abandon these practices, or at least adopt a system that is based on the antithesis of these ideas—a system where stability is preferred to liberty, where relationships are autocratic rather than democratic, where equality is superceded by special relationships? In just-in-time manufacturing stable, known-quantity relationships are developed with suppliers. The important factors are reliability, a willingness to cooperate, and proven performance. Conversely, American businessmen are accustomed to a system of competitive bidding, where new suppliers have the opportunity to prove their merit by winning a contract. As the chapter demonstrated, JIT has exhibited a great capacity to resolve conflict, but in the process we think it may produce a deeper conflict. Can Americans sustain a management system that is based on ideas opposite of their way of thinking? Can Americans embrace JIT and at the same time maintain the belief system that makes their culture distinctive from all others? That is the true paradox.

Other questions emerge when considering Eisenhardt and Westcott's discussion of JIT that might be amenable to empirical research. One general line of questioning revolves around explaining the impressive gains achieved in manufacturing performance through means other than JIT. Eisenhardt and Westcott's chapter might be attributing gains to JIT when, in fact, they are due to investment in equipment or layout. Some sort of Hawthorne effect might temporarily enhance JIT's impact. Another alternative is that firms which adopt JIT management practices do so because they have difficulties and have the most to gain. That would explain why they prosper so much after the transformation. A third consideration is that firms may transfer certain costs off their books by applying leverage on their suppliers to hold inventory. The apparent gain for the adopter of JIT does not produce overall gains in the economy.

More philosophical questions concern the long term feasibility of bringing JIT to the United States. The just-in-time philosophy assumes that workers are inner directed rather than incentive driven. This is most apparent in the setting of ultimate goals. Laborers are asked to get satisfaction by working toward goals, rather than by achieving measurable sub-goals. How pushing toward absolute goals affects laborers after a long period of fruitless pursuit is a problem that can be addressed empirically. Another, less measurable question is whether the United States is geographically suited to implement JIT. In Japan, a country smaller than the state of California, less than half of its area is used in any sort of economic exploitation. This makes practices of dealing with suppliers within a two-hour radius quite palatable. In the United States business has prospered by transporting raw materials over long distances to sites close to cheap energy sources or by dealing with suppliers who have developed economies of scale by serving wide geographic areas. Should American companies adopt JIT and ignore the advantages they have gained by being less provincial? Perhaps in conjunction with that question, managers should ask whether just-in-time is the only and/or best way of pursuing multiple goals, nurturing creative problem solving, and bring new perspectives to the problems that face American business.

In closing, the Eisenhardt and Westcott chapter does an excellent job of explaining JIT and holds out hope for promising applications to American manufacturing. We vigorously disagree that JIT resolves paradox, but the chapter has stimulated us and will stimulate others to think about the paradox concept and the potential value of JIT. The chapter developed an intriguing argument, and the research and practical implications of its ideas are enormous. We hope to see future work by these authors or by others who are stimulated by the research questions surrounding just-in-time manufacturing, paradox, conflicting goals, creative problem solving, and new technologies.

REFERENCES

Chandler, A.D. 1977. *The Visible Hand: The Managerial Revolution in American Business*. Cambridge: Harvard University Press.

Hall, W.K. 1980. "Survival Strategies in a Hostile Environment." *Harvard Business Review* (September-October): 75–84.

Lacey, R. 1986. *Ford: The Men and the Machine.* Boston: Little, Brown and Co.

Quinn, R.E., and K. Cameron. 1983. "Organizational Life Cycles and Shifting Criteria of Effectiveness: Some Preliminary Evidence." *Management Science* 29, no. 1: 33–51.

Quinn, R.E., and J. Rohrbaugh. 1983. "A Spatial Model of Effectiveness Criteria: Towards a Competing Values Approach to Organizational Analysis." *Management Science* 29, no. 1: 363–77.

Tilley, N.M. 1985. *The R.J. Reynolds Tobacco Company.* Chapel Hill: University of North Carolina Press.

6 LESSONS FROM FAMILY THERAPY
The Potential of Paradoxical Interventions in Organizations

Max Siporin and Burton Gummer

> "These are old fond paradoxes to make fools laugh i'
> the alehouse."
> —Shakespeare, *Othello* (II.i)
>
> "The truest sayings are paradoxical."
> —Lao-Tse

During the past several decades we have witnessed a growing interest on the part of psychotherapists in the use of paradoxical strategies and interventions. There is a growing literature on the subject, with approximately sixty books and articles on the topic appearing in 1980 alone (Seltzer 1986: xiii). There continue to be regular contributions to the literature and well-attended workshops on the uses of paradoxical strategies in a variety of therapeutic settings. Because therapy and therapists have become such a prominent feature of American life today, therapeutic notions about paradox have spread to other areas of our culture and to other helping professions, including that of organizational development.

The present paper seeks to bring developments in this field to the attention of students of organizational behavior with the hope that some of its insights and techniques can be used to improve organizational functioning. The discussion will begin with a clarification of the nature and functions of paradox within the individual personality as well as within families, groups, organizations, and other social systems. The development of paradoxical strategies will then be traced, with an exposition of how symptoms are understood as paradoxical in nature, and also how the helping process and interventions are similarly understood to be paradoxical. Consideration is then given to the differential use of paradoxical strategies and interventions to help treat organizational conflict and dysfunctioning and to facilitate organizational development and well-functioning.

PARADOX IN WELL-FUNCTIONING SYSTEMS

As Cameron and Quinn point out in their introduction to this volume, there is a definitional problem about the concept of paradox, with much difficulty among the general public in comprehending and defining the term. Ideas, statements, conditions, or actions that consist of contradictory elements may be logically incongruous but psychologically and factually true. The viewpoint of the perceiver is a crucial factor in determining a paradox.

From a psychodynamic point of view, paradox is a normal, inherent, and prevalent aspect of human nature. Conflicting feelings and attitudes of love and hate, attraction and rejection, affection and anger, co-exist simultaneously within individuals and in the relationships among members of families and other social systems. Desires and expectations are rarely completely satisfied, and interpersonal relationships are rarely completely compatible or complementary. Subjective feelings of regret, disappointment, loss, or resentment often accompany success, but are usually denied, repressed, sublimated, or just accepted. Rewards may be greater than costs in situations that are consciously assessed as not completely desirable, but as "satisficing."

A belief, statement, or action is paradoxical when component elements appear to be opposing or contradictory. Alternative impulses or feelings may not have or may lose subjective consistency and become conflicting for the person. They may be subjected to conscious, logical, linear, dichotomous thinking, in which premises and conclusions have to be explicitly consistent and conclusions are therefore either right or wrong. In such logical thinking, a paradox is "a contradiction that follows correct thinking from consistent premises" (Watzlawick, Beavin, and Jackson 1967: 188). "Be spontaneous" is a prime example of such a logical paradox. There is an important moral aspect of paradox, in that it essentially evaluates matters in terms of what is good or bad.

A psychological or psychodynamic viewpoint informs us that paradoxes have important positive functions as well as negative consequences. As von Oech (1983: 82-85) points out, a paradox involves ambiguity, allowing different interpretations and meanings, which—while they may cause communication problems—stimulate creative ideas. He states that paradoxes "whack you out of narrow thought paths, and force you to question your assumptions. . . . '[S]eeing the paradox' is at the crux of creative thinking." The dialectical struggle of thesis and antithesis can result in a creative synthesis. Metaphors and metaphorical communication often involve a paradoxical pairing of incongruous elements (e.g., "organized anarchies"). The incongruity of elements in a paradoxical statement or situation often appears comical and stimulates surprise and humor, yet may reveal a basic truth, such as Picasso's statement that art is a lie that makes us realize the truth.

From a systems perspective, the well-functioning of people and social systems depends on an adaptive fit between their attributes, expectations, demands, resources, and opportunities (Bertalanffy 1968; Dubos 1965; Siporin 1980a; Germain 1981). Individuals and social systems achieve this adaptive fit by containing and resolving the inherent dialectical forces and conflicting impulses for unity and autonomy that are characteristic of their functioning and development. This dialectical aspect is a central feature of work and other social organizations (Benson 1977; Cameron and Quinn, Chapter 1).

Well-functioning individuals, families, and organizations largely accept and indulge in paradoxical behavioral patterns. People may exhibit different identities and behave in apparently contradictory ways in different roles and social situations, as, for example, a man who is an indulgent father at home and a strict authoritarian at work. Many such people believe they act consistently and morally in accord with their value systems and situational demands as they perceive them (Gergen 1982).

Adaptive change often follows the ability to perceive the oppositional elements of a paradox and to deal with them. This calls for dialectical, divergent thinking of the kind that Rothenburg (1979) calls "Janusian thinking." This can lead to a deeper understanding of the complex polarities and competing values in problematic situations. It can facilitate different perspectives or insights into potentialities and alternatives for resolving a problem and stimulate creative innovation for progressive change. Such creative insight promotes an acceptance of one's own responsibility and capacity for choice and action to alter a painful, unacceptable situation. The tension of coping with contradictory impulses and desires may require resolution and thereby motivate change. Paradoxes can express a dialectical process of change, which can be facilitated and helped to achieve new syntheses of values, norms, relationships, and synergistic behavior patterns. Where change is not feasible, the acceptance of paradox also provides emotional comfort and enables tolerance of difficult, competing impulses and demands.

SYSTEM DYSFUNCTIONING AND DEVIANCE

The development and existence of paradoxical situations may have dysfunctional and pathological, rather than positive, meanings and consequences. Contradictory, opposing tendencies, beliefs, expectations, wants, and goals may result in system dysfunctioning, deviant behavior, and pathology. Pathology, such as "double binds" or "vicious circles," in turn, can lead to system disorganization, decline, and dissolution.

Dysfunctioning of individuals and social systems results from a mismatch or noncomplementarity of the attributes of people and their milieu. The capacities, needs, and aspirations of people may be discrepant from available resources, demands, and opportunities. Such a condition is aggravated in periods of social turmoil and change; obstacles, frustrations, losses become too great and costs outweigh rewards. The perceived oppositional polarities become too conflicting and stressful for people to accept. They develop anxiety or guilt about their inability to meet the demands of their situations, to the point that they define their situations as dilemmas, predicaments, crises, or disasters.

In severe problematic or crisis situations, maladaptive behavior, such as excessive drinking, may become persistent and pathological and find expression in psychic, role, and interpersonal conflicts, along with demoralization and disorganization. The persistent dysfunctioning is deviant in that it is norm- and rule-violating, deviating from the expectations of self and others for satisfying, approved performance of social roles and tasks. Such deviant, pathological behavior can take the form of mental disorder and criminality, social dependency, conflict, and violence at individual, group, organizational, and community levels.

Individuals can react to dilemmas and crises by constructively correcting the problem or by leaving the field. Or they may adopt such psychic defense mechanisms as denial, dissociation, indecisive ambivalence, sublimated compensatory behavior, or they may utilize alienated, disruptive, aggressive, and other types of maladaptive deviant behavior. Families, organizations, and communities may adopt similar interpersonal and collective defensive mechanisms. These may take such forms as group denial, goal displacement, group think, collusion, mystification, infantilization of a member, a sado-masochistic relationship, "triangulation" in using one member to preserve the group order, overt interpersonal conflict, "vicious circles" of chronic negative interaction, scapegoating, and outcasting. They also may resort to empire-building, ritualism, sabotage, exploitation, criminal or corrupt practices. A negative deviance process, if left unchecked, may lead to group or organizational dissolution.

Symptoms of dysfunctioning and deviance which become persistent and pathological, such as psychogenic hallucinatory behavior, compulsive hand washing, or chronic conflict, take on a paradoxical character. The person or group appears to communicate involuntary loss of control and inability to give up such behavior, while actually achieving certain desired purposes and rewards. Symptomatic behavior protects and defends the person against anxiety and guilt and enables the individual to avoid what is feared. The individual or group thus obtains secondary gains from the ostensibly self-defeating, painful behavior, including burial of the basic conflicts, sympathetic support, or desired distance from or closeness to others, as well as control of others to accord with the actor's needs. A misbehaving child gains desired attention from parents, and also may manipulate the parents to obtain rewards otherwise unobtainable from them.

The consequences of certain forms of deviant behavior may be as rewarding for the actor's family or social group as for the actor. The parents of a misbehaving child may put aside the conflicts in their relationship in focusing their attention on coping with the difficult child. The child may consciously be acting as a scapegoat, or may "triangulate" the relationship to avoid the painful fights between the parents. Similarly, an organizational work group may avoid dealing with an intragroup conflict by scapegoating or triangulating an inadequately performing or deviant member (Hirschorn and Gilmore 1980).

Paradoxically, the ineffectual effort to resolve a problem—the deviant, symptomatic behaviors—itself becomes a central contradictory element of the problem (Watzlawick, Beavin, and Jackson 1967: 212). The pain of the unresolved difficulty and the desire to escape it are still there, but the rewards of the defensive behavior bind the symptom firmly to the pain, and amplify it. The symptomatic behavior implicitly communicates the unresolved ambivalence and conflict (Haley 1963). It also serves to maintain the dysfunctional system as it is.

A person, group, or organization can thus become caught in a "pathogenic double bind." This consists of contradictory injunctions in that one is damned whether there is compliance or disobedience to the demand made; in addition, one cannot discuss or leave the situation or the relationship which is the source of the injunctions (Bateson et al. 1963). The classic example of a double bind is Joseph Heller's *Catch-22* where the combat aviators were trapped in endless tours of duty. They could not free themselves from a no–win situation in which their irrational behavior and claims of insanity were considered normal, "sane" reactions to combat flying experiences and not a justification for being sent home.

In a double bind, the reinforcement of symptomatic deviant behavior by social processes and self-categorizations helps establish a secondary type of deviation, in that behavior, interaction patterns, and social relationships are adopted on the basis of the protective functions of the deviant behavior, identity, and roles. The alcoholic's self-categorization as a "drunk" may be part of a "vicious circle" of self-fulfilling prophecy and deviance-amplifying reinforcement, in which significant others confirm the unworthiness of the alcoholic, while trying to save or look after him, thereby driving him to drink more, and so on. The long-suffering wife of an alcoholic usually is one who unwittingly reinforces her husband's alcoholism and the conflicts in their marital relationship are thus protected from efforts at direct resolution. This may obtain for members of an alcoholic's work group who are unable to deal directly with their own anxieties or group conflicts, so that these become displaced in caring for the troublesome, dependent, yet childlike member. The alcoholic gains the desired attention and care through the alcoholic behavior.

In these negative feedback loops, the painful, maladaptive behavior is continued because of the protection afforded against underlying anticipatory anxieties and guilt feelings. It acts against the stresses and strains for which alternatives are not perceived to be available. It yields valuable payoffs or secondary gains for the alcoholic and for family members or significant others, which reinforce the pathological interaction. The deviant actor and his or her significant others often resist and even sabotage corrective efforts. Part of the defensive mechanisms is the actors' views of the symptomatic, maladaptive behavior as involuntary and un-controllable. This perception is a significant element of the actors' cognitive world, of their definition of the reality of their life situations.

Masuch (1985) discusses such vicious circles in organizations based on frustrated, conflicting expectations and goals. He identifies several types: bureaucratic struggles about change; inflated status systems; biasing and counterbiasing communication systems; pathological growth; and conflict involving the installation of counter-bureaucracies. He also clarifies how such pathologies can lead to organizational underperformance, stagnation, fragmentation, decline, and collapse.

It is important to identify how pathological behavior is maintained by social reinforcements, with self-reinforcement mechanisms operating conjunctively. Attention to the systemic context of symptomatic, deviant behavior thus is extremely significant for any corrective program. Reinforcements from family, work, and other reference group members need to be directly assessed and the interaction networks dealt with in order to help resolve target problems.

THE FAMILY THERAPY MOVEMENT

The importance of paradoxical behavior in mental disorder was early recognized in medicine, the ministry, and other helping professions. Seltzer (1986: 10–15), who provides a helpful history of the development of paradoxical strategies in psychotherapy, observes that concern with the paradoxical nature of behavior has a long tradition in Eastern thought, as in Zen Buddhism and more recently in forms of psychotherapy developed in India and Japan. The resistance to getting well and giving up painful symptoms was a striking pattern of behavior emphasized by Freud as a central feature of mental disorder, to be analyzed in terms of the transference neurosis. Alfred Adler made direct use of paradoxical dynamics in analyzing neurotic behavior and in the use of what we now call paradoxical interventions with his patients (Weeks and L'Abate 1982: 7–9).

It was, however, in the development of family therapy in the United States during the 1950s and 1960s that the varied strands of influence from psychoanalysis, behaviorism, and systems theory came together to give prominence to the importance of paradox in understanding and treating mental disorders. Renewed concern with the sociocultural context for social pathology and mental disorder placed greater emphasis on helping programs with families. The expanding scope of traditional and family-centered social work (Gomberg and Levinson 1952; Sherman 1961; Scherz 1953; Siporin 1980b); the work of Bateson and his colleagues (Bateson et al. 1963; Watzlawick, Beaven, and Jackson 1967); Ackerman's (1958) psychoanalytic family therapy; the paradigmatic psychoanalytic therapy of Nelson and his colleagues (1968) and of Spotnitz (1969); the gestalt therapy of Perls (1971); the existential therapy of Frankl (1960) and of Satir (1964) with her emphasis on growth and communication; the behavior therapy of Dunlap (1932); Bowen's (1978) intergenerational therapy; Minuchin's (1974) structural therapy; the hypnotherapy of Milton Erickson (Haley 1967, 1973); Haley's (1963) strategic therapy—all contributed to a remarkable flowering of family therapy and the development of therapeutic strategies and techniques based on the paradox concept.

The family therapy movement, in turn, was influential in the spread of the theories and techniques involving paradox to therapies with married and unmarried couples. There have been some applications as well to helping programs with organizations (Hirschorn 1978; Hirschorn and Gilmore 1980). Although quite a number of theoretical approaches in family therapy now exist, there are certain general beliefs and practices that warrant a common identity for the movement as a whole (Broderick and Schrader 1981; Gurman and Kniskern 1981).

The focus on the paradoxical nature of pathology and therapy was initially characteristic of the strategic model of family therapy developed by the Bateson group (Haley 1963; Watzlawick and Weakland 1977; Bodin 1981). The initial concern was with schizophrenic disorders, with a controversial assertion that the double bind is a central feature of the pathology of this disorder. In time, it became evident that the double bind phenomenon was prevalent in many different types of behavior, and that other additional features seemed to be involved in schizophrenic reactions. Also, the initial applications to schizophrenia did not seem to have effective results. A shift then occurred to apply the therapeutic double bind to a wide range of problems.

The paradoxical strategy came to be explicitly adopted and employed in structural systems, gestalt, behavioral, and other approaches in the psychotherapy field as a whole. Seltzer (1986: 19, 151–56) and Weeks and L'Abate (1982: 17) observe that although paradoxical interventions are widely used in many different schools of therapy, they are often explained according to different theoretical orientations. A major, recent theoretical development is the integration of the structural systems and strategic-interactional schools (Stanton 1981b).

The family therapy movement contributed several important theoretical and procedural advances: in understanding the paradoxical nature of psychopathology, in developing a general paradoxical approach to therapy, and in generating a set of assessment and interventive technical procedures. We discuss these contributions in the following sections.

ADVANCES IN THEORY AND THERAPY

Family therapists have been instrumental in developing a view of deviant behavioral symptoms, including those of psychoses, as forms of paradoxical communication and behavior having particular systemic functions and expressing a need and potential for change, blocked and ambivalent as these might be. They also emphasize the family system and even wider social contexts as the locus of difficulty and focus for intervention. This view is in contrast to the formerly prevailing Freudian view of neurotic symptoms as reactive to unacceptable psychic impulses.

Family therapists also developed a general paradoxical strategy, consisting of a basic theoretical approach and a number of procedures to deal directly with chronic pathological behavior patterns that have become resistive to change. The Bateson-Palo Alto group evolved an approach featuring a "therapeutic double bind," in which clients are directed to behave in ways that place them in a different kind of bind, in relation to the therapist, than what their symptoms express. Haley (1963, 1976), Watzlawick, Weakland, and Fisch (1974), and Stanton (1981a) explain this strategy as addressing and siding with the resistive deviant behavior of the client or client group. The symptom is accepted, even praised for its altruistic functions (as in keeping the parents from divorcing), and the therapist encourages its continuation, and, in some cases, its intensification. However, this is done in ways that place the deviant actor and his or her group in a counter-bind, so as to stimulate change. The pathogenic double bind is countered by a therapeutic double bind. Thus, a couple is directed to increase the rate of their daily quarreling, but to do so at specific times of the day to increase its benefits. A woman who compulsively collected towels and was hospitalized for this compulsion was eagerly—rather than annoyingly—showered with a flood of towels by her ward attendants and nurses. A woman who cannot say "no" to what people ask of her is instructed and helped to say "no" to a series of requests made by other members of a therapy group and is thereby helped to change this behavior pattern.

These successful therapeutic results are achieved by certain operations of paradoxical helping procedures:

1. The prescription of the symptomatic behavior places the client in a bind: if he or she continues to use the symptomatic behavior in an effort to resist the therapist and the therapy, this then puts the therapist in control of the situation because the therapist has encouraged this behavior. Also, the client is ostensibly accepted as unable to control or change the involuntary behavior, yet is implicitly accepted as being able to help him- or herself (Haley 1963: 185). The client is therefore induced to assume a position where to maintain control over his or her own behavior, and to resist the therapist's control, the symptomatic behavior has to be relinquished.

2. Clients are thus stimulated to assume self-control. By recognizing that they do have voluntary control over their supposedly involuntary symptoms, they are able to modify their frequency or intensity.

3. Clients are helped to face their fears directly; paradoxically, the acceptance of their fears works to enable them to give up their symptomatic, deviant behavior. Their anticipatory and performance anxiety is confronted, perceived not to be so threatening, and thereby reduced, with less need for the irrational beliefs and the defensive and protective functions of the dysfunctional behavior. With reinforcements for the dysfunctional behavior thereby weakened, its occurrence is increasingly extinguished. The client's awareness of or insight into this process may or may not be necessary for this process to take place.

4. The client is stimulated to make a personal choice and take personal action for change, thus acting spontaneously and self-directedly, utilizing his or her own resources (Haley 1974: 20). The client is thus empowered to be self-motivated and take personal responsibility for his or her own life.

5. This kind of intervention initially may seem irrational to the client, but is psychologically rational and purposive in terms of the therapist's objectives. The client's expectations about responses to his or her behavior are generally frustrated, with consequent confusion or psychophysiological arousal that stimulates a breakdown of defenses and an openness to change, a point emphasized by Selvini Palozzoli and her colleagues (1978).

6. A shift in perspective, through the often humorous aspect of the intervention, and through relabeling of the symptomatic behavior, results in a reframing, or redefinition, of the contextual situation. The client thereby gains a certain degree of emotional detachment from the troublesome behavior and can appreciate its irrationality and unnecessary nature.

7. By attention to the systemic context of significant others and reference groups included in the interventive procedure, the situational, social reinforcement mechanisms are altered, so that systemic change is facilitated. Such systemic change in the rules and relationship patterns of a family or other social system is termed "second order change" by Watzlawick and his colleagues (1974), in contrast to the "first order change" of mere behavioral alteration.

TECHNICAL PROCEDURES AND DIFFERENTIAL USES

In order to operationalize this general approach, family therapists developed a host of innovative paradoxical strategies and procedures for work with family groups, couples, and individuals. Many of these techniques are similar or identical, though given different names and rationales in the various therapeutic schools. Thus Frankl's technique of "paradoxical intention," which encourages the continuation of the symptom in exaggerated ways (as in conscious, repeated hand tremor) is a form of symptom prescription or permission; it is applied in what is termed "flooding," "modeling," "exposure in vivo," or "induced anxiety," among other names (Frankl 1975: 232).

Paradoxical helping procedures have been grouped into two categories: symptom prescription and reframing (Haley 1963; Papp 1983; Selvini Palozzoli et al. 1978; Bandler and Bandler, 1982; Weeks and L'Abate 1982; Weeks 1985; Watzlawick 1978a; Watzlawick and Weakland 1977; Seltzer 1986).

Symptom prescription includes permission, modification, exaggeration, or redirection of symptomatic behavior, and the prediction or prescription of relapse. There also may be a restraining or discouragement of change, as in advice that the prognosis for change is poor and a couple should continue their quarreling. A symptom may be prescribed for performance under new conditions, as at a certain time, place, or frequency. For example, a family group may be instructed to follow a family rule that there continue to be no quarreling, but, in addition, to hide and deny any expression of anger (since the anger has been expressed nonverbally).

As another example of symptom prescription, a young boy who masturbates in front of his family is instructed to continue to masturbate in this way, but to do so a certain number of times and only on certain days of the week. He is told to follow this prescription in order to determine when this gives him the most pleasure. The mother and other members of the family are directed to follow their usual routines and to be very accepting of the boy's behavior as a way of being helpful during this period. The boy stops masturbating in front of his family as a way of breaking the therapeutic bind.

Reframing is a form of interpretation, though different from the psychoanalytic concern to provide insight into intrapsychic defenses. It includes the relabeling and redefinition of behavior and situation, as well as the consequent stimulation of different relationships, rituals and rules. There is a recognition that situational definitions are central determinants of a person's cognitive map of reality, and therefore of behavior and relationships.

As Coyne (1985) states, "Reframing involves a reconstruction of someone's sense of reality." It thus acts to

> change the conceptual and/or emotional setting or viewpoint in relation to which a situation is experienced and to place it in another frame which fits the "facts" of the same concrete situation equally well or even better, and thereby changes its entire meaning. . . . What turns out to be changed as a result of reframing is the meaning attributed to the situation, and therefore its consequences, but not its concrete facts. (Watzlawick, Weakland, and Fisch 1974: 95)

Paradoxical reframing (in contrast to other types) needs to have some illogical or contradictory feature, as with symptom prescription. For example, the constant quarreling within a group can be redefined as expressing mutual needs for greater closeness and understanding. Also the redefinition of behavior or situations needs to provide new meanings that have a positive quality, as in recognizing the intention to express concern for welfare of the other, even by seemingly hostile criticism.

> The redefinition of the situation that is shared with the client should indicate and clarify its elements of positive choice, that it is subject to one's influence and effort and has potential for some positive outcome. . . . [S]uch redefinitions need to be in accord with the actualities of the situation. (Siporin 1975: 309–10)

However, in some cases, if done effectively, providing a negative, pathological label for behavior (as opposed to the person), as in declaring behavior to be schizophrenic, can have positive results (Grunebaum and Chasin 1978).

In addition to direct statements, the use of metaphors, jokes, anecdotes, and stories are helpful in such reframing (Barker 1985; Wallas 1985; Rosen 1982). Thus, Erickson (in Haley 1973: 27) helped a couple resolve their sexual maladjustment by discussing with them how a mutually enjoyable meal could be constructed with consideration for their individual likes and dislikes, and then prescribing this meal, with its metaphorical meaning, for them. As another example, the members of a group are instructed to argue with someone when they get annoyed about something or when they want that person's attention, to help them make the connection between these two behaviors.

Paradoxical interventions have also been categorized as compliance-based and defiance-based. As Rohrbaugh and his colleagues (1981) explain, their use depends on an assessment of the potential for compliance or defiance on the part of the primary performer and/or client group to the helper's directives, and whether the target behavior is believed by the client or client group to be voluntary or involuntary. Compliant persons with avoidance type symptoms seem to benefit from tasks that call for performance of the target behavior scheduled at specific times and/or at a greatly increased frequency, with a rationale consistent with the client's beliefs, language, and life style. For example, the therapist can suggest that this would help the client know just when a symptom occurs or to better understand its conditions and benefits.

Defiance-based strategies are used to provoke an oppositional client to rebel against the therapist and to reject a task and also the target behavior. Thus, an overprotective mother may authoritatively be given the task of greatly intensifying her overprotectiveness so that this behavior becomes unacceptable to her and she gives it up altogether. Another defiance-based strategy, that of "restraining," may be used in declaring that change efforts are futile; this can cause a battling couple to turn against the therapist and prove him or her wrong. Although many resistive clients have oppositional traits that warrant the use of defiant-based techniques, differential distinctions need to be made for the appropriate application of these procedures.

Paradoxical procedures involve interpretations and directives formulated to provide tasks for the individual or group client. Where possible, these tasks should be metaphoric in implicit communications concerning the relationship with the accepting yet situation-controlling therapist and the voluntary nature of the target behavior. The tasks may be conveyed verbally or in written form, as in paradoxical letters (Weeks and L'Abate 1982: 152–70). They need to be based on an explicitly formulated problem and plan. A meaningful helping relationship must be established between the helper and the client or client group. The assigned tasks also have to be presented with a rationale for their performance that encourages the client or client group to carry out the tasks involved. They should be group directed in that both the primary actor and the family or group situation are addressed, so as to stimulate change in both individual behavior and situational relationships. As much as possible, where symptoms are to be exaggerated, the assignments should be given and explained in an atmosphere of good humor. Such requirements call for careful assessment and understanding of the psychodynamics and sociodynamics involved, as well as timing and modes of presentation that accord with the client's accessibility, readiness, and performance capacities. Where these conditions are lacking, the assignments have a superficial quality and do not work.

INDICATIONS AND EFFECTIVENESS

Paradoxical interventions have been applied for a variety of symptoms and problems from simple habits of thumbsucking, to enuresis, delinquency, insomnia, depression, and borderline personality disorder (Seltzer 1986: 274–81). The basic criterion for their use is the presence of resistance to change that has persevered in the past or perseveres at present despite corrective efforts. There also needs to be some expressed desire for change, as in seeking or requesting help. Where direct structural-systemic change efforts, such as advising the modification of family role expectations, do not work, paradoxical reframing procedures are indicated (Stanton 1981b).

Counterindications are those situations in which clients lack age, intelligence, and other capacities to carry out or even to reject tasks intentionally; where clients are not resistive, or are not involved or motivated to involve themselves in the therapeutic process; in acute crisis or chaotic situations; or with destructive, aggressively hostile, or paranoid individuals (Seltzer 1986). Yet, some therapists report success with retarded, suicidal, or other types of unpromising clients or situations, so that the expertness or other qualities of the therapist or unknown properties of the client's situation may operate to maximize therapeutic gains in unpromising situations.

The great popularity of paradoxical procedures is partly explained by their cost effectiveness. They are brief, short-term techniques, which accomplish radical changes quickly and dramatically, with clients doing most of the work. They are widely appropriate because people seek professional help when their symptoms have not resolved spontaneously or through their own efforts, and circular, reinforced, resistive patterns have been established. The challenge to the therapist is to be expert, in charge, directing others, and particularly creative in developing and prescribing ingenious procedures.

Research on the effectiveness of paradoxical interventions (Weeks and L'Abate 1982; Seltzer 1986) indicates that paradoxical interventions are effective and result in significant improvement in client functioning. This is supported by the widespread adoption of such techniques by therapists who provide anecdotal evidence of their effectiveness. Clients report that though they initially perceived their assignments as "weird" or "crazy," or a "dumb exercise," they later report that these exercises "stimulated some of the most important learning of my life," and "The results were amazing, the damn thing worked. Within three weeks I was functioning for most of my day at a reasonable level of efficiency and effectiveness" (Weeks and L'Abate 1982: 236–37).

Though there is an increasing number of empirical studies reported in the literature, including the use of follow-up post-therapy procedures, they mostly have not used controlled experimental designs. Clinical outcome studies present major difficulties, having to consider complex and interrelated variables, the control of which presents formidable research tasks. Seltzer (1986: 169) is pessimistic about the possibility of gaining evidence from controlled studies, believing that "the ambiguities and complexities of the therapeutic enterprise" make it "most unlikely that the ultimate truth" about paradoxical interventions can be demonstrated or disconfirmed. However, he finds that the available research evidence does support the effectiveness of paradoxical interventions used in behavior and system-strategic therapy approaches.

APPLICATIONS TO ORGANIZATIONAL BEHAVIOR

We turn now to a consideration of the applications of the understandings and technical procedures of paradoxical interventions in family therapy to the world of organizational development and functioning.

Although families and organizations seem to be quite different, there are important linkages and commonalities that indicate the presence and operation of the same kind of psychodynamics and sociodynamics. Both are social systems, as Parsons (1951) clarified, with the same needs for survival, growth and self-realization, adaptation, integration, boundary and pattern maintenance, and problem-solving goal attainment. The well-functioning and dysfunctioning of organizations and families depend on the complementarities among intra-system elements and between their characteristics and those of their environments. Both demonstrate the same paradoxical resistances to making adaptations for change, and they utilize similarly defensive, self-defeating, deviant behavior mechanisms out of their fears of change. Organizations therefore appear suitable for the helping approaches and paradoxical technical procedures identified above.

Although there have been only a few attempts to apply the techniques of paradoxical communication to organizational situations, the ones that have been tried so far point to opportunities and obstacles in the use of these approaches. Hirschorn and Gilmore (1980) used family therapy techniques, including the use of paradoxical injunctions, in work with a social agency experiencing what Hirschorn (1978) defines as "stalemate." This is a situation of blocked development, in which

> conflict within the agency increases, agency members withdraw to their own protective turf, blaming-behavior increases rapidly, and everybody generally feels impotent. . . . Ironically, the agency's past successes become at the same time the ground for its present failure. The same structures, attitudes, and organizational norms that once established its visibility and productivity now become the barriers to the agency's further development. (p. 426)

In order to break the stalemate, the organization must engage in developmental planning that permits the organization to locate itself in an evolving context, and then move to a new developmental phase in which the organization's goals and structure can be redefined and its behavioral patterns thus changed (Hirschorn 1978: 429–35). Developmental planning can thus be seen as an instance of reframing, aimed at "second-order change (Watzlawick, Weakland, and Fisch, 1974).

While Hirschorn and Gilmore (1980) had moderate success in helping the organization reframe and subsequently modify its goals and procedures, they identified several obstacles to the application of paradoxical techniques to organizations. Some of these obstacles arise from the differences between organizations and families. As Miller and Rice (1967) suggest, most organizations—especially work organizations—are infused with an ethos of competition: competition for jobs, salaries, status, and power. Many organizations accept the viewpoint that conflicts are to be stimulated and maintained because they provide the energy to drive the enterprise forward. In contrast, the driving force in a family is its unity—a unity based on norms and mechanisms that foster cooperative effort and help resolve conflict, as through compromise, or through sublimation, repression or denial.

Hirschorn and Gilmore (1980) identified several structural differences between organizations and families that impeded their efforts as consultants. Organizations contain more complex and diverse coalitions than families; organizations have more sources of authority and power, and organizations are more politicized than families. Consequently, it was more difficult for the consultants to establish their legitimacy in the organization than it would be for a therapist with a family. They were also less likely to identify and join completely with all the relevant coalitions within the organization. To the extent that this happens, the consultant can become part of the dysfunctional action sequences of the organizational systems. They believe that control of the timing of organizational interventions and the formulation of developmental tasks for organizations are more difficult than with families.

They also learned that the power of the consultant in this kind of intervention depends greatly on the prospective tasks (whether they are in the form of paradoxical injunctions) that the consultant gives to different coalitions. This requires great knowledge about the substantive content of the organization's work, the wider task environment, and a historical perspective in order to select tasks that are authentically developmental. Such tasks must not only help to meet current problems and restructure the organization, but also help the organization learn about the new issues it faces as it moves to a new stage of its existence.

It is evident that the particular properties of work organizations require specific adaptations in the application of paradoxical interventions to organizational problems. These differences need to be identified and differential applications of paradoxical prescriptions and reframing interventions tested for their applications to varied organizational problems. It is appropriate to use compliance-based as well as defiance-based interventions, depending on the authority structure of organizations, and the nature of organizational member relationships.

Blake and Mouton (1984) make a helpful distinction between an "Interpersonal Facilitator Model," and an "Interface Conflict-Solving Model," for resolving organizational conflicts and rebuilding trust and cooperation. They suggest that the facilitator model is useful when compliance with change directives can be expected, and that the conflict-solving model is indicated where involvement and agreement on the part of antagonistic contestants are necessary. Their case illustrations demonstrate that paradoxical directives (which they do not so label)—such as instructing contestants to continue doing their own thing, but in a "fishbowl" procedure in which they are under the observation of others—lead to attitude and behavior change that enables relationship patterns to be developed. Their conflict-resolving model relies on the development of an ideal design for organizational operations, the avoidance of coercion, and the stimulation of self-awareness and self-motivated change.

The use of defiance-based procedures would seem to fit with our adversary culture, with the anti-authority, pseudo-democratic, and egalitarian orientation prevalent in many organizations. This is an orientation popular with people who give high value to personal autonomy and self-direction. Paradoxically, many are very conformist in their reference groups and in regard to what is considered to be avant-garde fads and fashions. However, many such individuals can be responsive to challenges in which they are involved and committed for their own and some common good.

CONCLUSIONS

The effort to view organizations as analogous to families may be like "a description of a jungle using a theory of a farm" (Krupp 1961: x). There is a view that organizations in the United States are moving toward more bureaucratic, impersonal structures, and to a more materialistic, rationalistic, amoral ethos (Scott and Hart 1979). On the other hand, there is evidence of a more recent and increasing trend to humanize organizations, particularly work organizations, so that they constructively contain the tensions of competing values, devalue the competitive ethic, and take on the unifying norms and consensual, conflict-resolving patterns akin to those in families (Kanter 1983; Quinn and Cameron 1983; Bennis and Nanus 1985).

There is question about the appearance of solipsism in the use of the paradoxical approach by family therapists, in that reality seems to be viewed merely as a mental construct (Watzlawick 1978b). The concern with mental frames and subjective meanings can be misinterpreted to arrive at such a judgment. Essentially, however, the paradoxical strategies are based on a systemic perspective, which interrelates subjective, psychodynamic phenomena with situational contexts and interpersonal relationships. Symptom prescription and reframing procedures deal with the actualities of human dramas—with the needs for secure order and risky change; for deviance and dependency; the love and hate, passions, fears, ambivalences, and conflicts—that operate within and between people. It is these dialectical human dramas that lead to the traps and resistances for which paradoxical approaches are particularly indicated.

There also are ethical questions involved that merit further discussion than can be considered here. Deceitful manipulation of the client has been well discussed in the family therapy literature (Haley 1976: 195–221; Weeks and L'Abate 1982: 242–48). The issues are similar to those related to the use of behavioral modification techniques, though mechanistic, behavioral conditioning procedures are not involved. Paradoxical strategies are directed to stimulate the client's autonomy to act as he or she wishes, to clarify alternatives, and to generate motivation for self-directed change. The directiveness and lack of full disclosure about the paradoxical tasks are justified in that they oppose the client's manipulative, controlling actions that maintian the deviant, symptomatic behavior. In effective therapeutic binds, the therapist is required to control the helping situation, rather than the client, who is free to reject or comply with prescribed tasks. Defiance-based tasks, in particular, aim to stimulate and empower the client to break out of the pathogenic double bind and to assert his or her freedom.

Family therapists generally are able to avoid being sucked into pathological dynamics of dysfunctioning families and pathogenic double binds by emphasizing the importance of awareness of their own reactions and behavior, maintaining a systems perspective, a professional relationship and leadership role in relation to the family as a unit, and skillfully negotiating with and between family factions to achieve consensual objectives, values, and courses of action. The paradoxical role of the therapist or facilitator is a difficult one, in conveying acceptance of the client yet also directively influencing the client system to change its structure and behavior. Helping organizations through the use of paradoxical procedures requires special qualifications, knowledge, expertise, and training, which organizational leaders and consultants need to develop and obtain.

The obstacles that prevent organizations from resolving their problems and moving to new life stages lie not so much in the characteristics of organizations as in the character of their members and of the people in charge of them. As Saul Bellow remarked, "You get as much truth as you have the courage to approach." It requires a courageous kind of leadership to resolve resistances to change, and to provide paradoxical interventions through which members and organizations can face the truths of their actual situations, confront their fears, and move forward. Such a "transformative leadership," as Bennis and Nanus (1985: 225) suggest, "is not so much the exercise of power itself as the empowerment of others." They also suggest that this kind of organizational leadership overcomes resistance to change by achieving a voluntary commitment to shared values, integrating "those who must act with that which must be done, so that it all comes together as a single organism in harmony with itself and its niche in the environment" (pp. 185–86).

REFERENCES

Ackerman, N. 1958. *Psychodynamics of Family Life*. New York: Basic Books.

Bandler, R., and J. Bandler. 1982. *Reframing*. Moab, Utah: Real People Press.

Barker, P. 1985. *Using Metaphors in Psychotherapy*. New York: Brunner/Mazel.

Bateson, G.; D.D. Jackson; J. Haley; and J.H. Weakland. 1963. "A Note on the Double Bind—1962." *Family Process* 2, no. 1 (March): 153–61.

Bennis, W., and B. Nanus. 1985. *Leaders: The Strategies for Taking Charge*. New York: Harper & Row.

Benson, J.K. 1977. "Organizations: A Dialectical View." *Administrative Science Quarterly* 22, no. 1 (March): 1–21.

Bertalanffy, L. Von. 1968. *General Systems Theory*. New York: Brazilier.

Blake, R.R., and J.S. Mouton. 1984. *Solving Costly Organizational Conflicts*. San Francisco: Jossey-Bass.

Bodin, A.M. 1981. "The Interactional View: Family Therapy Approaches of the Mental Research Institute." In *Handbook of Marriage and Family Therapy*, edited by A.S. Gurman and D.P. Kniskern, pp. 267–309. New York: Brunner/Mazel.

Bowen, M. 1978. *Family Therapy in Clinical Practice*. New York: Jason Aronson.

Broderick, C.B., and S.S. Schrader. 1981. "The History of Professional Marriage and Family Therapy." In *Handbook of Marriage and Family Therapy,* edited by A.S. Gurman and D.R. Kniskern, pp. 5–35. New York: Brunner/Mazel.

Coyne, J.C. 1985. "Toward a Theory of Frames and Framing: The Social Nature of Frames." *Journal of Marriage and Family Therapy* 11, no. 4 (October): 337–44.

Dubos, R. 1965. *Man Adapting.* New Haven: Yale University Press.

Dunlap, K. 1932. *Habits: Their Making and Unmaking.* New York: Liveright.

Frankl, V.E. 1960. "Paradoxical Intention: A Logotherapeutic Technique." *American Journal of Psychotherapy* 14, no. 3 (July): 520–35.

——— . 1975. "Paradoxical Intention and Dereflection." *Psychotherapy: Theory, Research, and Practice* 12, no. 3 (Fall): 226–37.

Gergen, K.J. 1982. "From Self to Science: What Is There to Know." In *Psychological Perspectives on the Self,* edited by J. Suls, Vol. 1. Hillsdale, N.J.: Erlbaum.

Goldberg, M.R., and Frances T. Levinson, eds. 1952. *Diagnosis and Process in Family Counseling.* New York: Family Service Association of America.

Germain, C.B. 1981. "The Ecological Approach to People–Environment Transactions." *Social Casework* 62, no. 6 (June): 323–31.

Grunebaum, H., and R. Chasin. 1978. "Relabeling and Reframing: The Beneficial Effects of a Pathological Label." *Family Process* 17, no. 4 (December): 449–55.

Gurman, A.S., and D.P. Kniskern. 1981. "Family Therapy Outcome Research: Knowns and Unknowns." In *Handbook of Marriage and Family Therapy,* edited by A.S. Gurman and D.P. Kniskern, pp. 742–75. New York: Brunner/Mazel.

Haley, J. 1963. *Strategies of Therapy.* New York: Grune & Stratton.

——— . 1973. *Uncommon Therapy: The Psychiatric Techniques of Milton Erickson.* New York: Norton.

——— . 1976. *Problem-Solving Therapy.* San Francisco: Jossey-Bass.

Haley, J., ed. 1967. *Advanced Techniques of Hypnosis and Therapy: Selected Papers of Milton H. Erickson, M.D.* New York: Grune & Stratton.

Hirschorn, L. 1978. "The Stalemated Agency: A Theoretical Perspective and a Practical Proposal." *Administration in Social Work* 2, no. 4 (winter): 425–38.

Hirschorn, L., and R. Gilmore. 1980. "The Application of Family Therapy Concepts to Influencing Organizational Behavior." *Administrative Science Quarterly* 25, no. 1 (March): 18–37.

Kanter, R.M. 1983. *The Change Masters.* New York: Simon & Schuster.

Krupp, S. 1961. *Pattern in Organizational Analysis: A Critical Analysis.* New York: Holt, Rinehart and Winston, Inc.

Masuch, M. 1985. "Vicious Cycles in Organizations." *Administrative Science Quarterly* 30, no. 1 (March): 14–33.

Miller, E.J., and A.K. Rice. 1967. *Systems of Organizations: The Control of Task and Sentient Boundaries.* London: Tavistock.

Minuchin, S. 1978. *Families and Family Therapy.* Cambridge, Mass.: Harvard University Press.

Nelson, M.; M. Coleman; M.H. Sherman; and H.S. Strean, eds. 1968. *Roles and Paradigms in Psychotherapy.* New York: Grune & Stratton.

Papp, P. 1983. *The Process of Change.* New York: Guilford.

Parsons, T. 1951. *The Social System.* New York: Free Press.

Perls, F.S. 1971. *Gestalt Therapy Verbatim.* New York: Bantam Books.

Quinn, R.E., and K.S. Cameron. 1983. "Organizational Life Cycles and Shifting Criteria of Effectiveness: Some Preliminary Evidence." *Management Science* 29, no. 1 (January): 33–51.

Quinn, R.E., and J. Rohrbaugh. 1983. "A Spatial Model of Effectiveness Criteria: Towards a Competing Values Approach to Organizational Effectiveness." *Management Science* 29, no. 3 (March): 363–77.

Rohrbaugh, M.; H. Tennen; S. Press; and L. White. 1981. "Compliance, Defiance, and the Therapeutic Paradox." *American Journal of Orthopsychiatry* 51, no. 3 (July): 454–67.

Rosen, S., ed. 1982. *My Voice Will Go with You: The Teaching Tales of Milton H. Erickson.* New York: Norton.

Rothenburg, A. 1979. *The Emerging Goddess.* Chicago: University of Chicago Press.

Satir, V. 1964. *Conjoint Family Therapy.* Palo Alto, Calif.: Science and Behavior Books.

Scherz, F.H. 1953. "What Is Family-Centered Casework?" *Social Casework* 34, no. 8 (October): 343–49.

Scott, W.G., and D.K. Hart. 1979. *Organizational America.* Boston: Houghton Mifflin.

Seltzer, L.A. 1986. *Paradoxical Strategies in Psychotherapy.* New York: Wiley.

Selvini Palozzoli, M.; L. Boscolo; G. Cecchini; and G. Prata. 1978. *Paradox and Counterparadox.* New York: Jason Aronson.

Sherman, S.N. 1961. "The Concept of the Family in Casework Theory." In *Exploring the Base for Family Therapy,* edited by N.W. Ackerman, F.L. Beatman, and S.N. Sherman, pp. 14–29. New York: Family Service Association of America.

Siporin, M. 1975. *Introduction to Social Work Practice.* New York: Macmillan.

——— . 1980a. "Ecological Systems Theory in Social Work." *Journal of Sociology and Social Welfare* 7, no. 4 (July): 507–38.

——— . 1980b. "Marriage and Family Therapy in Social Work." *Social Casework* 61, no. 1 (January): 11–21.

Spotnitz, H. 1969. *Modern Psychoanalysis of the Schizophrenic Patient.* New York: Grune & Stratton.

Stanton, M.D. 1981a. "Strategic Approaches to Family Therapy." In *Handbook of Marriage and Family Therapy,* edited by A.S. Gurman and D.P. Kniskern, pp. 361–402. New York: Brunner/Mazel.

——. 1981b. "An Integrated Structural/Strategic Approach to Family Therapy." *Journal of Marital and Family Therapy* 7, no. 4 (October): 427–39.

Von Oech, R. 1983. *A Whack on the Side of the Head.* Meno Park, CA: Creative Think.

Wallas, L. 1985. *Stories for the Third Ear.* New York: Norton.

Watzlawick, P. 1978a. *The Language of Change.* New York: Basic Books.

——. 1978b. *How Real Is Real?* New York: Vintage.

Watzlawick, P., and J.H. Weakland, eds. 1977. *The Interactional View: Studies at the Mental Research Institute, 1965–1974.* New York: Norton.

Watzlawick, P.; J.H. Beavin; and D.D. Jackson. 1967. *Pragmatics of Human Communication.* New York: Norton.

Watzlawick, P.; J.H. Weakland; and R. Fisch. 1974. *Change: Principles of Problem Formation and Problem Resolution.* New York: Norton.

Weeks, G.R., ed. 1985. *Promoting Change through Paradoxical Therapy.* Homewood, IL: Dow Jones-Irwin.

Weeks, G.R., and L. L'Abate. 1982. *Paradoxical Therapy.* New York: Brunner/Mazel.

PARADOXICAL INTERVENTIONS FOR TOP MANAGERS AND TROUBLEMAKERS

Ralph H. Kilmann

The major lessons that emerge from the family therapy literature on paradoxical interventions can be summarized as follows:

1. although the client requests help, he or she resists change and continues to perpetuate a vicious cycle of double binds that result in dysfunctional behavior;
2. the interventionist focuses on the symptoms, not the causes, of the dysfunctional behavior by requesting, in fact, that the client intensify such dysfunctional behavior—but according to specified times and locations;
3. if the client can be induced (manipulated) to behave according to these prescriptions, the dysfunctional behavior necessarily becomes self–controlled by the client and, in order to continue resisting the interventionist, the client gradually extinguishes the dysfunctional behavior precisely because that behavior (and its intensification) has been explicitly requested by the interventionist.

Thus, the initial double binds that have locked the client in one vicious cycle of dysfunctional behavior after another, which presumably were not under the client's control, become transformed into new double binds between the client and the interventionist. These new double binds

229

result in a reframing of the behavior (its meaning) and a loss in motivation to persist in the dysfunctional behavior.

The immediate appeal of paradoxical interventions is their counter-intuitive quality: rather than directly seeking to decrease the incidence of dysfunctional behavior, these interventions first seek to intensify them, subject, however, to controlled conditions for their expression—thus defying the "laws of logic." The client, if he or she knew of the plan, might very well feel manipulated, since it does not seem that full disclosure about the intervention and its rationale is provided. Rather, the client is led to believe that his or her behavior is being rewarded and encouraged to continue—actually, to *increase* in its occurrence. The only price to pay for this new lease on life is that the intensification of the troublesome behavior must follow the constraints imposed by the interventionist. Importantly, the interventionist works to control the constraints, not the behavior. Probably all other efforts to control the client's behavior have focused on the behavior itself—to decrease its occurrence—which sets in motion subsequent efforts at resistance, defensiveness, and a new cycle of dysfunctional behavior. In the case of paradoxical interventions, the client is "tricked" into gaining self-control and thereby develops a sense of responsibility for the behavior, while losing the impetus for enacting the behavior in the first place.

The application of this type of intervention to organizational settings is not treated in depth by Siporin and Gummer; the main purpose of their chapter seems to be summarizing the literature and principles of paradoxical interventions. Although a brief discussion of the differences between families and organizations is provided, it is up to the reader to consider when and how to use paradoxical interventions in organizations. Therefore, the remainder of this rejoinder is an attempt to augment the application of the family therapy material by highlighting two areas in which I believe paradoxical interventions to be quite relevant and important:

1.   managing the inner circle of top managers in order to alter their obsession with quick-fix changes in the organization, despite fundamental and pervasive changes in the business environment; and
2.   managing the organization's troublemakers—those individuals who continually enact dysfunctional behaviors toward other members in the organization, thus limiting efforts at trust, risk taking, and innovative behavior, precisely what is needed for success today.

These two organizational domains are not unlike what has been experienced in a family context: the nonadaptive family that is unable to adjust to changed circumstances (e.g., a separation or divorce) and the family's reaction to a troubled member (e.g., an alcoholic parent).

BURSTING TOP MANAGEMENT'S BUBBLE

All members in every organization have heard the message: the world has changed. Yesterday's protected marketplace made the world seem rather stable and predictable; today's global marketplace makes the world seem mostly dynamic and turbulent. Why, then, do top managers resist transforming themselves and their organizations into market-driven, innovative, and adaptive beings for today's world? Why do top managers work so hard to convince themselves that what worked in the past—and made their organizations so successful—will also work in the future? Will top managers take responsibility for revitalizing their organizations for the long haul, or will they continue to wait for the world to become simple and stable once again? What does it take to burst top management's bubble?

Many of today's CEOs rose to the top in yesterday's world; thus, the behaviors that made them so successful—extreme dedication, persistence, attention to detail, and precision—are precisely what prevents them from being effective in today's world. How are these executives likely to deal with the anxiety that now confronts them? They will demand guarantees before they take even one step forward into the unchartered, global, competitive marketplace. They will insist on quick-fix solution to today's complex problems. Anything that smacks of uncertainty, such as a long-term program for revitalization, is not likely to be accepted.

Typically, CEOs surround themselves with a strong band of colleagues—an inner circle—composed of the senior executives of the firm. Most often, this inner circle acts much like a family: first, they protect themselves, and second, they do what is best for the larger organization or society. The worst case is for the CEO to have an inner circle with a very narrow range of talent. Most often, in fact, I find that the inner circle is purposely composed of top managers who see the world just as the CEO sees it. Not surprisingly, this group comes to easy agreement on any decision or action. In addition, if the CEO views loyalty as blind acceptance of his ideas, the inner circle will provide strong support for solving the wrong problem in the wrong way. This situation illustrates a *dysfunctional* inner circle, and seems to be present in most organizations.

Non-paradoxical interventions would seek to convince the CEO and his inner circle to minimize resistance to change, to relinquish their complete power and hold over the organization, to engage in a different sort of behavior—proactive, risk-taking, and innovative—that could benefit the whole organization and society more than themselves. Such advice, in my experience, often falls on deaf ears even amidst great pain and discomfort regarding the future prospects of the organization. It seems that group denial is a much stronger force of resistance to change than individual denial. Again and again I have witnessed a variety of vicious cycles and double binds in top management groups that defy logic (Kilmann 1984).

A paradoxical intervention in these circumstances offers the promise of changing the double bind, developing self–control and responsibility on the part of the inner circle, and gradually extinguishing the dysfunctional behavior that locks an organization in the past. If an external consultant can gain the trust of the top management group, and if this group does desire to change in some way (because the members do recognize, if only individually, that the behaviors of the past must be altered), then the interventionist can apply non-intuitive methods to break the spell. Briefly, the interventionist can stage a series of workshops for the inner circle to intensify their efforts at maintaining the status quo at all costs. Members could role play, using more extreme forms of denial of external events, extreme put-downs of any statements intended to see the situation differently, and strong resistance to hearing any new ideas or new approaches to managing the organization in a different way. This role playing among the members of the inner circle should illustrate their dysfunctional behavior face to face, which might enable them to detach themselves from it long enough to reframe and modify their perceptions and emotions. By self-controlling this dysfunctional behavior in staged settings, they are more likely to control it in the course of their everyday meetings. In addition, perhaps the intensification and corresponding emotional detachment might enable them to decrease the need to resist change at all costs. Rather, the inner circle can begin to realize that risk-taking behavior is not as fearsome as it first unconsciously seemed.

MANAGING THE TROUBLEMAKERS

In every organization I have ever encountered, there are one or more troublemakers. These individuals create havoc by their disruptive and self-serving behavior. Troublemakers are not especially concerned with efficiency and effectiveness; they are preoccupied with enhancing their own power and glory, often at the expense of all other members. Thus, troublemakers are not well-intentioned individuals who simply express disagreement with company policy. Rather, troublemakers enact rather unhealthy and even destructive forms of behavior: lying, cheating, stealing, harassing, intimidating, and purposely hurting other people. These behaviors kill the organization's spirit and performance. We need all our energy to manage the critical problems imposed by the organization's environment, with no surplus to divert to unnecessary problems created by any of its own members. Yet, when troublemakers are allowed to act out their destructive tendencies on others, it is difficult to have an open and meaningful discussion on important problems. Does every organization have to tolerate such behavior? Or can the troublemakers be managed so that all members can concentrate on high performance rather than worry about defense tactics?

The non–paradoxical intervention that I have developed to manage the troublemakers consists of a four-step process whereby the interventionist provides constructive feedback to the identified troublemaker (Kilmann 1984). The feedback consists of sharing other people's feelings regarding the troublemaker's behavior (in general terms to protect the source's anonymity)—for example, what it feels like when the troublemaker talks to a subordinate in a derogatory and demeaning manner in the presence of others or even privately. Weekly one-on-one sessions between the interventionist and the troublemaker continue with the hope of enlightening the latter to the impact of his behavior on others and to discuss alternative ways to interact with superiors, subordinates, and peers. The assumption is, of course, that such feedback eventually will decrease the dysfunctional behavior and gradually will replace it with more effective, adaptive behavior.

In most cases, however, the interventionist conducts many such counseling sessions to review what has transpired with the troublemaker, but to no avail. Often the same discussions are held over and over again. The troublemaker insists that he has changed his behavior—why can no one else see this? He claims that he is a victim of circumstance, of a series of misunderstandings. If only others knew how much he cares about them and about the organization, surely they would understand. He just does not see how his motives and behaviors can be so misconstrued. Perhaps other members are simply jealous of his energy, intelligence, and accomplishments.

During these sessions, the interventionist sees creativity at work as the troublemaker plays out the dysfunctional behavior and serves to reinforce the double binds. Troublemakers can turn, twist, rationalize, distort, and justify almost anything. These individuals, because of their wartime tactics, have learned to define and create reality so that it matches the image they have of themselves. If the facts do not fit their needs, they change the facts. They come up with a new reality to explain the value and worth of their net contributions. The most vivid example of these distortions is illustrated by the troublemaker's insistence that he likes and cares for certain individuals—who just happen to be the very same ones who have been hurt by the troublemaker time and time again. Often these mentioned individuals are the ones who complained about the troublemaker in the first place. Such is the power of psychological compensation, vicious cycles, and double binds.

The paradoxical intervention for managing troublemakers would, of course, be quite different. Here the interventionist would encourage the troublemaker to intensify his dysfunctional behavior in particular settings—ideally, in carefully contrived workshop settings—where the dysfunctional behavior will not actually hurt subordinates and peers with whom the troublemaker must still interact. As long as everyone in the setting is aware of the purpose of examining day-to-day interaction styles in a focused manner, the role playing behavior can proceed. Eventually, just as in the case of the top managers, the troublemakers will gain a sense of self-control over their own dysfunctional behavior, previously judged uncontrollable. Because that behavior has been exaggerated for open inspection, the troublemakers will develop some emotional detachment to see the behavior for what it really is. Perhaps, under these circumstances, the former troublemakers will begin to extinguish the dysfunctional behavior that is now under their control and to substitute a different style of interacting with organizational members that is not based on "uncontrollable" fears and urges.

CONCLUSIONS

In suggesting how paradoxical interventions that were learned from family therapy can be applied to these two organizational domains (top managers and troublemakers), we must keep in mind that considerable research and experimentation are required before such interventions are adopted on a large scale. To intensify behavior in settings that are not purely family in nature is potentially dangerous, especially if the other aspects of the organization might reinforce the intensification of dysfunctional behavior. For example, the culture of the organization, reward systems, and strategies and structures might support the intensification effort even when individuals, on their own, would prefer to decrease their dysfunctional behavior following the paradoxical intervention. Furthermore, as with any effort to change people, a more elaborate discussion on the ethics of the method, including how much of the method should be disclosed to the client, is in order. Nevertheless, the powerful impact that top managers and troublemakers have on organizational success and the quality of life within the organization certainly should encourage continued examination of these rather new efforts of paradoxical interventions for organizations.

REFERENCES

Kilmann, R.H. 1984. *Beyond the Quick Fix: Managing Five Tracks to Organizational Success.* San Francisco: Jossey-Bass.

7 TEACHING MBAs TRANSFORMATIONAL THINKING

Gareth Morgan

Paradox and transformation can be important concepts and tools in the helping professions. This is particularly true in teaching. At least, it is true when the teacher's intention is to change the capacity to understand and comprehend rather than just impart information and facts to be comprehended. If the intention of a teacher or any other kind of helper is to modify the assumptions, deep structures, or paradigms of another person, then "telling" is a futile method. In this paper I wish to explore how paradox can be used to transform thinking about organization and management, with particular reference to my experience in teaching organizational analysis to MBA students.

I work from the hypothesis that there are strong parallels between the mindset of the "average MBA" and that of the typical bureaucrat. Thinking tends to be fragmented in that knowledge of organization is "departmentalized": into distinctions between organizational behavior (OB), strategy, accounting, finance, marketing, etc. And, as a result, expectations about legitimate spheres of discourse, perceived relevance, and the relationship between problems and solutions tend to fall in line with an over-bureaucratized view of the world. In addition, MBA conceptions of organization are often dominated by a bureaucratic view, gleaned from early work experience, introductory courses on management, or familiarity with texts that equate organization with a clarity of structure and control. This often leads them to see the process of "getting organized" as one of developing clear, rational structures of tasks and activities, rather than of understanding organization as an open-ended, flowing process that demands the management of many contradictory strains and tensions.

My primary aim in teaching the art of organizational analysis is to transform this fragmented and over-bureaucratized view into a more open-ended appreciation that will allow the student to understand the complex and paradoxical nature of organizations and the problems of managing them. In essence, I strive to teach a style of critical thinking that recognizes how analysis and management are always based on an interpretative process that can take many forms according to the paradigms, images, or metaphors that are used to frame inquiry (Burrell and Morgan 1979; Morgan 1986).

My favored approach is to use the method of "reading" developed in *Images of Organization* (Morgan 1986), which encourages students to generate multiple views and interpretations of situations before arriving at judgments and prescriptions. The aim is to create an element of paradox and tension that will challenge their taken-for-granted assumptions, and lead them to entertain and develop new ways of thinking, and eventually, new ways of organizing and managing.

It is impossible to describe the complete method in a short chapter such as this (the author can provide further details on request). Its essence rests in the attempt to transform thinking by getting students to appreciate that:

1. our favored ways of seeing are based on images or metaphors that provide partial and one-sided viewpoints;
2. a comprehensive understanding of any situation always rests in an ability "to see" from multiple perspectives; and
3. it is necessary to integrate the insights thus provided.

The subject matter of the course is organized around readings and cases that illustrate the role of different metaphors in organizational analysis, integrated through a practical project applying all the ideas to the analysis of a real organization (usually the one in which the students work, or have worked in the recent past).

To illustrate the approach and the kind of transformation in thinking that I try to achieve, the rest of this chapter focuses on the very first class of my course, which uses a case study designed to help students reveal their taken-for-granted ways of thinking about organization, and some alternatives. The function is to show how we typically impose assumptions, biases, and knowledge on the situations that we are attempting to understand, and how a fuller understanding, or "reading of the situation," requires that we remain open to the possibility of other interpretations as well.

To illustrate, consider the following case, which I typically introduce with the question: *How would you explain the events at Eagle Smelting?*[1]

THE EAGLE SMELTING CASE

The Eagle Smelting Company has a number of smelting and refining operations in various sites across North America. The firm usually ships its finished product—aluminum ingot of various qualities—directly from its smelters to its customers, heavy industry manufacturers around the world.

Eagle's Northtown smelter is just outside a small port town on the Pacific coast. Raw materials are brought in by ship to the all-weather harbor and unloaded at the company dock, which is linked to the smelter by a private railroad. Any breakdown in the railway is a very serious matter, as it can disrupt both production and shipping schedules. Also important to the smelter's operation is the firm's fleet of land vehicles which are, for the most part, maintained on-site. To keep all this machinery in repair the company has a full-time crew of mechanics and a well-equipped machine shop, capable of fabricating most needed parts.

Don Macrae, a professional engineer, is the plant manager. Macrae, fifty-three, has been with the company for twenty-four years. He was plant engineer for four years before being named plant manager eighteen months ago.

The current plant engineer is John Holt, also a professional engineer. Holt, thirty-six, has been with Eagle for thirteen years. He was transferred to the Northtown smelter when Macrae became plant manager.

Holt is responsible for all engineering-related activities at Northtown, and is therefore involved in a variety of tasks, both at the plant and the nearby town site. Sometimes his work takes him even farther afield. One of his responsibilities is the plant's machine shop, but only a fraction of his time is actually spent there.

Ed Smith, a master mechanic, is foreman of the machine shop. Under him are three trainers, a half dozen semiskilled workers, and five fully qualified mechanics. The machine shop operates regular daytime hours, except when overtime work becomes necessary. Job requests are usually submitted to the shop by section heads, and requests are often supported by drawings or lists of specifications. Smith assigns tasks each day, but usually the work itself requires only a minimum of supervision.

One sunny Friday morning in June, events at Northtown got off to a bad start. The smelter's locomotive broke down while carrying a "rush order" to the dock. The breakdown was reported to the dock captain, Luke Hardy, just as he was leaving for the "morning conference," a short daily meeting with the plant engineer and the plant manager, held to discuss and deal with routine operational problems. Hardy raised the matter immediately when the meeting began. Holt, after hearing details, realized a part would have to be fabricated, and promised delivery of it by 1:45 that afternoon. Allowing for proper installation, this meant that the locomotive would be running again in time to catch the final shipment of the day.

The arrangement called for swift action, but Holt was confident that his target could be achieved even though special problems were involved in the fabrication of the required part. The special lathe needed for the job had recently become unreliable. While still functioning well at low RPMs, it tended to vibrate badly when operated at normal or high speeds. This vibration made precision work difficult and would, Holt feared, soon ruin the machine itself. The service representative from the manufacturer was due to visit the smelter to repair this lathe the following week, and Holt had hoped to keep it out of service until then. The present emergency, of course, made its use unavoidable. He felt, however, that the job could be done satisfactorily at low speed without risk to the machine and thus did not raise the problem for fear of lengthening the meeting.

As the job was urgent, Holt decided to leave the meeting early, and went straight to the machine shop to get work started. Foreman Smith, having made his daily work assignments, was over at the payroll department looking into a complaint by his men that too much was being deducted from their paychecks for the company's pension plan. Knowing that he was likely to be there a while, Holt decided that the work being done by Lee Curtis, one of the senior mechanics, was not urgent, and assigned Curtis to the job.

Curtis, a fully qualified mechanic and one of the most experienced and skilled men in the shop, had at one time been considered for the post of machine shop foreman. However, Macrae and Holt both preferred

Ed Smith, another excellent mechanic who, at forty-eight, was just a few years younger than Curtis. At first, Curtis had taken the missed promotion badly, but he soon seemed to settle down and accept the situation.

In assigning the priority job to Curtis, Holt specified that the machining should be done at a low speed. Curtis knew the machine well and had, in fact, reported the problems in operating the lathe just two weeks before. Holt was thus quite confident that Curtis could do a high quality job, as he had on so many other "rescue operations" in the past.

After giving Curtis his directions, Holt left the machine shop to attend to his other duties. Most Friday mornings took him to Northtown, where it was his custom to stop by his bank to deposit his weekly paycheck, and sometimes do a little shopping for the weekend. He felt free to do this as he often started early and worked late into the evening without overtime when his job required.

In the late morning, Macrae, on one of his frequent walks through the smelter, happened to stop by the machine shop. Seeing that Curtis was at work on the locomotive part, he stopped at his work station, where he discovered that Curtis was operating his machinery at low speed.

"Where's your foreman?" asked Macrae.

Curtis said he didn't know.

"How about Mr. Holt?"

Curtis replied that he didn't know where he was either. Macrae muttered to himself, told Curtis to "speed up the damn job," and hurriedly took off for his office.

Holt returned to the machine shop a little after noon, and dropped in on Smith, who, after returning from the Payroll Department and making a rapid tour of the machine shop, had gone straight to his office to deal with a backlog of paperwork. Holt explained the trouble with the locomotive, and after a brief conversation they decided to visit Curtis's work station to check on progress. The lathe was vibrating badly, and making an unpleasant whining sound. The part being tooled by Curtis was obviously not going to meet the required specifications.

"You knew the lathe shouldn't be run at this speed," said Holt in a fury. "You've messed up this job on purpose. You're fired." Turning to the foreman he told him to make arrangement for Curtis's severance pay and to see that someone else took over the priority job. He then returned to his office.

A few minutes later Smith sought him out there, and told him that he was not justified in firing Curtis.

"He speeded up the job because Macrae ordered him to," explained the foreman. "He says Macrae is the boss, and he did what he was told."

Holt, on hearing this explanation, strode over to Macrae's office and burst in without knocking. "By sticking your nose in this morning you've ruined the rush job on the locomotive part and probably scrapped an expensive lathe to boot. If that's the way you run things here, then I quit."

"You're right," Macrae shouted back. "That locomotive job was a top priority, so why weren't you or Smith overseeing it? Was it in danger of interfering with your personal business? I know your Friday morning routine! I accept your resignation."

A CASE ANALYSIS

How, then, are we to explain the events at Eagle Smelting?

The case is a very rich one, and many different interpretations are possible, each suggesting different kinds of managerial solutions. Consider, for example, the following:

1.   *A case of chaotic organization and poor communications?* Shaped by assumptions that Eagle Smelting is a bureaucratic organization that is functioning inefficiently, various problems can be highlighted, for example, violation of the chain of command, poor information exchange, overlapping job responsibilities, and sloppy adherence to prescribed roles. The solutions to the perceived problems are, of course, *bureaucratic* ones: "tighten up" the organization in all these respects.
2.   *A case of poor planning?* The failure and problems can be subscribed to the machine breakdown, and the lack of an effective stock of spare parts, or set of contingency plans. The solutions thus become highly *technical* ones: better machinery, more spare parts or better inventory control, clear emergency procedures, etc.
3.   *A case illustrating the dysfunctions of authoritative management?* Macrae is a highly authoritarian manager. Holt also likes to give instructions. No one asks questions. There is no evidence of participation or "bottom-up" influence. Curtis has been conditioned to a "do as you're told" mentality. This analysis leads toward some kind of *human relations* solution to the problems at hand, involving more participation, a "flatter," less hierarchical form of organization, a better match between individual and organizational needs, or to

some form of *contingency approach* emphasizing the importance of matching tasks, structure, and people to create "good fit."

4.   *A case of the plant manager doing his old job?* Macrae is acting as the area engineer. He wants Holt to do the job exactly as he used to do it. He has interfered with his colleague's responsibilities. He is "managing by walking about," but in a "hands in" rather than "hands off" style. This interpretation of the case sees the problem as resting with Macrae. He needs to change his *managerial style,* or be replaced by someone who can do the plant manager's job in a broader way.

5.   *A case of "awkward" or clashing personalities?* Relations between Macrae and Holt are frequently hot and emotional. Tempers are quick. Curtis may be seething with resentment about a missed promotion. Many managers would say he has "an attitude problem." Others might say he is alienated and fed up with his work, or dislikes authority. This kind of interpretation leads back to some kind of *human relations* solution calling for more participation and better communications, or to some kind of *fire and hire* solution.

6.   *A case requiring a "search for villains"?* Who's to blame? This approach leads one to prescribe solutions that involve *firing* key offenders. The trouble is that a case can usually be made against almost everyone. Macrae can be blamed for his meddling. Holt can be blamed for not staying on top of the job. Curtis can be blamed for deliberately wrecking the job. And even Smith can be "fingered" for spending so much time away from the machine shop.

7.   *A case of organizational politics?* Are Macrae and Holt in competition with each other? Does Holt have an eye on Macrae's job? Does Macrae feel insecure and threatened by his younger colleague, who does things in such a different way? Do they have personal dislikes and quarrels? Does this have an adverse influence on the work relations between the two managers? Is Curtis truly seething with resentment about the missed promotion? Is he looking for a way to get revenge? Has he deliberately engineered Holt's dismissal? Has he been waiting for an opportunity to use the conflict between Macrae and Holt for his own ends? Has he been waiting for the perfect opportunityy to make his move? Are Smith and Curtis in collusion? Are their actions part of a preconceived plan to move against Holt and Macrae: disgruntled workers making a protest against incompetent management? Was Hardy involved

in the plot? Was the locomotive sabotaged? Some of these questions may seem farfetched. The case is ambiguous and does not
speak to these points in a specific way. But all identify possible
situations. This line of questioning leads to a *political* interpretation of the case, favoring forms of conflict management that
recognize competing interests and power relations.

8. *Is this a case of a fragmented corporate culture?* There appear to
    be few shared norms and values. Should those responsible for
    managing the organization attempt to develop an overarching sense
    of shared meaning that would bind people in the organization
    together in a meaningful way? This interpretation of the situation
    directs attention to solutions involving *the management of meaning.*

9. *Is this a case of a radicalized organization?* Are there deep divi-
    sions between management and workers? Even though there is no
    mention of a militant union, perhaps relations are antagonistic
    and conflictual. Are there divisions between the professional out-
    siders (Macrae and Holt) and the local workforce? Are there im-
    portant social and cultural differences between management and
    workers? Such interpretations would lead to solutions that recognize
    the immediate problem to be *a symptom of a much deeper his-
    torical, socio-economic problem,* and lead to strategies that at-
    tempt to bridge the gulf in some way.

The above discussion is by no means exhaustive. But it does serve
to illustrate the complexity and potentially paradoxical nature of what,
at first sight, seems to be a relatively straightforward situation. All the
above interpretations, which are all partial, and which all depend on
a degree of "reading into" the situation, especially where information
is vague and incomplete, and may be simultaneously correct. They may
all be combined in the very nature of the situation.

The task of the organizational analyst, or the reflective manager, is
to unravel this complexity in the best way he or she can. It involves an
awareness of the fact that we typically read and understand situations
in partial ways, and that a comprehensive understanding demands the
kind of framing and reframing process evident in the line of questioning posed above.

Effective managers and organizational analysts often develop the
knack of reading situations intuitively. Some talk about gaining "a feel"
for a situation, or "grabbing it with their guts," or trying to "smell" its
key dimensions. Each case involves an interpretative process that attempts

to understand the essence of the situation at hand. The process simulated above, and explored in further detail in Morgan (1986), can be used to achieve the same results. By being open to the possibility of making multiple interpretations of any given situation, we create alternative models for understanding, alterntive patterns of explanation, and set the basis for alternative modes of action, problem formulation, and problem solutions.

For example, mechanistic interpretations of a situation almost always result in mechanistic approaches to problem solving. The manager whose basic conception of organization is bureaucratic almost always looks for solutions that involve changes in the structure and design of organizational tasks and activities. The manager who is more open to negative thinking will be much more sensitive to issues of "process," the conditions required for evolution and change, and unsatisfied needs. The manager who has been influenced by the latest books on corporate culture is more likely to tune into the symbolism, and the construction and management of meaning. And those with a political bent will probably see wheeling and dealing everywhere.

The problem is to provide ways of balancing and integrating these insights, and of knowing when they provide the basis for effective action. By broadening one's ability to understand the different dimensions of the situations with which one is dealing, one's approach to management can become much more reflective, and transformative in its effects. New and broader forms of understanding can provide the basis for new kinds of organization to emerge.

TRANSFORMATION IN THE CLASSROOM

The seeds for this kind of transformation begin in the class setting in the disjuncture between the views of organization brought into the classroom and the views with which the students leave. The typical student analysis of the Eagle Smelting case is usually a very limited one. Most often, students interpret the case as presenting a problem that must be solved, and proceed to analyze the case in terms of a quasi-mechanistic frame of reference identifying problems with the organization's systems of communication, job design, line of command, definitions of responsibility and authority, managerial styles, and poor human relations. Sometimes discussion points towards the politics of the situation, especially in terms of "personality conflicts" and "feelings of alienation."

But when it comes to "solution time," the political problems are usually seen as a product of the structural problems referred to above. Solutions thus focus on clarifying structures, lines of command, job responsibilities, improving human relations skills, and so on.

The learning generated by this case really gets underway when the students have formulated their solutions, and the instructor begins to use the case analysis as a kind of mirror in which they can see their own assumptions and biases. For example, as the models and metaphors of organization that have been implicitly adopted as a basis for analysis and prescription are reflected back to the class, different interpretations of the case are quickly identified. And, as the paradoxes and contradictions highlighted by competing interpretations are explored, students quickly see that their prescriptions and solutions may be quite limited or inappropriate. The paradoxes can be clearly illustrated by focusing on the contrasts between quasi-mechanistic and political interpretations of the case. If the case is truly rooted in the kind of conflicts highlighted under points seven and nine of the earlier analysis, it is extremely unlikely that they can be resolved through the quasi-mechanistic or human relations approaches typically favored by the majority of the class. The political dynamic within the organization will merely take a new form.

This class session is often a dramatic one. Conventional assumptions are challenged. The existence of alternatives is clearly demonstrated. And the course is set on a voyage of discovery through which these alternatives will be explored. Subsequent weeks focus on the systematic interpretation and reinterpretation of organizations and organizational problems through the variety of metaphors explored in *Images of Organization*. The process, illustrated each week through case-based discussions in class, is also grounded in student projects involving the ongoing analysis of a real organizational situation that must be interpreted from different viewpoints. After each alternative perspective is applied, it is not uncommon for students to feel that they have at last arrived at *the* answer, the one that truly makes sense of the situation. However, after the fifth or sixth week, the transformation glimpsed in that very first class, but usually pushed to the sidelines for ease of mind thereafter, at last reoccurs.

There is no one theoretical frame that can provide the definitive answer. There are usually many possible answers, or combinations of answers, that need to be carefully evaluated against the many possible meanings and interpretations inherent in the situation being studied. As this message hits home, students begin to realize that organizational analysis is ultimately a complex interpretive process that deals with paradoxes and tensions of many kinds. Rather than reach for simple "off-the-shelf" interpretations and solutions, they are encouraged to realize that there is no substitute for solid diagnosis that grasps and integrates the various aspects of the situation.

This process also illustrates that managers in everyday situations face similar problems. They too must arrive at appropriate interpretations and understandings of the situation being managed, and engage in actions that fit those situations. Students thus begin to appreciate the key role of interpretation in the management process, and how managers must learn to be their own theorists and diagnosticians, developing the kind of critical thinking that will broaden their range of understanding and action opportunities.

In this way, students are encouraged to understand and explore the paradoxes and ambiguities inherent in organizational analysis and the management process generally, and to broaden their capacity for creative thinking about situations that were previously taken for granted. And ultimately this transformation in thinking helps to provide a basis for a transformation of action. For seeing and understanding organizations in new ways helps to create a capacity for one to manage them in new ways.

NOTE

1. The case is introduced without any prior discussion about the course, and before any course outlines or handouts have been distributed. The case is based on a description of unknown origin; key details have been changed; and the case has been written to place it in a North American context.

REFERENCES

Burrell, G., and G. Morgan. 1979. *Sociological Paradigms and Organizational Analysis.* London and Portsmouth, N.H.: Heinemann Educational Books.

Morgan, G. 1986. *Images of Organization.* Newbury Park: Sage Publications.

TRANSFORMATIONAL THINKING SEEN FROM A DEVELOPMENTAL PERSPECTIVE

William R. Torbert

I strongly agree with Morgan's opening comments that the mindset of average MBAs and managers can be described as "departmentalized." Indeed, this impressionistic description dovetails with data on MBAs' and managers' ego development from three separate studies by different investigators, all using Loevinger's well-validated measure of ego development (Torbert 1987). All three studies show that the modal level of MBAs' and managers' (whether the managers be supervisors, middle managers, or senior executives) is the Technician stage. As the word "departmentalized" suggests, at the Technician stage a single, internally consistent logic (whether it be the logic of accounting, computing, engineering, or sailboating) is viewed as the source of meaning, coherence, and validity.

Given the mindset of average MBAs, what should we teach them? Certain facts and functional skills? Yes, of course, as I am sure Morgan would agree. But these are likely only to reinforce the already "departmentalized," "technical" mindset.

Virtually all MBA programs make some efforts that Morgan does not mention to transform this mindset: for example, they overload students with day-to-day work so that they cannot succeed if they stick too closely to a solitary, methodical, perfectionistic approach to learning (all elements of the *Technician*'s approach). Most MBA programs also force students to deal with ambiguous, multifunctional business

249

cases and to work in groups where their favored approach will clash with others'.

These conditions may encourage students to transform to the next developmental stage, the *Achiever* stage. At the Achiever stage a student/manager seeks to achieve, not internal purity of logic, but rather external goals. To achieve external goals in organizational settings requires responsiveness to negative feedback from constituencies that can influence goal attainment, whether or not their logic agrees with one's own. Hence, the Achiever stage involves implicitly coordinating multiple logics on a pragmatic level. (Each developmental stage is described in much greater detail in Torbert [1987].)

THE TRANSFORMATION THAT INTERESTS MORGAN

But this transformation from Technician to Achiever is not enough for Morgan. The intellectual perspective that Morgan advocates and the teaching methodology that he illustrates in his chapter both encourage students to transform beyond the Achiever stage of development to the *Strategist* stage. (The developmental research already cited shows that fewer than 10 percent of MBA students and managers move to this stage, so there is certainly room for more encouragement of this sort.) At the Strategist stage, students/managers become aware—explicitly and intellectually, not just implicitly and pragmatically—that different persons make different assumptions in interpreting reality. This intellectual awareness of paradigm differences among persons permits a manager to develop theories or strategies about how to work with, around, and through these differences. It is only at this stage that critical thinking— thinking that recognizes the limitations of its own and others' assumptions—begins.

This is what Morgan wishes to teach: critical thinking, multiple views of a situation, recognition that many or all views may be simultaneously correct, recognition that no view is gospel, no view is always and exclusively right. His way of developing multiple interpretations of "The Eagle Smelting Case"—particularly his twist of discussing the case prior to offering any course outlines or handouts—nicely dramatizes this issue in a concrete instance. The case method helps make what could all too easily be, for MBAs, an unpalatably abstract approach undeniably relevant to specific "real life" situations.

Using a pedagogy or management system that counters the natural inclination of one's perspective or personal style—as Morgan does here in inviting student perspectives on a concrete case to introduce his very abstract "perspective of perspectives"—is to enact an intentionally paradoxical process. Such intentionally paradoxical processes, which reach across from the leadership's perspective to others', are crucial to the possibility of transforming students or other subordinates. Such processes do not distance and deauthorize those who do not share the leadership's perspective, but rather invite them into the conversation. Such intentionally paradoxical processes cannot, therefore, be easily stereotyped and rejected. By the time students realize that they are in over their heads (that the conversation is not just about physical events, but also about metaphysics) they *are* in over their heads. At that point, even getting out as fast as they can may be a transforming experience (Torbert 1978).

Morgan's most recent book, *Images of Organization* (1986), wonderfully supports his multiperspectival approach, showing how work in the field of organizational behavior during this century represents multiple metaphors or paradigms. His reinterpretation of Frederick Taylor's life and work, for example, is a tour de force that shows how the various metaphors live themselves out even in those who are consciously devoted to but one. If a teacher of organizational behavior wishes to survey the field, this book is an infinitely more lively, provocative, and intellectually significant way of doing so than any textbook currently available.

THE LIMITS OF MORGAN'S PERSPECTIVE

By now, Morgan the writer and Morgan the teacher are sounding almost too good to be true. But the seasoned reader who has already learned Morgan's lesson about multiple perspectives suspects that, however true all that I have so far said may be, it is not the whole truth. There must be some perspective that includes all of Morgan's perspectives while keeping itself outside them. Such a perspective would reveal any incompleteness, inefficacy, or even evil in Morgan's "perspective of perspectives." One such perspective is the developmental perspective, already introduced in this rejoinder in the references to the Technician, Achiever and Strategist perspectives.

According to developmental theory, Morgan's perspective itself corresponds to the relativistic Strategist stage of development. Certain difficulties characterize this stage. The Strategist struggles to develop an explicit theory of change to guide him and her in action, because all perspectives seem equally valid and equally arbitrary initially. Hence, the relativistic Strategist has a hard time developing a unitary view of phenomena and committing to action based on a given set of values. Note, for example, that though Morgan seems to claim that his teaching leads toward an "intuitive," unitary "feel" for situations, he does not describe at all how this occurs. Indeed, the transformation that he does illustrate lightly is a transformation in what appears to be the opposite direction from a unitary feel, namely a transformation *toward* taking the fact of multiple perspectives seriously. Note, also, that though Morgan claims that "transformation in thinking provides a basis for the transformation of action," he offers no illustrations of this, nor describes how this latter transformation occurs. In particular, effective action is timely action, yet there is nothing about Morgan's multiperspectival approach, nor about his pedagogy as he has described it, that addresses the issue of timing. Note, finally, that though Morgan claims his teaching provides a basis for transforming organizations in fundamental ways, he again offers no illustrations either of relevant pedagogical techniques or of actual effects on organizations.

The developmental perspective suggests that Morgan is in one sense perfectly correct in speaking of his teaching as providing *a basis* for a fully adequate unitary perspective, for committed action that recognizes the fact of multiple perspectives, and for fundamental organizational transformation. According to developmental theory, persons must reconnoiter the Strategist perspective before transforming to still later developmental stages that resolve the dilemmas of creating ethical priorities amidst a legitimate multiplicity of perspectives, of committing to irreversible action in a timely fashion, and of successfully cultivating fundamental organizational transformations. But the developmental perspective also highlights the fact that these are in no direct way consequences of developing the Strategist perspective. They do not follow from it like a ball rolling down a chute. Indeed, these consequences are no more likely to follow from Morgan's approach than is multiperspectival thinking itself likely to follow from a normal MBA case-oriented course.

Quite the contrary—each of these further steps will require pedagogies as inventive as Morgan's and developmental transformations that are as hard-won as the one he outlines for us.

Actually, it is very unlikely that many of Morgan's students actually make the transformation to the Strategist stage during his course. Those starting at the Technician stage may learn something about unforeseeable complexities of action situations that helps them move toward the pragmatic Achiever perspective. And many of those already at the Achiever stage will focus on consolidating their performance at that stage (e.g., picking up that Morgan wants multiple perspectives and skillfully finding them for him), rather than on opening toward a new ontology and epistemology. To date, reasearch on ego development has uniformly found that single courses do not result in systematic developmental change in students.

This last point raises questions about where Morgan's approach is best placed within an overall MBA curriculum (I would suggest in the third semester Business Policy/Strategic Management course), and about how an MBA program as a whole might plan its courses and pedagogies if the development of transformational thinking and action are among its aims. These questions go beyond the scope of his article and therefore also beyond the scope of this rejoinder.

REFERENCES

Morgan, G. 1986. *Images of Organization.* Beverly Hills, Calif.: Sage.

Torbert, W. 1978. "Educating Toward Shared Purpose, Self-Direction, and Quality Work: The Theory and Practice of Liberating Structure." *The Journal of Higher Education* March/April: 3–23.

——— . 1987. *Managing the Corporate Dream: Restructuring for Long-Term Success.* Homewood, Ill.: Dow Jones-Irwin.

8 CRAFTING A THEORY OF PRACTICE
The Case of Organizational Paradoxes

Chris Argyris

If paradoxes are an important phenomenon for administrators, (Barnes 1981; Argyris 1985), why is it that the prominent theories of administration or organization do not have them as a central focus? What would it require to craft theories where paradox has a primary role?

LOGICAL AND BEHAVIORAL WORLD PARADOXES

I should like to differentiate between logical paradoxes and paradoxes that result from human action. Philosophers have focused on logical paradoxes for many years. A logical paradox occurs when the meaning embedded in the words used contains its own contradiction. For example, if I say "I am lying," then that statement is true. But if the statement is true, I am not lying; then the statement is false. In this example, the existence of the paradox can be identified by examining what the person said. We need no further data. The contradiction is embedded in the statement "I am lying."

The paradoxes that exist in the behavioral world, strictly speaking, do not have the same properties. Most paradoxes that I have observed occur because individuals designed and produced inconsistent meanings and disguised the fact that they were doing so. The resultant actions appear to be paradoxical because we do not know all the facts.

255

For example, assume that A said to B "I trust you." Assume also that A did not trust B but hid his true views because he did not wish to upset B. We have a situation where the "action" has at least three components. The first is what A said. It could be caught accurately by a tape recorder. If we stopped with the first component, the statement by A that "I am lying" is true. We then have the basis for the logical paradox.

The second component of the action was what A thought and did not say. A knew that he did not trust B, but he did not say so because he did not wish to upset B.

The third component was that A acted as if he were not withholding any views. He acted as if he were not lying. If we focus on components two and three, then A is still lying. However, there is no paradox because the thoughts and actions explain the cover up. The behavior appears paradoxical because we did not know what was covered up.

One step further. Let us assume that A covered up because he intended not to upset himself by being responsible for upsetting B. Under these conditions, it is likely that A will not allow any discussion of the cover-up because to discuss it would upset B and A and would lead to a contradiction. Let us also assume that B senses that the cover-up cannot be discussed and he goes along, but B also covers up what he senses. We now have two individuals acting in ways that are undiscussable, and their undiscussability is undiscussable.

All these consequences not only maintain the original action paradox, but they make it unlikely that the paradox will ever be discussed. The actions are not only self-maintaining; they are also self-sealing. But if they are self-maintaining and self-sealing, and if this cannot be discussed, and if their undiscussability is undiscussable, then they are not manageable.

We now have a second-order paradox. The intention of management is to manage, yet it is not possible to manage actions that are not manageable.

We must study these actions paradoxes because, I believe, they are endemic to the way most organizations are managed. Organizations are designed and managed in order to make management less difficult, but human beings act in ways that make management more difficult. I am suggesting that unlike the physical science universe where Einstein insisted that nature would not play tricks, in the universe of the behavioral world, tricks may be a key characteristic. How does one theorize about a tricky universe? Are there features of the tricks that can be stated in the form of disconfirmable propositions? If so, in what sense are they tricks?

WHERE TO STUDY PARADOXES

Paradoxes of the kind that concern us develop as a result of programs in peoples' heads and norms in the culture in which they are embedded. What would lead individuals to produce such actions?

One of the richest hunting grounds for paradoxes is in the routines that exist to defend against embarrassment or threat, be it at the individual, small group, intergroup, or organizational levels. Organizational defensive routines may be defined as any policy or action that prevents someone (or some system) from experiencing embarrassment or threat, *and* simultaneously prevents anyone from correcting the causes of the embarrassment or threat. Organizational defensive routines are antilearning and overprotective.

Although they are related, it is important that we differentiate organizational defensive routines from the well-known individual psychological defenses that clinicians have identified. Organizational defensive routines differ from psychological defensive routines in that:

1. they are taught through socialization;
2. they are taught as strategies to deal effectively with threat or embarrassment;
3. they are supported by the culture of the organization; and
4. they exist over time even though the individuals (with different psychological defensive routines) move in and out of the organization.

An Example of an Organizational Defensive Routine: Mixed Messages[1]

Built into any organization is the age-old dilemma of autonomy versus control. Subordinates wish to be left alone but held accountable. Superiors agree but do not want surprises. The subordinates push for autonomy asserting that leaving them alone is the best sign that they are trusted by top management. They push for a solution that combines trust with distancing. The superiors, on the other hand, push for no surprises by using information systems as controls. The subordinates see the control feature as confirming mistrust.

The point is not how to get rid of the dilemma. That will never occur; it is built into the concept of decentralization. The point is how to deal with it effectively.

Mixed messages are the most frequently used strategy to deal with this dilemma. The top keeps saying "We mean it—you are managing your show." The divisional heads concur that the message is credible except when the division or corporate gets into trouble or when a very important issue is at stake. In the eyes of the divisional heads, corporate begins to interfere precisely when they want to prove their metal. In the eyes of corporate, they intervene precisely when they can be of most help, that is when the issue "requires a corporate perspective."

Divisional heads described the mixed messages they received as:

"You are running the show, however . . ."

"You make the decisions, but clear with . . ."

"That's an interesting idea, but be careful . . ."

The Logic Embedded in the Mixed Messages.   Mixed messages contain meanings that are simultaneously: ambiguous and clear; imprecise and precise.

Anyone who deals with mixed messages experiences the dilemmas that are embedded in them. The designers know that constructing a message to be clearly ambiguous requires skill and knowledge about the receiver. They know that to be vague and to be clear is inconsistent. Furthermore, to be clearly vague is not only inconsistent, but designed inconsistency. To design inconsistency makes the designer vulnerable unless the receiver does not question the inconsistency.

The Logic and Rules of Mixed Messages.   There are therefore four rules about designing and implementing mixed messages. They are:

1. Design a message that is inconsistent.
2. Act as if the message is not inconsistent.
3. Make the inconsistency in the message and the act that there is no inconsistency undiscussable.
4. Make the undiscussability of the undiscussable also undiscussable.

The Consequences of Mixed Messages.   The first-order consequences of mixed messages is that they are based on rules that require inconsistent actions. They produce advice that is paradoxical: to be consistent, act inconsistently, and act as if that is not the case. To manage, act as if you are not managing. To make some issues discussable, make others undiscussable, and act as if this is not the case.

CRAFTING A THEORY OF PRACTICE

In order for human beings to act, they must first understand what is going on and why. In the case of defensive routines, this leads to a second-order consequence. Individuals create attributions to explain each others' actions. The attributions are often wrong, or at least incomplete. But, following the logic of mixed messages, the attributions are neither discussed nor tested publicly. As a result, any distortions or errors that may result are not corrected; indeed, they are often magnified and enlarged. This feeds back to reinforce the use of mixed messages as well as the rules about undiscussability and nontestability.

The third-order consequence is that the organizational defensive routines, in this case mixed messages, become unmanageable and uninfluencable. This, in turn, leads to a fourth-order consequence which is a set of operating assumptions or beliefs about defensive routines. Individuals express, on the one hand, a sense of despair and cynicism about the defensive routines ever being changed. On the other hand, individuals may come to believe that engaging defensive routines can be dangerous, because doing so will open Pandora's box. Consequently, individuals distance themselves from engaging the defensive routines. The rule is to bypass them and act as if you are not bypassing.

The fifth-order consequence is that defensive routines take on a life of their own. They maintain, reinforce, and proliferate themselves; hence, they become unmanageable.

WHAT ARE THE FEATURES OF THEORIES THAT DEAL WITH PARADOXES?

A theory about paradoxes must explain why human beings create a world that is contrary to the world they intend, or if they do intend the world, then how do they explain their actions by asserting that they are forced to act as they do? In either case, we are dealing with inconsistencies that appear to be designed. The first feature, therefore, of a theory to understand paradoxes that result from defensive routines is to describe the differences between what human beings espouse and how they act. After all, if the consequences are not what they intend, then what did they intend? What beliefs or theory of their practice do they hold and espouse?

The discrepancy between what human beings espouse and what they actually produce should be viewed as the result of a describable, systematic, nonrandom process. In other words, if paradoxes exist, if individuals behave in accordance with them, if their behavior is contrary to what they espouse, then there must be some theory of action in which this contradictory behavior is not contradictory.

The fundamental assumption, to return to the Einstein remark, is that there is a rational theory to explain the tricks even though the individuals may not be aware of it. One such theory is presented in the next section.

A theory that purports to explain human paradoxes is also a theory about self-responsibility. Human beings are causally responsible for their actions. The theory must help to explain the reasons that underlie human beings' reported denial of personal causal responsibility in creating and maintaining paradoxes. For example, the theory should explain the predisposition to blame others for the defensive routines, to insist that one is helpless to change them, and to be unaware of one's own causal contributions.

The theory should make explicit the relationship between personal causal responsibility and the creation of the larger social entities such as groups, intergroups, and organizations. There are at least two important types of explanations that the theory should provide. One is how the individuals create a universe that is consistent with and protects the inconsistency and the bypassing required by defensive routines. This explanation should also provide the basis for empirical research that would disconfirm important aspects of the theory. For example, it should not be possible to observe individuals producing defensive routines, and at the same time, producing them in a context that does not reward or sanction such defensive routines.

The second explanation should be related to the conditions under which a change in the context that does not sanction defensive routines would indeed reduce them. For example, if individuals are personally causally responsible for their actions, if they are "against" creating defensive routines, if they necssarily create systemic conditions that support the defensive routines, how could changes in the systemic features of defensive routines alter how the individuals act?

Again, the processes that answer these questions should lead to ways to test the theory empirically. For example, it should not be possible to get individuals to reduce defensive routines without providing them with a new set of skills and a theory of action that they can use to reduce defensive routines. Supplying these features should not be easy, because even if we knew what they were, their effective use would go against the skills that human beings presently use.

The theory that can be used to explain paradoxes should be part of a more general theory of human behavior in the context of administration and organization. Paradoxes exist in a universe where there is much that is nonparadoxical. The theory should deal with both sets of phenomena.

A THEORY OF ACTION

Donald Schön and I have begun to create a theory that meets these criteria. We began by interviewing people, obtaining as many examples as possible, to construct theories of action. Because we also tape-recorded some meetings, we found that there was a systematic discrepancy between what people espoused and how they actually behaved, and that they were unaware of the discrepancy.

But this finding by itself was not new. Our new finding was that the discrepancy was designed, and the unawareness was also designed. In other words, the respondents held a theory that they never said they used to design and implement whatever they espoused. The individuals programmed themselves to remain unaware of the discrepancies. We called this theory of action the theory-in-use.

We began to study theories-in-use empirically. To our surprise, we found that although most individuals (across age groups, cultures, economic or educational status, and gender) held varying espoused theories, they all held the same theory-in-use.

The theory-in-use was modeled and called Model I. It contained three basic components: the governing variables or values; the action strategies; and the consequences of the first two on the behavioral world (Argyris and Schön 1974).

The consequences of using Model I theory-in-use (or the opposite of Model I) were the same. These could be described as miscommunication, self-fulfilling prophecies, self-sealing processes, and escalating error. Mixed messages, for example, are excellent examples of Model I action strategies to advocate one's position and to use face-saving in the service of such governing values as unilateral control, and win-and-do-not-lose (Argyris 1982, 1985).

If most individuals are programmed with a Model I theory-in-use that leads to the creation of behavioral worlds, then the repetitive use of this theory-in-use leads to systems or patterned structures that necessarily reinforce it. We have called these O-I (for organization) learning systems. They are the systemic or organizational counterpart to individual theories-in-use. They contain features that simultaneously encourage and protect the use of defensive routines. Like their individual-oriented counterparts, they are systems for limited learning, escalating error, defensive routines, and defensive loops (Argyris and Schön 1978).

Models I and O-I can be used as an explanation of the source of paradoxes. The explanation stated simply is as follows:

- Human beings seek, in an interaction, to control the relationships in such a way as to attain their intended consequences (Bandura 1977; de Charms 1968; Heider 1958; Strong and Claiborn 1982).
- The theory of control embedded in Model I and reinforced by O-I is one of unilateral control. We gain control by taking it away from others. No one should be able to use the reciprocal of Model I theory-in-use and design actions that are consistent with Model I.
- Acting in ways to control that takes away the control of others triggers others' defensive routines. These, in turn, protect the parties involved, and at the same time, blunt the defensive routines or inhibit the attempts of individuals to act effectively. All parties now use defensive routines that escalate error, and create self-fulfilling and self-sealing processes.
- The result of mutually reinforcing defensive routines is to combine wishful thinking (Jones 1977) (systematic overestimation) with anticipatory face-saving (systematic underestimation) which, in turn, results in systematic distortions. These distortions result in paradoxical consequences because, as we have seen, they result in conditions where individuals (or social entities) are effective and ineffective; they experience success and failure; the consequences are productive and counterproductive.

All theories of human nature are based upon a thesis of rationality or reasonability (Rescher 1977). Human beings are rational in that they keep their actions in consonant alignment with their beliefs. They coordinate their actions and expectations in the light of the best information they have (p. 85).

Our view is that there is rationality in the espoused theories and in the theories-in-use. The rationality of actions is to be uncovered by examining the theory-in-use. This makes understanding rationality more complex because, as we have seen, the rationality embedded in the theories-in-use is often counter to the rationality embedded in the espoused theories.

A theory of reasonability assumes that we are not systematically perverse. We do not act counter to or in disregard of our beliefs. Yet our research suggests that we are systematically perverse. A theory of reasonability also assumes that we do not act counter to, or without regard for, our intentions. Yet our research suggests that we do.

The apparent violation of the thesis of rationality and reasonability can be explained by differentiating between espoused theories and theories-in-use at the individual and organizational levels. It is the latter theory that makes us perverse, and at the same time, leads to defensive routines that prevent situational rupture but may lead eventually to systemic rupture.

DEALING WITH THE BYPASS PHENOMENON

Defensive routines are created to bypass embarrassment or threat to individuals or systems such as groups, intergroups, or organizations. In order for them to work, the individuals acting as agents for the systems must act as if they are not bypassing. In order to accomplish these requirements, individuals must be highly skilled, and the context in which they are operating must reward such actions. If the actions are highly skilled, and if they are culturally sanctioned, then they will be taken for granted. This means that not only the bypassing will be taken for granted, but the bypassing of the bypassing will also be automatic and taken for granted.

Social scientists who intend to focus on paradoxes require theories that alert them not to take for granted the bypass activities that are taken for granted. Let me give an example. During a meeting of the top line and corporate staff officers in a large decentralized organization, the CEO asked why line and staff were having problems in working effectively. As a result of the discussion, at least four causes were identified by all present:

- The philosophy and policies about how the organization is managed are inadequate.
- Corporate staff roles overlap and lead to confusion.
- Staff lacks clear-cut authority when dealing with line.
- Staff has inadequate contact with top line officers.

The CEO appointed two task forces to come up with solutions. Several months later, the entire group met for a day and hammered out a solution that was acceptable to all.

There are two important features about this story. First, the staff-line problems are typical. Second, the story has a happy ending: the causes of the problems were reduced.

However, there is a bypass problem here. Why did line and staff officers adhere to, implement, and maintain policies that were inadequate, roles that produced confusion, and contacts that were insufficient?

But why address this question if we have solved the problem? If we have not reduced the defensive routines that made it possible for executives to adhere to, implement, and maintain what, by their own judgment, were errors, these organizational defensive routines will remain alive and healthy, ready to undermine this solution or to cover up other problems.

For example, some corporate staff members said that they tried to discuss these issues with line but felt the line did not wish to discuss them. Some line officers denied ever hearing such a request. Some staff officers acknowledged this by admitting that they asked "indirectly." Other line officers reported that they heard the request and deflected it because they had experiences where the staff went to the CEO after a visit to the divisional officers and communicated information they should not have passed on. The CEO looked surprised and asked why people censored their conversations. Because, responded some line officers, he (the CEO) tended to shoot from the hip, causing unnecessary trouble. The divisional presidents had learned how to shape messages and how to time them correctly; the staff unknowingly sabotaged this.

All these actions are highly skilled; they are based on concern for people, on what the administrators conceive of as being realistic, and they are all self-sealing.

When dealing with any issues that contain defensive routines, we must study the substantive problem, be it technical or human. We must also study the bypass problems to learn why individuals adhere to, implement, and maintain the causes over time.

WHAT DRIVES DEFENSIVE ROUTINES IN ORGANIZATIONS?

By their very nature, organizations will produce conditions that tend to activate Model I theories-in-use and especially the by-pass phenomena. First, the theory-in-use of the pyramidal structure is consistent with Model I. For example, unilateral control over others is central to the concept of superior-subordinate relationships.

Second, most organizations are managed by the rule of exception. The rule instructs superiors to define performance standards and to manage the employees by inspecting carefully those who deviate from the performance standards. The performance of an effective organization, under this rule, would always tend to cluster around the standards already defined—there would be no surprises. Under these conditions, individuals would seek to protect themselves from deviant performance. And, as the world is unlikely to produce no surprises, individuals then have to protect themselves against this possibility. Protection tactics include camouflaging surprises, bypassing them and acting as if not doing so, and surfacing them in a form that is acceptable, which usually means down–grading the surprise.

Third, surprises can also be produced by the very finiteness of the human mind. It is difficult to know everything that may be required. There are always gaps of information and, hence, there is vulnerability. Model I theories-in-use tend to produce distorted information and escalating error; this exacerbates the vulnerability.

The human mind must assemble information by using abstractions to aggregate many individual cases. For example, management information systems take on the "chunking" feature of the human mind. But in doing so, they may eventually create a world of injustice which, in turn, will be threatening to the players, which, in turn, will activate the bypass mechanisms, which, in turn, can lead to a distortion of valid information, which would produce consequences contrary to those intended.

Let us examine the nature of information required by those who use it at the highest levels versus those who use it at the lowest levels of the organization. The top, who are distant from the point of action, require information that is abstract, objective, in which the logic is explicit, and in which the data can be compared and tracked. The first line or local level use data that is concrete, subjective, in which the logic is tacit, and in which the data cannot be compared or tracked. These information characteristics produce worlds with different views about what is effective and what is just. The relevant parties, using the logic inherent in the information they use, create conditions of misunderstanding and distancing from each other. The difficulties and injustice escalate as the rationality deteriorates (Argyris 1979).

We may now examine two other assumptions that are embedded in organizations that create more puzzles and a higher likelihood of vulnerability. First, hierarchies are based on the rule that exceptions are major errors and that effective management means few or no major errors. Surfacing major errors will not be threatening.

Second is the assumption of a puzzling view of trust. The superior will trust the subordinate as long as errors are not produced. The subordinates, in turn, will feel trusted if the superior leaves them alone. The puzzle is that trust appears to exist under the unlikely conditions that errors will not be produced. If errors are produced, the superior will stay away (precisely when he or she intends to intervene and may be of help).

WHAT CHANGES WOULD BE REQUIRED IN THE PRACTICE OF CRAFTING AND TESTING THEORIES?

The nature of theory would not change—a theory would still be a set of logically interrelated concepts that were operationally defined in such a way that any hypotheses derived from the theory could be tested by a set of operations that were independent of the theory. Theories of action would therefore still be concerned with issues such as threats to internal and external validity.

Social scientists will have to pay more attention to creating theories about universes that do not exist currently, normative theories about how to produce rare events, such as the reduction of mixed messages.

Normative theories, by the way, do not automatically become prescriptive in the sense that they advise administrators how to act. In the first stage, a normative theory has to be tested. The individuals use the theory tentatively in order to see if it works, and if it does, there may be unintended consequences. Only after they are satisfied that the consequences are desirable would the normative theory become prescriptive.

Theories that purport to explain paradoxes may require different views about human nature than those presently held. For example, I believe that most scholars assume that the actors should be able to produce what they intend if they have the requisite skills, if they wish to do so, and if the context in which they are embedded does not create insurmountable barriers. These theories assume a sense of personal causality (Deci and Ryan 1985; de Charms 1968; Heider 1958) and efficacy (Bandura 1977).

Our research indicates a more complex relationship. On the one hand, we too accept the notion of personal causal responsibility, which, in turn, assumes that the actors' intentions are relatively transparent and that a sense of self-efficacy is crucial in designing whatever the actors consider appropriate actions. On the other hand, we are also suggesting that holding a Model I theory-in-use and being embedded in an O-I learning system often makes individuals unaware of the discrepancy between their espoused theories and their actions *and* of the mental theory-in-use programs that keep them unaware. The result is a paradox. The individuals have designed nontransparency and a built-in tendency for a reduction in self-efficacy as a result of a design to maintain and increase self-efficacy. They are personally causally responsible for acting in ways that reduce their sense of personal causal responsibility, yet they are, in fact, causally responsible. For example, recall that individuals express a sense of hopelessness and cynicism about changing defensive routines, the same routines for which they are responsible.

Paradoxes are related to meanings that are contradictory. Therefore, we must first identify the meanings. Because it is empirically true that there are systematic, nonrandom differences between the meanings people espouse and those embedded in their actions, and because it is also the case that actors are unaware of these discrepancies, then it is the researchers' responsibility to differentiate between meanings embedded in attitudes, espoused values, and beliefs from those embedded in actual behavior.

The first modification, therefore, would be the emphasis placed upon the importance of conversation or other relatively directly observable actions (from which meanings could be inferred). The theory-in-use can only be inferred from what individuals actually say and do as observed by others or as audio or video tape-recorded.

Conversations would no longer simply be anecdotal events to be somehow analyzed and scored according to a preestablished scheme of categories. Every act of conversation with meaning is the result of a micro-causal theory in the mind of a creator. Meaning produced in the form of conversation is never random; it is systematic.

All conversation, in turn, has at least two meanings embedded in it. The first is the meaning that comes from asking the question: what did he actually say? For example, a superior and a subordinate can both agree that the superior's words on tape were such and such. They could also agree, for example, that the superior was telling the subordinate that his performance was inadequate. The subordinate could disagree on that conclusion and still agree that the superior communicated that meaning.

The next level of meaning would be the inferences made by either party on the effectiveness with which the first meaning was communicated. For example, it could have been done thoughtfully or bluntly.

The first meaning (your performance is unacceptable) is the result of a design and an implementation of that design by the superior. Embedded in that design is a micro-causal theory about what the superior believed he had to say to the subordinate. The second meaning is the result of a causal theory in the superior's mind about how to communicate the message effectively.

So far we have found that the micro-causal theories are not infinite in variety. They all appear to be derived from the theory-in-use held by the actors. Because there is very little variance in the theory-in-use, it becomes possible to develop generalization across actors and contexts as well as within a given actor in various contexts.

Recall that defensive routines are the result of complicated patterns of processes. The patterns should be described in enough detail to explain how they maintain and proliferate themselves.

For example, in Model I, there are action strategies such as making attributions or evaluations without illustrating them or testing them publicly. In our early research, we developed quantitative patterns of such behavior based on interobserver reliability score of over 90 percent accuracy. These scores were used to illustrate quantitative patterns of categories of Model I.

We learned, however, that the scores by themselves told us little about how these categories developed into patterns of organizational defensive routines, how the defensive routines led to paradoxes, how the paradoxes were bypassed, and how the bypassing activities were bypassed. In other words, the quantitative pictures of the frequency of the units of behavior kept in a black-box status the causes of the defensive routines, the processes by which they maintained themselves, and the processes that produced the paradoxes. From the point of view of a science of paradoxes, the most important information had yet to be developed.

The same was true from the clients' viewpoint. For those who wanted to change their Model I behavior, the quantitative picture provided them with information that they already knew. Changing their actions required the very information that was kept in black-book status.

There is another important issue that we are currently facing in trying to decide what are the appropriate units of analysis. This issue surfaced as we observed what units of analysis humans used whenever they tried to act on our data. As scientists, we were interested in the covariance of variables. For example, did changes in untested evaluations vary systematically with changes in untested attributions? We were able to plot many such relationships.

As we fed these data back to the individuals who wished to alter their actions, we learned that variance of variables that remained within Model I theory-in-use did not help them. They were prepared to alter their Model I theory-in-use. Once they understood the reasoning processes and the skills they used to produce Model I actions, providing them with quantitative relationships of various combinations that were consistent with Model I proved redundant.

We are now asking ourselves the following question: If Model I theory-in-use is what actors use to organize, store, and retrieve information in order to act, then is knowledge of the ways the variables within Model I vary empirically redundant? For example, individual A may have a pattern of 20 percent unillustrated attributions and 80 percent unillustrated evaluations. He could have quantitative figures reversed. From the point of view of creating defensive routines, the reversal of the scores makes no difference, because both patterns are Model I action strategies that lead to defensive routines.

Perhaps individuals require two different types of information. One is those quantitative patterns which, if they existed, would lead to a change in Model I. But that, according to our theory (and so far it is not disconfirmed by our research) is not possible. No imaginable combination of Model I variables can lead to states that are so different that they reduce defensive routines and their resulting paradoxes. Model I actions are self-sealing.

The second type of information is a model of the processes that produce the defensive routines and the subsequent paradoxes; a model of a new set of processes; and a model of how to get from here to there.

In short, we are beginning to believe that the units of study should be maps of processes from which it is possible to produce predictable consequences, not quantitative maps of how the variables such as action strategies within a given model might vary empirically.

The fifth change in emphasis will be a move toward producing maps of these multilevel processes (Argyris 1985; Argyris, Putnam, and Smith 1985).

Let us take an example of a map an individual developed to understand her pattern of bypassing and bypassing the bypass pattern (Figure 8–1). The map describes the context, the action strategies, and the consequences. The map purports to describe the bypass routines and the

Figure 8–1. Nested Propositions about Bypassing.

CONTEXT	STRATEGY	CONSEQUENCES
When asked to provide an evaluation	ignore client's question	client defensiveness
	act as though I am not ignoring it	reduced learning for both
	reflect back the client's statement	remain blind and blame client
When asked again	ask client what he wants	escalating client frustration
	attribute privately he should know	little learning
	ignore that he has told me what he wants	
When asked again	unilaterally advocate an opposing view	client becomes angry and gives up
	do not make reasoning explicit	little learning
	do not invite inquiry	remain blind

paradox that results, namely that the individual acts in ways that are counter to her own intentions of being helpful.

The map may be used in several ways. First it organizes a set of complicated processes into an explanatory model. Second, the model can be more easily stored and retrieved from the human mind. The map may also be used to predict that the individual will continue to behave in these ways because there are no actions that can be used to interrupt and to reduce the counterproductive features of her pattern. All the feedback processes reinforce the pattern. The prediction not only helps the individual understand the consequences of the model: it becomes a test of the validity of the map. For example, we could observe or tape-record the individual's behavior in similar situations, after the map was developed by her (with the help of others). We should observe action strategies that are consistent with those described in the map. We should not observe action strategies where she engages the client's questions productively. These tape recordings could be analyzed by competent analysts who have no idea of the map as well as by the individual and those helping her to change. The analysis would be made separately.

These types of analysis are now standard operating procedure in our work. We use them to test features of the theory and to help individuals reflect on their practice, to organize their reflections in the form of maps that explain and predict their actions. Finally, we also use the maps as the basis for changing the actions.

In evaluating the toughness of the test, we should keep in mind that in most cases, individuals believe that they can alter the actions once they have mapped them. The tape recordings indicate otherwise. Their prediction that they could alter their actions was disconfirmed even though the actors created the maps, knew about the changes, and intended to produce the changes.

These types of maps can also be crafted for groups and other social systems. For example, a group of personnel administrators (PAs) in a very large organization complained that the line managers acted in ways that disempowered them. They complained that the PAs were often asked by the line to perform inappropriate tasks and that the PAs' role had a low status.

The vice president of human resources formed a twenty-person task force to study the problem. After some fifteen hours of deliberations, the task force found that it had documented the complaints but that it did not know what to do about them. They explained their dilemma by their disbelief that line management would wish to change. Asked one, "What's the sense of working to produce ideas for change if you know the ideas are not likely to be taken seriously by the line?"

With their assistance, we implemented the following experiment. We asked the task force members to assume that they could have access to any line manager they wished, and to assume also that the line managers would be willing to listen genuinely to their ideas. We then asked them to write a case that would illustrate what they would actually say and do if they had this opportunity.[2] What actions would they take to change the line managers?

The PAs then met to discuss their cases. In every instance, the PAs concluded that the actions designed in their cases were counterproductive. They decided that if given an opportunity to change line managers, they would act in ways that disempowered themselves. As one PA put it, "I now realize that we shoot ourselves in the foot."

We then analyzed the tape recordings of these sessions and developed a map of how the PAs disempowered themselves (Figure 8–2). The map was distributed to the PAs for their confirmation or disconfirmation. Some of the PAs showed the map to other PAs and to other line managers for their reactions. There was no one who disagreed with the paradoxical results predicted by the map. The only changes that were made were editorial or additional examples.

The PAs decided that it would be highly unlikely that they could reverse the processes described in the map without some reeducation. This decision was significant: they had to say in the report to the vice president, "Not only do we disempower ourselves while trying to reduce our disempowerment, but we do not believe we have the requisite skills to change this situation." The PAs requested a reeducation program.

The vice president was delighted for two reasons. As a line executive for many years he always felt that the PAs were their own worst enemy but he did not deal with this issue openly because he could not see a constructive consequence. But, if the PAs did develop the skills, then they could use them to change the line managers who, the VP agreed, did treat the PAs unjustly.

The PAs now had a map that described their actions that disempowered them. How can this map be tested?

The first test of the map is to observe the tape recorded interactions between line and PAs. The tapes should show either actions that do disempower or actions that are not relevant to the issue. The tapes should not indicate any actions that would engage defensive routines in ways that reduce disempowerment. The second test of the validity of this description is to ask the PAs who participated in the seminar to confirm or disconfirm its validity. In our experience, individuals in the position similar to the PAs do not confirm the map easily. Their self-esteem is on the line; confirming the map indicates that they are not as competent as they should be. They are, after all, human resources specialists who are supposed to help others, not to create conditions of disempowerment.

A third test is to show it to other PAs who did not help to develop the map. A fourth test is to show it to line managers. All the test situations are tape-recorded.

The tapes can be used for further tests. First, if the map is disconfirmed, then we must examine carefully the reasoning behind the disconfirmation. Second, under certain conditions, the reaction used to test the map could be a test. For example, in some cases PAs who did not participate in producing the map disagreed that they disempowered themselves. The way they disagreed with their fellow PAs led to conditions of disempowerment between them. Moreover, the examples that they used and the way they defended them illustrated defensive routines. Third, the tape recordings can be available to fellow researchers who might wish to listen to the processes by which we assert the maps were not disconfirmed.

Another series of tests is developed by studying the training program designed to reeducate the PAs. For example, the participants develop their own maps based on their individual experiences. The actions to be changed are then derived from the map. If, for example, the PAs learn the new skills, then they should be able to design new actions that they agree are more effective. They could test these inferences by role playing with each other or by inviting in some line managers.

A more powerful test would be to tape-record or observe the PAs in action with the line managers in nontraining situations. This is not difficult, because PAs have regularly scheduled meetings with their line superiors. The PAs introduce the tape recorder or the observer by saying that they are participating in a training program to increase their effectiveness. So far, individuals in the position such as line managers have cooperated. Indeed, many of them become intrigued and involve themselves in learning about how they create defensive routines.

THE VALUE OF CRAFTING THEORIES THAT DEAL WITH PARADOXES

There are science-building and practice-building reasons for crafting theories that deal with paradoxes. A comprehensive theory of administration and organization includes the understanding of paradoxes because they are part of the universe. Social scientists would not be fulfilling their stewardship if they did not describe the universe as is. If paradoxes are especially activated when attempts are made to change the underlying patterns in our universe, then a full description of the universe as is would require the production of propositions about how the patterns react to varying degrees of change. Descriptions of how the status quo reacts to fundamental change is part of the description of the world as is.

Turning to the practice-building reasons, if the future problems of administrators will focus especially around gaps, inconsistencies, dilemmas,

Figure 8–2.   PAs Disempowering Themselves.

Situational Givens		Consequences		Strategies to Deal with Barriers
High Ambiguity				Tear/Wear Them Down
-Organization in time of transition		Frustration		-Showdown: Stand up to God
		Tension		-Be the Lone Ranger
				-Work my needs
-Personnel Administrators report to two different bosses who often have conflicting view of what PAs should do.	Desire to change role of PAs to be change agents and to raise status of Personnel in the organization	PAs encounter barriers to their intended change, particularly from line.		Maneuver Around Them
Personnel is Perceived as Low Status				-Don't confront if I get my way
-PAs asked to do inappropriate tasks.				-Wait for time to pass
				-Match my style to the manager
-PAs asked to function as peacemakers; to smooth over conflict; to apply bandaids to symptoms instead of getting at root causes.				-Privately time interventions

Source: Argyris and Argyris (1985).

Strategies about Strategies	Dilemmas	Consequences
	-If I confront line they may distrust me and maintain their negative view	-Confirms line's prejudice about Personnel
-Keep use of strategies private	-If I maneuver around line, I do not challenge line's negative view of Personnel and they maintain it. ⟶ sense of disempowerment	-Does not model for line strategies they don't already know
-Base beliefs about effective strategies on feelings ⟶		-Does not create opportunities for PAs to learn about how they may contribute to line's negative view
-Do not test	-If I maintain one style, I may reduce the range of managers with which I can work.	-Does not create opportunities for line to learn how they create barriers for PAs
	-If I switch styles, I may weaken my own and others' sense of Personnel identity.	-Neither line nor Personnel learns about any validity in their view of each other
		-Reinforces fragmented "chameleon" identity of Personnel
		-May create skepticism on both line and Personnel's parts that Personnel can become change agents.

and paradoxes, then we have an obligation to help human beings understand and solve these types of problems. Dealing with paradoxes may lead to significantly different theories of explanation and change. For example, the "inhumane" features of formal organizations that I described in *Personality and Organization* (1957) were caused, in important ways, by human features of human beings such as the information processing limits of their minds (Argyris 1978). This awareness not only led to a different set of propositions about the world as is; it also led to different theories of intervention.

THE DILEMMA TO CONDUCT ACTION SCIENCE

There is an important dilemma that social scientists will have to face if paradoxes are to be studied and reduced. The dilemma is created by the fact that the theory-in-use of normal science actions to minimize threats to internal and external validity (Campbell and Stanley 1963) are consistent with Model I. Social scientists may be producing generalizations that have the same features of mixed messages and defensive routines (Argyris 1980). In order to overcome this dilemma, we may have to focus on research that conceives of subjects as clients to be helped to reduce the defensive routines and therefore combines description with intervention. The intervention becomes the context for testing the description.

Several years ago, I conducted a colloquium with faculty and graduate students on intervention. After a while, the concerns of the faculty and graduate students about intervention began to surface. Most of the concerns, it seemed to me, were defensive routines. For example, would not interventions cost more because they take longer? We compared their budgets with mine, and mine were significantly less. Moreover, the organizations that I have studied were willing to pay more if we remained.

Did the interventionists become biased by the organization that paid them? I had published an analysis of the work of such scholars as Blau, Perrow, and Thompson. Although the work that I cited was primarily supported by government funding agencies, their theories, I tried to show, were more consistent with traditional managerial values than were the theories of scholars like Likert, McGregor, and myself (Argyris 1972).

A young female assistant professor raised what I believe to be a critical question. She said that the problem she had in combining description and intervention was that she was never trained to do it, and it scared the hell out of her. Donald Schön and I have been conducting seminars in European and American universities during the past ten years on conducting action science. We have found that her comments reflected the causes better than the other concerns.

During the past ten years, we have also been conducting seminars to teach graduate students and younger faculty action science skills. To date, these students experience three surprises early in the seminars. First is our insistence on meeting the normal science criteria of generalizability and disconformability. We do seek to change the role of subjects to clients, for example, but not at the expense of muddling the research. The second surprise is that their theory-in-use is consistent with Model I; that they experience the same embarrassment, bewilderment, and frustration that their prospective clients do when faced with this finding.

The third surprise is that the skills for dealing with defensive routines, their own as well as the clients', are learnable, and with about as much or as little difficulty as they experienced in learning regression analysis. The key issue was whether they genuinely wanted to create research conditions where they would experience a greater sense of vulnerability than would be the case when conducting research where the task was primarily descriptive. We have begun to design graduate seminars where students can be exposed to learning the skills and then make up their minds as to what directions to take in their own future research (Argyris, Putnam, and Smith 1985). In our experience to date, most strive to include features of intervention in an incremental manner. They design action science research that is consistent with their skills. As the research succeeds, then they up the ante.

NOTES

1. For a more complete discussion, see Argyris 1985.
2. See Argyris and Schön 1974, and Argyris 1982 for the instructions to produce these types of cases.

REFERENCES

Argyris, Chris. 1957. *Personality and Organization.* New York: Harper and Brothers.

Argyris, Chris. 1972. *The Applicability of Organizational Sociology*. London: Cambridge University Press.

Argyris, Chris. 1978. "Is Capitalism the Culprit?" *Organizational Dynamics,* Spring: 21–37.

Argyris, Chris. 1980. *Inner Contradictions of Rigorous Research*. New York: Academic Press.

Argyris, Chris. 1982. *Reasoning, Leaning and Action.* San Francisco: Jossey-Bass.

———. 1985. *Strategy, Change, and Defensive Routines.* Boston: Pitman Publishing.

Argyris, Chris, and Donald Schön. 1974. *Theory in Practice.* San Francisco: Jossey-Bass.

———. 1978. *Organizational Learning.* Reading, Mass.: Addison-Wesley.

Argyris, Chris; Robert Putnam; and Diana M. Smith. 1985. *Action Science.* San Francisco: Jossey-Bass.

Bandura, A. 1977. "Self-Efficacy: Toward a Unifying Theory of Behavioral Change." *Psychological Review* 85: 191–215.

Barnes, Louis. 1981. "Managing the Paradox of Organizational Trust." *Harvard Business Review* March/April: 107–16.

Bonn Working Group Conference on Information Systems Environment. 1979. "Some Inner Contradictions in Management Information Systems," June.

Campbell, D.T., and J.C. Stanley. 1963. *Experimental and Quasi-Experimental Design for Research.* Skokie, Ill.: Rand-McNally.

de Charms, R. 1968. *Personal Causation.* New York: Academic Press.

Deci, Edward L., and Richard M. Ryan. 1985. *Intrinsic Motivation and Self-Determination in Human Behavior.* New York: Plenum Press.

Heider, Fritz. 1958. *The Psychology of Interpersonal Relations.* New York: Wiley.

Jones, Russell A. 1977. *Self-Fulfilling Prophecies: Social Psychological and Physiological Effects of Expectancies.* Hillsdale, N.J.: Lawrence Erlbaum Associates.

Rescher, Nicholas. 1977. *Methodological Pragmatism: A Systems-Theoretic Approach to the Theory of Knowledge.* New York: New York University Press.

Strong, Stanley R., and Charles D. Claiborn. 1982. *Change Through Interaction,* New York: John Wiley.

ON THE CRAFTING
OF A THEORY

Philip H. Mirvis

That apprentices and masters go about their craft differently became apparent to me when touring an exhibition of Leonardo da Vinci's sketches at the Buffalo campus of the State of University of New York. I was struck by a portion of the exhibit that featured one of Leonardo's sketches alongside copies of it by later artists. To my eye, many of these followers were imitating Leonardo's work, painstakingly matching his brushstrokes, striving to master the craft by remaking, in exacting detail, his masterly work. By contrast, a few subsequent artists instead seemed to be emulating da Vinci: their brushstrokes bore their own mark; their imagery reflected their own interpretations; and their finished sketches, while paying homage to Leonardo, also bore witness to their own virtuosity.

I have made a comparable distinction while reading the texts of scholars these past several months on the subject of paradox in organizational theory. Many of the tracts begin with a philosophical discourse and diagram the components of paradoxical statements, such as that of Epimenides, that "All Cretans are liars." Their authors then recount how animals simultaneously signal submission and superiority, and revisit the work of theoreticians and therapists to trace the origins of paradoxical thought and intervention. In my estimation, there is more to their recitation than a review of the literature, and I suspect that its purpose is not solely to introduce otherwise uninformed readers (like me) to the subject at hand. My belief is that these scholars are undergoing an apprenticeship and are trying to master paradoxical theory by imitating its originators and reliving their discoveries.

Certainly this is one way to master a subject and a way that I (and many others) have followed in our intellectual and professional development. At this point, several organizational scholars have gained their own voice on the matter of paradox and a few have contributed seminal ideas to the broader theory base. My intent, then, is not to derogate their path of apprenticeship nor to diminish in any way their eventual contributions. I would only contrast their methods with that of Chris Argyris, the author of the preceeding chapter, who seems to me to have sketched his contributions in more craftsmanlike fashion. His chapter illuminates paradox on the basis of his own experiences, describes its components through his own interpretive framework, and speaks to the subject of crafting theories of practice with reference to his own mastery of "action science."

CRAFTING PARADOX AT WORK

As evidence of the sureness of his craft, consider three of his "sketches" of paradox at work. Argyris's first illustration shows how mixed messages can put recipients into a classic "double bind." His description of how communicators "design a message that is inconsistent" and then "act as if the message is not inconsistent" exemplifies how *negation* figures into paradoxical communications. The senders are acting consistently with reference to their inconsistent message.

In the specific example, top management sends a consistently inconsistent message to division heads about their autonomy and accountability. The division heads are damned if they do "manage their own show," because they may be undermined; and they are damned if they don't take charge, because they may appear weak to subordinates. That this is undiscussable means that there is no way to clarify the motivational and situational underpinnings of the mixed messages. And because that undiscussability also cannot be talked about, there is seemingly no way out of the negation.

In another illustration, Argyris shows how errors in *logical typing* can produce paradoxes. Signals from a management information system may yield one set of implications for operational managers, he notes, and a contrary one for senior management. He makes the case that management information at the operative level is concrete and subjective and is generally analyzed tacitly and idiosyncratically. In turn, MIS data reported at top levels in a company is abstract and objective and is most often analyzed through an explicit and comparative logical framework. That this creates "difficulties and injustices" is plain enough. A paradox emerges when (1) "exceptions" from expected results are encountered; (2) top and operative managers operate on data from distinct frames of reference; and (3) there can be no "meta-level" discourse through which to reconcile the meaning of these exceptions or their import.

In Argyris's example, exceptions are deemed either good or bad, depending upon the level of trust between operating and top managers. We learn further that trust is reliably untrustworthy. The only way out of this paradox is to reframe the consequences of erring and to redefine the relationship between top and operating managers at a "meta-level."

Finally, Argyris shows how people play an active role in creating their own paradoxes. His depiction of powerless personnel administrators suggests that they may be *projecting* their own self-doubts on to line managers, thereby creating a "schism" in the organization. Line managers may, in turn, be *introjecting* this definition. Thus, *reflexivity* arises in the relationship of the personnel administrators to line management. The administrators are "stuck" not simply because their strategies to become powerful are ineffective, but also because their self-image is reflexively contributing to and dependent upon line manager's perceptions of them.

How can they break out? The route to escape lies in seeing that they are "shooting themselves in the foot." The personnel administrators need to embrace their own powerlessness and see how concealing their stratagems to gain power only furthers their inefficacy. More broadly, Argyris suggests that they must work among themselves and with line managers to sort through "maps" of their behavior and its consequences ultimately to redefine their self-image and reformulate their relationship to the line organization.

In crafting these illustrations, Argyris has not sought to explicate paradoxical processes in this arcane language. Nor has he tried to represent them in symbolic logic (*a* and *not a*) or with detailed reference to other's formulations of these concepts. I suspect that Argyris has read the classical sources and has no doubt mulled over the ideas of negation, reflexivity, and logical typing, and how they contribute to paradoxes. My point is that a master of a craft works ineluctably from his or her own base of knowledge and experience when approaching a subject. In this chapter, Argyris has brought the puzzle of paradox into his own frame of reference and, more crucially, into his own behavioral world. The examples he offers of paradox in organizations come from his own experiences and ruminations thereupon. He probes sources of paradox contrasting espoused theory with people's theory-in-use and recommends that the crafting of such theories is best accomplished through methods of "action science."

The immediate implication, to me, is that theory building begins with oneself and one's understandings of human nature. Certainly study of the masters and practice of the master's craft are essential. But it is when these are "put aside" that craftsmanship begins. As the subject here is "crafting" theories of paradox, my intent is to look at specific facets of Argyris's craft and consider what they imply for building theories of practice.

LIVING IN THE BEHAVIORAL WORLD

To begin, it should be noted that Argyris is concerned with paradox in the "behavioral" as opposed to the "logical" world. He makes the point that logical paradoxes are distinct from those found in the behavioral world. Logical paradoxes rest upon contradictions between elements in a relationship wherein the elements are self-reflexive and their relationship is self-sealing. Paradox in the behavioral world is also defined by contradictory elements but these are shaped in a psychic subterrain, wherein people (consciously and unconsciously) conceal their true intentions and thus obscure the meaning of their relationships with others. They become harder to escape in a social super-structure wherein it is neither permissible to discuss the concealment nor to discuss the indiscussability.

Life in the behavioral world of organizations is governed by people's predilections to avoid embarassment and embrace pretense, as well as by organizational norms to cover-your-ass and to sweep-things-under-the-rug. Much as these are "part of the game" in organizational life, people can often make sense of conflicting messages, can figure their way through codeterminous consequences, and can maintain reciprocal relationships with their bosses, peers, and superiors based upon some reasonable *quid pro quo*. In essence, they can live with paradox and cope with being simultaneously effective and ineffective. There can come points of high conflict or turbulence when these tacit understandings and agreements unravel and a painfully problematic behavioral paradox is produced.

What is important to note is that logical paradoxes are inescapable within their formulation. To break out of them requires second order change—a reframing of the propositions at another level of abstraction and analysis. By comparison, behavioral paradoxes are made inescapable by the acts of seemingly logical people and organizations. Such paradoxes cannot be resolved solely through creative turns of the mind: they and their resolution must be lived.

DRAWING INFERENCES ABOUT
THE BEHAVIORAL WORLD

What produces paradoxical behavior in organizations? Argyris acknowledges that it may be in part traceable simply to human limits in information processing, another variant on bounded rationality, and to particular turns of the human mind, as Abelson and Rosenberg (1958) noted when distinguishing analytic logic from "psycho-logic." Argyris, however, puts these mental functions into the rubric Model I where he finds a systematic discrepancy between people's espoused theories and their theories-in-use. There is "rationality" behind intentions and behaviors, he notes, but the rationality behind people's theory-in-use is consistently driven by a desire to lessen threat and avoid embarassment, and thus produces what he calls defensive routines. These routines negate intentions, yield mixed messages, and are variously projected on to and introjected into groups in organizations, producing self-reflexive and sometimes self-exciting schisms.

That these defensive routines become part of the culture of an organization Argyris attributes to norms of "bypassing" that develop in the pyramidal, control-oriented organization wherein mixed messages and misunderstanding are all part of the game. In a sense, bypassing is not only part of the behavioral game in organizations, it is how the game is defined and regulated. This makes re-framing ideas and re-forming relationships all the more problematic. In other papers and books, Argyris prescribes the development of Model II behavioral strategies and relationships as the primary means of breaking out of Model I loops. At this "meta level" of thinking and relating, people can discuss the undiscussable and experiment with new behaviors without fear of shooting themselves in the foot.

STUDYING THE BEHAVIORAL WORLD

To craft theories of this sort, Argyris contends that scholars must visit "universes that do not exist" and must entertain assumptions about human nature beyond the ordinary and commonplace. Plainly, this means exploring a world undefined by linear-causal logic and seeing human nature as something other than a product of stimulus-response learning. It also means, necessarily, reformulating, or abandoning, the analytic methods and research procedures that reproduce such understandings of people and the world.

How can scholars cultivate such thoughts? Certainly there is a connection between the processes of creative thinking and the construction of a creative view of the world. Bateson (1979) makes the point that mind and nature "co-evolve," and as scholars give freer reign to their thoughts they may be sufficiently "freed up" from preconceptions to discover a new view of human nature and the social world.

This sort of theory building is, in one sense, fundamentally a "mind game" and can, as logicians over the ages reveal, yield a view of a universe based upon either ordered causation (one game) or countless sorts of "tricks" (another one). But while it may be very "heady" it can also be heartfelt. Compare, for example, Hofstadter's (1979) elegant analyses of the "strange loops" created by paradox with Laing's (1969) rather more down-to-earth descriptions of the "knots" people create for themselves. When it comes to theories of practice, Watzlawick and his associates, pioneers in the development of paradoxical interventions, make it plain that the traditional scientific search for "why" is itself only one means of illuminating human behavior. My tastes, for instance, run to the creation of "art works" and "stories" as a means of describing the human condition. But Argyris is dedicated to crafting "why's" and in furtherance of this he has crafted "action science" to develop and test theories about unknown universes and heretofore unknown human characteristics.

Argyris states that to discover new worlds researchers must be "close" to their data, either through direct observation or analysis of tape recordings. In this sense, they must immerse themselves in data. Clifford Geertz (1973) has made a comparable point in calling for "thick descriptions" in analysis of cultures. It would be stretching Argyris's prescriptions to say that researchers must *live with and in* their data. Personally, I find such immersion, when accompanied by introspection, a fruitful source of insight. Argyris insists, however, that insights must be tested. His broader point, then, is that abstraction must be grounded in the concrete.

Furthermore, Argyris states that analyses should focus upon "patterns," rather than episodes, of behavior. Bertrand Russell's (1913) formulation of the hierarchy of logical type implies that there is a distinctive pattern to patterns that can be discerned from "looking down" upon them from a higher level of abstraction. Alfred Korzybski (1958) urges the use of such analyses in distinguishing between words and things, the map and the territory, where the focal point of analysis concerns their relationship. The larger point is that paradoxes cannot be discerned through Model I forms of inquiry. We need methods based on Model II.

Action science requires that the researcher and the research participants become co-creators of data. As Argyris has been interested in crafting theories of practice, much of his research has been undertaken in the context of helping people to break out of Model I modes of conduct and operate in the Model II mode. There is a useful extension of Kurt Lewin's (1948) dictum that the best way to study behavior is to change it. The act of creating new data and behaviors, it seems to me, may be the best way to yield insights into both stability and change.

CONTINUITY VERSUS CREATIVITY

It needs to be asked, however, whether Argyris has himself discovered the "new." Gunther Stent (1972) makes the point that scientific discoveries are often premature and seldom unique. Certainly Argyris's pioneering studies on the misfit between traditional organization and human personality were "ahead of their time." Today he also has many contemporaries in fashioning multilayered models of human behavior, governed by reciprocal causality, and in advocating new methods of scientific inquiry and analysis.

The broader question is to what extent Argyris's current contributions to theory represent continuity versus creativity. Some may read Argyris's work as a "rehash" of old ideas. Certainly there are signs of continuity between his early studies of the fit of human personality with formal organization, the mismanagement of MIS systems, and the unintended consequences of rigorous research and their reconceptualization using Model I and Model II precepts (Argyris 1957, 1970; Argyris and Miller 1952; Argyris and Schön 1974). Yet Argyris himself reports that these new conceptions were the result of "surprises" and, to my mind, reflect a deeper appreciation of human nature and the behavioral world.

His contributions do not strike me as a matter simply of revising old ideas or, less graciously, repackaging them. I believe them instead to be a reflection of his lifelong commitment to understand and ameliorate the "inhumane" conditions posed by organizational and interpersonal life and to do so while remaining true to the central tenets, not to say governing traditions, of scientific orthodoxy. In that sense, his work shows continuity.

However, by continuing to delve deeper into the "whys"—exploring basic assumptions about human relations and refining action science to the point of transferability—Argyris has arrived at what I regard to be "new" insights into the human condition. To illustrate, his early studies of the problems encountered in human relationships traced them to inter-personal *incompetence*. Now by studying people's theories-in-use, he traces them to *skilled* defensiveness. Argyris's initial practice theories aimed at promoting more humane organization through the use of laboratory training and organizational development. It was assumed both could "free up" the emotional and structural barriers people encountered that blocked their development and effectiveness. Today Argyris advocates a distinctive set of Model II interventions and works in a decidedly new type of laboratory seeking to reduce people's defensive routines.

Neither his theories nor his methods seemed to me to have been overly determined by nor even predictable from his days of apprenticeship. Changes in Argyris's ways of thinking about and looking at the behavioral world go beyond "first order change" and might be construed as "breakthroughs." This brings me to a final point about Argyris's craft: collaboration.

DISCOVERY VIA SELF AND OTHER

I do not know much about Argyris's collaboration with Donald Schön nor can I do more than speculate about what it has meant for development of his scholarly craft. Few of his articles and none of his books published before 1974 were co-authored, though I'm told Argyris was a valuable colleague and able mentor to other faculty. I suspect, however, that the depth of his collaboration with Donald Schön figured prominently in his creation of the "new."

Speaking to this general point, I have followed with interest the maturation of Kenwyne Smith's voice on the matter of paradoxes in group and organizational theory. Frankly, Smith's (1982) early writings on the subject seemed to me to be apprentice-like and somewhat stilted. (They read rather like this review.) In his newest volume, with collaborator David Berg, Smith has gained a steady and evocative voice (Smith and Berg 1987). He and Berg offer interesting and self-reflective commentary on their collaboration which suggests to me that their relationship —marked by cooperation and competition and by symbolic and substantive gamesmanship—enabled them to live paradox and probe it, and provided them with invaluable "grist for the mill." That their relationship was "discussable" and that they developed a workable modus operandi while discussing it only furthers my contention that the act of collaboration, of living content in the context of an interpersonal relationship, can bring forth synergy and spark the new.

It may be that Schön and Argyris were "light" and "shadow," that they were Yin and Yang, that their relationship was marked by Model I dynamics, resolved in discovering Model II. I can only speculate that whatever dynamics marked their collaboration, they proved "discussable" and that "discussability" has marked Argyris's collaborations in the past several years. I will conclude by adding that Argyris and I discussed this view in preparation of his chapter and this commentary. I was routinely defensive.

REFERENCES

Abelson, R.P., and M.J. Rosenberg. 1958. "Symbolic Psychologic: A Model of Attitudinal Cognition." *Behavioral Science* 3: 1–13.

Argyris, C. 1957. *Personality and Organization.* New York: Harper.

———. 1970. *Intervention Theory and Method: A Behavioral Science View.* Reading, Mass.: Addison-Wesley.

Argyris, C. and F.B. Miller. 1952. *The Impact of Budgets on People.* New York: Controllers Foundation.

Argyris, C., and D. Schön. 1974. *Theory in Practice.* San Francisco: Jossey-Bass.

Bateson, G. 1979. *Mind and Nature: A Necessary Unity.* New York: Dutton.

Geertz, C. 1973. *The Interpretation of Cultures.* New York: Basic Books.

Hofstadter, D.R. 1979. *Godel, Escher, Bach: An Eternal Golden Braid.* New York: Vintage Books.

Korzybski, A. *Science and Sanity: An Introduction to Non-Aristotelean System and General Semantics,* 4th ed. Lake Shore, Conn.: Institute of General Semantics. This reference is drawn from C. Hampden-Turner, *Maps of the Mind* (New York: Collier Books, 1982).

Laing, R.D. 1969. *The Politics of the Family*. New York: Vintage Books.

Lewin, K. 1948. *Resolving Social Conflicts*. New York: Harper & Row.

Russell, B. 1913. *Principa Mathematica*. Cambridge: Cambridge University Press. This reference is drawn from G. Bateson, *Steps to an Ecology of the mind* (New York: Ballantine, 1975).

Smith, K.K. 1982. "Philosophical Problems in Thinking about Organizational Change." In P. S. Goodman and Associates, *Change in Organizations: New Perspectives on Theory, Research, and Practice*. San Francisco: Jossey-Bass.

Smith, K.K., and D. N. Berg. 1987. *Paradoxes of Group Life*. San Francisco: Jossey-Bass.

Stent, G. 1972. "Prematurity and Uniqueness in Scientific Discovery." *Scientific American* 227: 84–93.

9 PARADOX AND TRANSFORMATION
A Framework for Viewing Organization and Management

Robert E. Quinn and Kim S. Cameron

The purpose of this book is to help explore and evaluate the power of paradox as a metaphor for analyzing organization and management. In this book we do not seek to develop a predictive theory of paradox. Rather, we seek to develop a paradoxical perspective or framework. The major contribution to be made is not a set of specific, testable hypotheses explaining paradox, but rather a stimulus for asking new and richer questions. An analog is the introduction of the open-systems theory in the early 1960s. The open-systems approach did not provide a micro theory of behavior; instead it provided a new perspective for viewing organizations. Since that time, the variables and questions investigated in organizational research have been greatly influenced by the open-systems view. In a similar fashion, we believe that the introduction of a paradoxical persepctive will allow us to focus better on the contradictory, dynamic, and transformational phenomena in organizational life.

In writing this concluding chapter, we decided that we would not attempt to summarize, critique, or draw implications from the other chapters in the book. The rejoinders do that. Here, instead, we attempt to clarify our understanding of paradox and show how the paradoxical perspective might influence and enrich our thinking about organization and management.

The chapter is divided into four sections. In the first we consider paradox as contradiction and explore the implications of contradiction

289

for thinking about organization and management. In both the second and third sections we consider the dynamics associated with paradox, focusing on negatively perceived vicious circles in the second and on positively perceived virtuous circles in the third. Fourth, we return to an exploration of the implications, in this case evaluating the utility of the dynamic perspective for organizations and management.

PARADOX AS CONTRADICTION

One of the problems with paradox is that the definition is slippery. Not all the authors in this volume agree on the definition of paradox or use the term in the same way (see, for example, Chapter 5 and the rejoinder). The simplest definition, going back to the Latin root, says that a paradox is an apparent contradiction. A paradox is an observation in which two apparently contradictory elements are seen as present or operating at the same time. In Chapter 1, we show how the contradiction associated with paradox differs from other similar concepts such as dilemma, irony, inconsistency, dialectic, ambivalence, and conflict.

As Starbuck points out in the rejoinder to Chapter 2, every force in a social system tends to initiate an opposing force. While constantly changing organizations are filled with polarities, it is natural to ignore the oppositions in a social system and to see only the elements to which we, as observers, are predisposed (Festinger and Carlsmith 1959; Simon 1945; Quinn 1988). The employment of a paradoxical perspective leads us to a much increased awareness of the polarities that exist in organization phenomena.

Sutton (1987), for example, used the paradoxical frame in his analysis of dying organizations. He identified several pairs of polar demands that simultaneously occurred after the announcement that the organization would close. These included:

1. keeping members from leaving so the work of disbanding could get accomplished, but at the same time moving members out of the system;
2. maintaining client and customer relationships in order to last out the disbanding process, while at the same time severing relationships with clients and customers;
3. keeping objects such as office equipment and inventories in order to maintain orderliness and minimal services, while at the same time moving out such objects through going-out-of-business-sales;

4. taking away security of employment in order to help employees begin to search for alternative jobs, while at the same time maintaining security of employment so that employees would stay to help with the disbanding process and so that the best employees might even be reassigned within the broader organization.

Organizational ethics provide another example. The development of ethical standards in organizations almost always results from a violation of ethical behavior (e.g., harm to a customer). Yet, while organizations must develop standards of ethical conduct in response to violations, they simultaneously have to deny that they will need the guidelines or that they have violated them in the past. This helps organizations avoid the image of being unethical. The development of standards of ethical conduct, therefore, paradoxically enhances the image of ethical behavior and simultaneously destroys that image for an organization.

This is illustrated by the 1987 crash of Northwest Airlines flight 255 in Detroit killing 158 people. The airline almost immediately put into action a procedure used the year before by Delta Airlines. A company employee was assigned to the family of each victim to help with transportation, funeral arrangements, and even counseling. The assignments lasted for as long as the family required assistance. Financial compensation in excess of $300,000 per victim was offered to the families by the company. The fact that the procedure had been used before, however, and that Northwest seemed prepared to implement it, created criticism that the company was not ethical or socially responsible at all, just interested in saving itself from the lawsuits that normally follow airplane crashes (and that frequently produce larger settlements than $300,000 per victim). The existence of the guidelines produced an organizational paradox in the minds of some people in that the guidelines simultaneously helped engender socially responsible behavior and eliminate it.

In organizations, a similar paradox arises with regard to formal policies and procedures. Such policies and procedures are required in organizations to reduce exceptions, increase efficiency, and improve competitiveness. (The alternative is an adhocratic free-for-all in pursuit of individual objectives.) Yet, if employees in a manufacturing firm, for example, adhere strictly to the policy manual, they can soon shut down the firm because of inefficiency. Work slowdowns by union members, for example, are frequently just strict adherence to formal policies and procedures. Innovation and creativity, which by definition imply the violation of current practices and procedures, are inhibited by adherence to organizational policies. So, despite the need for social control through formal organizational policies, all organizations expect, even encourage, members to violate the policies in order to achieve effective performance, efficiencies, and innovativeness. Formalized social control mechanisms are, paradoxically, both functional and dysfunctional for organizational performance.

The point is that nearly all values—for example, predictability—have a polar opposite value that is also positive—for example, spontaneity. Effective functioning in organizations requires balancing polarities such as these. Several common prescriptions have been identified for coping with and managing these kinds of paradoxes in organizations. Economists suggest optimizing or satisficing strategies, psychologists advocate holding multiple mental realities (neuroses) or sequencing. By and large, however, most individuals seem prone to merely ignoring one side of the paradox or the other. In order to maintain a rational, logical view of organizational action, the complexity of simultaneous contradictions is frequently managed by ignoring one side of the contradiction and maintaining a simple linear perspective. Examples in organizational theory include maintaining that productivity and satisfaction are positively related, environmental turbulence and organic structures are positively related, and so on. The probability that the exact opposite is also simultaneously true is generally ignored.

The paradoxical frame, then, can serve to make our analyses richer and more complex. It leads us to ask what we are valuing in our analysis and what is the opposite positive value. What, for example, is the positive opposite of creativity, and what is the relationship between creativity and its positive opposite? This orientation also might lead us to look for the oppositions within a seemingly neutral concept. What are the polarities, for example, within the concept of communication? Is it possible to develop a competing values model (see Chapter 1) of concepts like communication or motivation? We think it is, and such efforts would greatly enrich our understanding of these concepts.

PARADOX AS A DYNAMIC PROCESS: THE NEGATIVE PERSPECTIVE

Some authors who have written on paradox work from another definition. They see paradox as a circular, self-referential, or dynamic process. Usually, they see this process as a problem. When paradox is defined in this way, authors tend to focus on processes and issues in organizations that lead to negative or positive outcomes. In the next two sections we explore some of these outcomes, first from a negative view and then from a positive view. We begin with illustrations of paradox as a dynamic problem. These illustrations are actual cases reported in Quinn (1988). We use them to illustrate this alternative perspective on paradox.

Case 1: An Individual.   Our first illustration is the case of a young man who went through a five-year engineering program in four years. Finishing with a 4.0 grade point average, he was hired by a major corporation, and became known for his technical brilliance and his personal aggressiveness. He regularly came up with technical proposals and problem solutions that resulted in increased savings and profits. He also pushed his people hard and often accomplished things that others considered difficult or impossible. Promoted rapidly, he was seen as a fast-tracker. After a major promotion, however, he began, for the first time, to encounter difficulties. His boss gave him negative evaluations, and he was passed over for a promotion.

In many ways it seemed to be an illustration of the Peter Principle. He seemed to have reached a level at which he was no longer competent. He complained that his technical proposals would go upstairs and come back watered-down or rejected by people who did not understand the technical world. He complained that his boss wanted him to "attend cocktail parties and to kiss people's butts." This he found most wasteful, complaining, "That political stuff is just not real."

He explained his problem by arguing that he had a bad boss. He tried to prove his worth by working harder still. He wrote more proposals and pushed them harder than ever. He also increased the pressure on his own people to be more productive. Unfortunately, the more he did these things, the more his problems increased.

Case 2: A Group.   A new commissioner was appointed to direct a large department of parks and recreation. She quickly discovered a huge schism between the "parks people" who maintained and ran the grounds and equipment and the "recreation people" who designed and ran the programs in the parks. The parks people regularly complained that the recreation people had no sensitivity to the problems of physically caring for a park. The recreation people regularly complained that the parks group would only be happy if "no one was ever allowed to enter one of our parks." The conflict between the two groups was intense and destructive.

Once aware of the problem, the Commissioner called a meeting of all employees. In a well-prepared speech she pointed out the difficulties created by the intergroup conflict, and outlined a program for improvement. When it failed miserably, she turned to more directive and controlling strategies. Unfortunately, her every effort to increase cooperation resulted in greater conflict.

Case 3: An Organization.   Some years ago, the director of a mental health center had a vision for delivering a new model of care. He built his organization on the values of teamwork, creativity, and growth. His people showed deep commitment and impressive versatility. The organization grew rapidly. Soon the top management team began to note a wide array of pressures to alter the open, responsive culture and to increase structure and control. There were pressures to develop procedure manuals, MIS systems, more precise job descriptions, and promotion criteria. The top management team responded by defending and fostering the uniqueness of the organization, by issuing exciting challenges, and attempting to inspire new levels of commitment and energy. The more they did this, however, the more the organization grew, and the more they experienced demands for the structures that would undermine the growth of the organization.

Characteristics of the Negative Dynamics

The above cases illustrate some characteristics of paradox from a dynamic problem perspective. The problems share several important attributes:

1. The person or people experiencing the problem are using an exclusive, either/or logic and are caught in a vicious circle.
2. The problem is lodged in the assumptions being made by the person and not in the logic that follows from the assumptions. Therefore, the cause of the problem is projected outside the focal person or group.
3. The problem is impermeable to rational instruction from a helper.
4. The problem must be resolved through reframing.

Either/Or Logic and Vicious Circles.   A problem occurs when an individual adopts an exclusive, or either/or frame. That is, when a person seeks to pursue some desired outcome, one particular strategy is chosen and the opposite strategy is labeled bad. This is known as a hierarchical logic characterized by the assumption that one alternative is good and the opposite is bad. (See Van de Ven and Poole's discussion of purposive action, Chapter 2, and Starbuck's rejoinder.) In adopting this logic the individual pursues a consistent strategy that may eventually generate a vicious circle (Masuch 1985). That is, an action continues to create negative outcomes which, in turn, lead to the same action again. The strategy may not lead immediately to the vicious circle. It may involve what Hofstadter (1979) calls a strange loop—the strategy may lead initially toward the desired outcome, but then, over time, a shift occurs so that the strategy generates something opposite to that which is desired.

The top management team of the mental health center, for example, wanted to grow so that they could better accomplish their new vision. They pursued this objective through involvement and creativity. The strategy worked; their logic was correct. They believed in it enough to take risks, and the faith in their logic was reinforced by big doses of success. They had evidence to support the rightness of their approach. What they could not understand is that in finding the right strategic fit with their environment, they were changing themselves and their environment. They were co-evolving (Ford and Backoff, Chapter 3). Soon elements of both the environment and their own evolving system would pressure them toward the implementation of structure. The implementation of structure would move them in a direction opposite from where they wanted to go.

This either/or logic is the foundation of rational action. It is not bad. It is the most efficient way to cope with the problems we face in daily life. It is used regularly without entering into vicious circles. It is for this reason so natural that when people get into a vicious circle, they find it most difficult to get out. Because it sometimes leads to the splitting of polarities and the loss of creative tension, the rational model is what gets us into the dynamic problems associated with paradox.

Projection.   Once in a vicious circle, an individual has difficulty getting out because the solution is counterintuitive. But it is not the logic that is at fault (Sipporin and Gummer, Chapter 6); rather, it is the assumptions, values, or world views underneath the logic that are at fault. These are deeply rooted and difficult to change. (See Kimberly's Rejoinder to Chapter 4.) When individuals note unintended outcomes, they reexamine their strategy to see if there is some logical flaw. They conclude, correctly, that there is not. They tend to conclude, therefore, that the problem lies in an outside source, in the environment. The problem is projected outward, and as individuals increase their efforts to alter the outside source instead of the assumptions, the problem intensifies.

The engineer in case 1 was successful in performing technical analysis and directing productive action. At lower organizational levels this was valued and rewarded, thus reinforcing his world view. But, as he was promoted to higher levels in the system, the political and interpersonnel aspects of work became increasingly important. He was less skilled at performing them. Because they were less tangible, he rejected them as unreal. As he experienced the vicious circle that comes with doing more of what has worked in the past but perpetuates the problem in the present, he became frustrated and projected his problems onto his boss, claiming that his boss did not practice good management.

In the entrepreneurial organization case, it was clear to the top management team at the mental health center that the problem was not with them. External agencies such as the Division of Budget and the Department of Audit and Control wanted reports beyond the capability of the system, were insensitive to what made the organization successful, and had to be distracted or ignored. New employees who wanted structure and policies did not understand the "true mission" of the organization and needed to be more fully socialized and challenged. These rationales, however, only intensified the problem.

Instructional Impermeability.   The individual who is caught in a vicious circle cannot be instructed out of it. Indeed, as Argyris argues (Chapter 8), it is often entirely undiscussable. In any case, to attempt to instruct someone out of the problem often merely reinforces the problem (Sipporin and Gummer, Chapter 6, and Kilmann's Rejoinder). To tell the person that the source of the problem is not in the target system but is in his or her own assumptions is threatening, even offensive. It flies in the face of that of which the person is most sure. The credibility of the helping person is often discounted, and the individual tends to defend the original position. The initial conclusion is reasserted more strongly. In attempting to instruct the person out of this vicious circle, the helper becomes part of the problem.

In the parks and recreation case, the two groups were caught in a vicious circle. When the commissioner called a meeting and tried to "instruct" them out of the problem, she became less credible. Each group immediately defined her as an outsider who did not understand them.

In their self-justification, they also reinforced their perspective that the other group was at fault. The commissioner, as she increased her efforts to resolve the problem, now created a second vicious circle. The more she sought cooperation through instruction, the more the two groups became conflictual.

Impermeability to instruction also seems counter to normal assumptions. It seems logical that when a problem exists, the manager's job is to define the problem and to instruct people on how to solve it. So pervasive is this assumption that seldom can an alternative approach even be conceived.

Reframing.   In interpreting the world, in imparting meaning, or in imposing structure on some situation, people use mental frames, schema, or templates (Bartunek, Chapter 4). They have implicit assumptions or governing rules that order their perceptions and strategies. Reframing involves taking on a new template. This is a deep, "qualitative, discontinuous, second order or double loop shift in the understanding of some domain," not an incremental shift in the previous level of understanding (Bartunek, Chapter 4). It is a dramatic change that results, not from instruction, but from discovery. It comes with "acting one's way out of a problem" (Thompson's Rejoinder to Chapter 3, and Mirvis's Rejoinder to Chapter 8). It often leads to new and seemingly counterintuitive ways of behaving. New assumptions and behaviors may reflect a more novel and more appropriate way of relating to the situation.

In the parks and recreation case, for example, a consultant was called in. His strategy was to help members of both groups come to an understanding of the futility of refusing to discuss their differences. Through intergroup conflict resolution processes (French and Bell 1984: Chapter 11) and reframing techniques, they were helped to realize that most of their criticisms and cynicism about the other group was a product of long-held myths, not actual behaviors. By the end of the two-day workshop, the groups had developed a new set of shared assumptions that allowed them to work together in mutual reinforcing ways. They developed novel and more appropriate interpretations of their situation. They began to communicate at a "meta level" and help create a new reality (Mirvis, Rejoinder to Chapter 8).

Because constructing a new frame often leads to a better fit with the environment, reframing is a change that often results in high energy and synergistic outcomes. This fact leads us to another perspective on the dyamics of paradox.

PARADOX AS A DYNAMIC PROCESS: THE POSITIVE PERSPECTIVE

In the previous section we considered the situation where individuals are trapped within a vicious circle. From that perspective, paradox is a problem to be solved. Many of the authors who have written about paradox in organizations take such a perspective in that they describe paradoxical problems. Less frequently do they identify paradoxical virtues. That is, instead of producing a vicious circle, paradox can help individuals become energized and propelled ahead. In this situation there is not a vicious circle that drags the person deeper and deeper into frustration but an energizing spiral that elevates the person to higher and higher levels of performance and feelings of exhilaration (see Ford and Backoff, Chapter 3, and Thompson's Rejoinder). It is an inversion of the vicious circle phenomenon. It produces a synergistic or "flow" state (Csikzentmihalyi 1976) that is entered after reframing. In this state complex contradictory forces are as present as they were in the problem state, but they produce a source of creative energy.

This positive dynamic is one way to account for excellence or peak performance (Eisenhardt and Westcott, Chapter 5). In describing this phenomenon, Dee Hock, the CEO at Visa International stated:

> In the field of group endeavor, you will see incredible events in which the group performs far beyond the sum of its individual talents. It happens in the symphony, in the ballet, in the theater, in sports and equally in business. It is easy to recognize and impossible to define. It is a mystique. It cannot be achieved without immense effort, training, and cooperation, but effort, training and cooperation alone rarely create it. Some groups reach it consistently. Few can sustain it (Schlesinger, Eccles, and Gabarro 1983: 486).

When individuals recount performance at their very best, at the peak of their experience, they often describe a synergistic state where such statements as, "I was high" or "I was on a roll," are used. They often report moving from a feeling of stuckness to a feeling of flow. In fact, in a study of peak experiences, Csikszentmihalyi (1976) coined the term "flow" to describe the feeling of being energized. He reported finding "flow" in all kinds of activities. In order to better understand what flow is, and how it relates to paradox, we will again consider some examples.

One example is provided by Bill Russell (1979), the former center for the Boston Celtics basketball team. Occasionally a Celtics game would "heat up" to the point that it would become "more than a physical or even mental" experience. Play would rise to an extraordinary level. It would start with three or four of the best players on each team making outstanding plays. Then a special feeling would spread across both teams. Each person on the floor would push himself harder and harder. At this level, what Russell calls "magic" would occur:

> At that special level all sorts of odd things happened. The game would be in a white heat of competition, and yet somehow I wouldn't feel competitive—which is a miracle in itself. I'd be putting out the maximum effort, straining and yet nothing could surprise me. It was almost as if we were playing in slow motion. During those spells I could almost sense how the next play would develop and where the next shot would be taken. Even before the other team brought the ball in bounds, I could feel it so keenly that I'd want to shout to my teammates, "It's coming there!"—except that I knew everything would change if I did. My premonitions would be consistently correct, and I always felt then that I not only knew all the Celtics by heart but also all the opposing players, and that they all knew me. There have been many times in my career when I felt moved or joyful, but these were the moments when I had chills pulsing up and down my spine. (177)

Hurst (1984) described a similar phenomenon at the organizational level. He pointed out that as a result of a major crisis, his company developed two contrasting management philosophies, one classic and hierarchical, the other holistic and fluid. By recognizing and employing both, Hurst claimed that amazing things happened. (See Ford and Backoff for a discussion of this point, Chapter 3.) An improved sense of timing emerged. A spirit of cooperation among senior managers became intense, and the organization seemed to "get lucky." Hurst described this phenomenon as "magic," the same term used by Russell, and claimed that when it occurs, "there is a tremendous sense of joy."

Several points can be made about this state of "flow," peak performance, or "magic":

1. It is paradoxical.
2. Reframing is a prerequisite.
3. It eventually leads to routinization and the imposition of the rational model.
4. Some individuals experience the state more frequently than others.
5. It may involve holonomic information processing.

Paradoxical. Csikszentmihalyi (1975) described the flow experience as one where individuals, groups, and organizations take on paradoxical characteristics. There is no split, he claimed, between the self and the environment, the stimulus and the response, the past and the present. Action and awareness are merged. There are no dualisms. Self-consciousness disappears. Individuals in flow seem to be both controlled and free.

For Bill Russell, the same paradoxical elements were described. The flow state (magic) was competitive but not competitive, excruciatingly painful but without pain, filled with surprise that surprised no one, an intense but delicate process that could be brought to a halt by the simplest mistake by any player on the floor.

In each case a mental reframing takes place. Individuals become more attuned to their environment, and a synergistic relationship with it occurs. In this relationship, oppositions seem to converge. Polarities are joined in self-reinforcing tensions that drive performance to higher and higher levels.

Reframing Is a Prerequisite.   Individuals normally follow a logical sequence in solving problems and reacting to their environments. In doing so, they tend to employ a narrow goal focus which assumes that they are to act upon the environment or task. After entering flow experiences, however, they report a more interactive perspective in which they see themselves acting with, rather than upon, the environment. The movement from the first to the second frame suggests movement from the application of rules based on a known paradigm to the discovery of a new paradigm that better fits the problem or situation and is yet to be routinized. It is a time of challenge, discovery, creative feeling, new direction, and reinforcement or synergy.

Bill Russell, for example, describes the role of the transformational leader in getting a group to go through this reframing process. He cites Oscar Robertson as a prime example of a player who could stimulate magic among his team members. At a certain time in the game, usually in the third quarter, Robertson would determine that it was time for his team to leave the normal rhythms of play and move to a higher level of performance. He would take five seconds and dribble the ball at the top of the key while he would swear intensely at his teammates. Russell claims that for the next few minutes you had to be careful to not get swept off the floor by the play of Robertson's team. Richard Hackman describes similar behavior in his analysis of Don Burr at People Express Airlines. Hackman provided an in-depth analysis of the behavior Burr used constantly to take his management team to higher levels of challenge, vision, and performance.

Another example of strategic reframing is provided by McDonalds. That firm shifted from having a self-identity focused on cheap hamburgers, to having the fastest hamburgers, to having the cleanest restaurants, to having the friendliest hostesses, to being a fun place for the family, to being a breakfast stop. Each shift in how the business was defined had a reenergizing and renewing effect on the corporation.

Peak Experience Eventually Leads to Routinization and a Return to the Imposition of the Rational Model. As Hock observed, the flow state cannot be sustained indefinitely. The high energy, high exertion experience must be routinized or the capacity of the system degenerates. Individuals and organizations all must return to normal levels of performance in order to avoid exhaustion. Excellence, by definition, is a deviation from normally observed processes. No organization can sustain it indefinitely. Therefore, organizations may continue to renew themselves by shifting or replacing the interpretive framework. Whereas peak performance will naturally produce exhaustion and eventual deterioration in a system, it can be overcome by routinization.

Many individuals and organizations become stuck in an exclusive, either/or frame (i.e., "we're either this or that, not both"). (See Thompson's discussion of thinking on the margin, Rejoinder to Chapter 3.) The engineer, the commissioner, and the entrepreneur in our three cases are examples of being stuck in a single framework that produced a vicious circle. It is also possible, however, to become stuck in blind pursuit of positive outcomes such as stimulation, innovation, and growth. In this condition, individuals may negatively define stability and consistency. This may lead to the unfortunate fate of Don Burr of People Express, or other entrepreneurs such as Steve Jobs at Apple, who were decoyed by their unwillingness to define positively and adopt an opposing framework. In the case of Burr and Jobs, they appeared to reject the positive values associated with formalization and routinization processes and seemed to refuse to couple them with innovation and clan qualities to renew a high performing system. Because they negatively defined hierarchy and control, they could go up the creative ladder, but they could not come down. They resisted the routinization process until the system rejected them. A virtuous circle turned into a vicious circle.

Organization and management theory tends to reinforce rather than resolve the problem of getting stuck in a single framework. For example, in the managerial literature, three illustrations can be cited: McGregor's (1960) differentiation of Theory X and Theory Y; Zaleznik's (1977) differentiation of management and leadership; and Burns' (1978) differentiation of transactional and transformational leadership. In each case, there is a predisposition to devalue one alternative and to value the other alternative. Theory Y, in contrast to Theory X, has become defined as new and enlightened management. Leadership, not management, is what is really needed in modern firms. Transformational leadership is more valuable than transactional leadership. In each case the either/or logic is imposed on the alternatives, and the possible identification of a dynamic relationship between the two is lost. The possibility of both, simultaneously, residing in and required by the same system is not consistent with mainline organization theory (Bass 1985; Quinn 1988).

Renewal in systems, then, requires that individuals adopt multiple frameworks, particularly paradoxical frameworks. Instead of becoming steeped in a single framework and rigorously defending and perpetuating it, the most effective organizations and leaders will make themselves free to adopt additional perspectives when circumstances warrant. Having multiple frameworks available, in fact, is probably the single most powerful attribute of self-renewing individuals and organizations.

> A good sense of relevance and timing is often treated as though it were a "gift" or "intuition" rather than something that can be learned, something spontaneous rather than something planned. The opposite is nearer the truth. One is more likely to "capture the moment" when everything one has learned is readily available. . . . Perhaps it's our training in linear cause-and-effect thinking and the neglect of our capacities for imagery that makes us so often unable to see the multiple potential of the moment. Entering a situation "blank" is not the answer. One needs to have as many frameworks for seeing and strategies for acting available as possible. (Herbert Shepard 1983: 420)

Some Individuals and Groups Enter the Flow State More Frequently than Others. Several streams of recent research suggest that the ability to acquire and shift among multiple mental frameworks is characteristic of relatively few people. Dreyfus and Dreyfus (1986) developed a five-stage model that explains how people move from being a novice to being a master. In the early stages of an activity, the novice learns facts and rules. Over time, as the person moves through the various stages, the activity itself is eventually understood to be a dynamic process. Hierarchical logic fades as the task is engaged in a more holistic, fluid, and dynamic way.

Torbert (Rejoinder to Chapter 7) presents a developmental model that suggests that many managers get stuck in a single, narrow framework and that only a few eventually move to a stage in which they can think paradoxically. In a similar vein, Streufret and Swezey (1986) report that the more capacity a manager has to think in complex and flexible ways about a system, the more effectiveness he or she can produce in that system. Finally, Quinn, Faerman, and Dixit (1987) reported that only a small percentage of managers have the ability to employ a variety of frames and behaviors that allow them to renew themselves, repeat peak experiences, and avoid exhaustion.

The Flow Experience May Involve Holonomic Information Processing. Holography is a type of photography that generates a three-dimensional image. In normal photography, light flows through a lens and is stored in a point-to-point relationship on the film in the back of the camera. The developed film is used to project a two-dimensional image. In holography light is transformed in a way so that the entire image is stored on every element of the film. If a piece of the film is torn away and then projected, the whole image still appears. The information stored in every element is perfectly redundant. Pribram's research suggests that the brain stores information in this fashion and Bradley, using data from communes, argues that human collectivities may do so also.

Recently work on holography in physics (Bohm 1980) and in brain research (Pribram 1982) has suggested some interesting applications to the study of individual and organizational peak experience.

Holonomic information processing may be descriptive of what happens to information during the process of "flow." There is a kind of understanding, action, communion, and creation of reality that transcends normal logic. Polarities and oppositions are experienced as one. There is an understanding beyond verbal interaction. The Celtics, their opponents, and the crowd became one self-reinforcing system. Together, they reach new levels of performance. Bill Russell claimed to "know" every other player and what will happen in the immediate future. In such cases a communion and a kind of information processing exists that exceed the assumptions of a single, rational framework. It appears to be, as Bradley suggests, holonomic information processing in that all cues in the environment are processed at once, multiple perspectives are available, and sequential actions seem to lose their time-bound quality.

IMPLICATIONS OF THE DYNAMIC
PROCESS DEFINITIONS

Earlier, after reviewing the first type of definition, we asked what might be the payoffs of employing the paradoxical frame? Our answer was that the frame leads to richer analyses in which we are forced to look more deeply than usual, and to ask about the positive opposites that might not be recognized in a given situation. Also we might be led to explore the creative tensions within our major concepts and categories. As we considered the second definition, just discussed, or the dynamic perspective so often associated with paradox, we might again ask what the implications are.

The paradoxical frame suggests that organizations are dynamic. They exist within and are themselves dynamic streams of energy which are constantly transformed (Ford and Backoff, Chapter 3). These energy flows are constantly taking material forms which, from the human time perspective, may be seen as permanent. The change process, however, is continuous both inside and outside the organization. While the transformations can take the form of vicious circles, they can also take the form of virtuous circles. When both of these phenomena are simultaneously recognized, we have a dynamic, paradoxical frame that allows us to understand transformation.

While transformation occurs naturally, the process can also be molded and designed intentionally through purposive logic. All successful strategic action reflects this proposition. Humans constantly mold and design the energy flows within which they exist. Purposive strategies of action tend toward goal accomplishment in the short term and system collapse, through entropy, in the long term. This proposition reflects the negative dynamics discussed above. Over time the single-minded, purposive pursuit of any value will begin to destroy the balance between polarities (Starbuck, Rejoinder to Chapter 2). In contrast, reframing strategies tend toward peak performance in the short term and system collapse, through exhaustion or negentropy, in the long term. This proposition reflects the seldom considered outcome of the positive dynamics discussed above. Reframing leads to the rebalancing of polarities and to peak performance. It, however, if exclusively pursued, will lead to exhaustion of resources and collapse of the system.

The above observation can be illustrated in Figure 9–1, which is adapted from Quinn (1988). In the middle circle or positive zone are eight general sets of effectiveness criteria. These are taken from the

Figure 9-1. The Transformation of Positive Values.

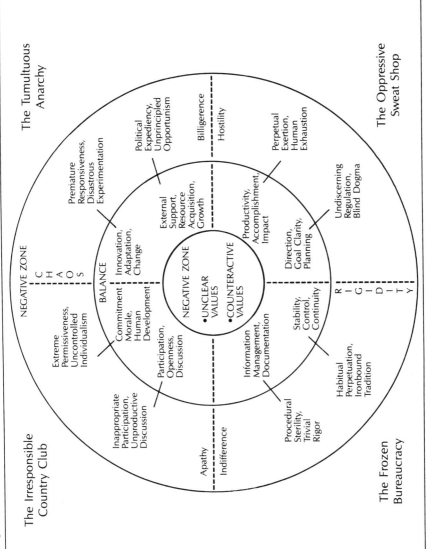

Source: Quinn (1988). Permission granted.

competing values model (see Cameron and Quinn, Chapter 1), and can be seen as polarities by observing the points farthest from one another. Stability, control, and continuity, for example, are contrasted with innovation, adaptation, and change, the values in the farthest point in the same circle.

Each set of criteria is positively defined. While any set of criteria might be emphasized at a given time, if any one is pursued exclusively, the creative tension between polarities may be lost, and the positive value can become negative. This is illustrated in the relationship between the positive and negative zones. In moving from the positive to the negative, a strange transition occurs. Stability, control, and continuity, for example, become habitual perpetuation and ironbound tradition. Innovation, adaptation, and change become premature responsiveness and disastrous experimentation.

The four labels on the outside of the circle suggest four negative situations that might arise (Quinn 1988). An organization characterized as a well-ordered hierarchy might become a frozen bureaucracy. A responsive adhocracy might become a tumultuous anarchy. A cohesive team or clan might become an irresponsible country club. An intensely profit-focused firm might become an oppressive sweat shop. In each case, the positive values in a particular quadrant are severed from their positive opposites and a strange loop occurs. In each case, by pursuing good through too narrow a frame, unintended negative consequences are created.

This conceptualization suggests that long-term survival depends upon the balancing of polarities through transformational strategies. According to the theory represented in Figure 9–1, a manager must avoid entering the negative zone, where he or she can be trapped in a vicious circle. Instead, the manager must operate within the tensions of the positive zone. Thus, the skilled manager can pursue one or more values in the positive zone while remaining sensitive to the need to consider polar values. By building the creative tensions between polar values, the manager can occasionally reach peak performance or the flow state, and then, eventually move back to routinization and control.

The process described in the above paragraph is predicated on a developmental learning process at both the cognitive and behavioral levels. In order to master such an approach, one must have the cognitive capacity to use multiple frames, and the behavioral capacity to use skills that match the frames (Argyris, Chapter 8). Few, if any, of our theories or schools of management are oriented to developing such capacities

(Morgan, Chapter 7 and Torbert's Rejoinder). The research discussed earlier suggests that the development of mastery comes through painful experience, and is enjoyed by only a small minority. Those who develop mastery have the capacity to balance polarities in a way that is difficult for someone to understand when they are mired in the either/or frame.

While there is still much work to be done on the paradoxical frame, it seems to us to have much potential for expanding our capacity to think about management and organization. We hope the works in this book will stimulate others to engage in such development.

REFERENCES

Bass, B. 1985. *Leadership and Performance Beyond Expectations*. New York: Free Press.

Bohm, D. 1980. *Wholeness and the Implicate Order*. London, Boston, and Henley: Routledge and Kegan Paul.

Burns, J.M. 1978. *Leadership*. New York: Harper and Row.

Csikszentmihalyi, M. 1976. *Beyond Boredom and Anxiety*. San Francisco: Jossey-Bass.

Dreyfus, H.L., and S.E. Dreyfus with T. Athanasion. 1986. *Mind Over Machine: The Power of Human Intuition and Expertise in the Era of the Computer*. New York: Free Press.

Festinger, L., and J.M Carlsmith. 1959. "Cognitive Consequences of Forced Compliance." *Journal of Abnormal Social Psychology* 58: 203–10.

French, W.L., and C.H. Bell. 1984. *Organizational Development: Behavioral Science Interventions for Organizational Improvement*, 3d ed. Englewood Cliffs, N.J.: Prentice-Hall.

Hofstadter, D.R. 1979. *Godel, Escher, Bach: An Eternal Golden Braid*. New York: Vintage Books.

Hurst, D.K. 1984. "Of Boxes, Bubbles, and Effective Management." *Harvard Business Review* 62, no. 3: 78–88.

Masuch, M. 1985. "Vicious Circles in Organizations." *Administrative Science Quarterly* 30: 14–33.

McGregor, D. 1960. *Human Side of Enterprise*. New York: McGraw-Hill.

Pribam, K.H. 1982. "Localization and the Distribution of Function in the Brain." *Neuropsychology After Lashley*, edited by J. Orbach, pp. 273–96. Hillsdale, N.J.: Earlbaum.

Quinn, R.E. 1988. *Beyond Rational Management: Mastering the Paradoxes and Competing Demands of High Performance*. San Francisco: Jossey-Bass.

Quinn, R.E.; S.R. Faerman; and N. Dixit. 1987. "Perceived Performance: Some Archetypes of Managerial Effectiveness and Ineffectiveness." Working paper, Department of Public Administration, State University of New York at Albany.

Russell, B. 1979. *Second Wind: The Memoirs of an Opinionated Man.* New York: Ballantine.

Schlesinger, L.A.; R.G. Eccles; and J.J. Gabarro. 1983. *Managerial Behavior in Organizations: Texts, Cases and Readings.* New York: McGraw-Hill.

Simon, H. 1945. *Administrative Behavior.* New York: Free Press.

Streufert, S., and R.W. Swezey. 1986. *Complexity, Managers and Organizations.* Orlando: Academic Press.

Sutton, R.S. 1987. "The Process of Organizational Death: Struggling, Disbanding and Reconnecting." Working Paper, Department of Industrial Engineering, Stanford.

Zaleznik, A. 1977. "Managers and Leaders: Are They Different?" *Harvard Business Review* 55, no. 5: 67–80.

NAME INDEX

SUBJECT INDEX

ABOUT THE EDITORS

Robert E. Quinn is a professor of organizational studies and of public administration at The State University of New York, Albany, and is currently on a two year visit at the University of Michigan Graduate School of Business. His particular areas of interest are in organizational change, organizational effectiveness, and managerial effectiveness. He is the author of numerous journal articles and books, the most recent of which is the forthcoming *Beyond Rational Management: Mastering the Paradoxes and Competing Demands of Management.*

Kim S. Cameron is an associate professor of organizational behavior and department chair at the University of Michigan Graduate School of Business. A specialist in organizational effectiveness and organizational decline, he has written numerous articles and books on these subjects. He is also the co-author of a text on managerial skill development. He also holds a bachelor's and a master's degree from Brigham Young University and a Ph.D. from Yale University.

ABOUT THE CONTRIBUTORS

Chris Argyris is the James Bryant Conant Professor of Education and Organizational Behavior at Harvard University. He was awarded the A.B. degree in psychology from Clark University (1947); the M.A. degree in economics and psychology from Kansas University (1949); and the Ph.D. degree in organizational behavior from Cornell University (1951). From 1951 to 1971 he was a faculty member at Yale University, serving as the Beach Professor of Administrative Sciences and as chair of the Administrative Sciences department during the latter part of this period.

Robert W. Backoff is associate professor of public administration management and human resources, and political science at The Ohio State University. He received his B.A. degree from the University of Illinois, his M.A. from Johns Hopkins University and his Ph.D. in political science from Indiana University. His current research is in the strategic management of public sector organizations and in organizational transformation and evolution. His recent publications appear in the *American Journal of Planning,* the *Public Administration Review,* and *Technological Forecasting and Social Change.*

Jean M. Bartunek is an associate professor of Organizational Studies at Boston College, where she has taught since 1977. She received a

Ph.D. in social and organizational psychology from the University of Illinois at Chicago in 1976 and served as a visiting assistant professor in organizational behavior at the University of Illinois at Urbana-Champaign from 1976 to 1977. Her writing has focused on participative decisionmaking, conflict management, and, primarily, planned and unplanned organizational change. She is a member of the editorial boards of *Administrative Science Quarterly,* the *Academy of Management Journal,* and the *Journal of Applied Behavioral Science* and is on the executive committee of the Organization Development division of the Academy of Management.

Victoria Buenger is a doctoral student in management at Texas A&M University. Her research interests include strategic management, organizational theory, and business history.

Richard L. Daft is the Hugh Roy Cullen Professor of Business Administration at Texas A&M University. He has published six books and numerous articles in journals such as *Administrative Science Quarterly,* the *Academy of Management Journal, Managemenet Science,* and *Academy of Management Review.* He has served as associate editor of *ASQ* and is co-editor-in-chief of *Organization Science.* His research interests are in the areas of organization theory, organizational information processing, organizational innovation, and strategy implementation.

Kathleen M. Eisenhardt is an assistant professor in the Industrial Engineering and Engineering Management Department at Stanford University. Her research interests are in the organizational issues created by high-velocity, high-technology environments. Her work includes studies of the strategic decisionmaking of top management teams in the microcomputer industry, and the success factors of new ventures in the semiconductor industry. Her publications have appeared in *Management Science, Organizational Dynamics,* and *California Management Review.*

Jeffrey D. Ford is associate professor of management and human resources, and public administration at The Ohio State University. He received his B.S. degree from the University of Maryland and his MBA and Ph.D. in organizational behavior from The Ohio State University. His current interests include strategic management, strategic change, organization design, and organizational transformation and evolution.

His recent publications can be found in the *Academy of Management Review* and the *Academy of Management Journal.*

Burton Gummer, M.S.W., Ph.D., is an associate professor at the School of Social Welfare, Rockefeller College of Public Affairs and Policy, The University at Albany, State University of New York. His field of interest is the organization and administration of social agencies, with an emphasis on the role of organizational politics. He has published widely in this area and is currently writing a book entitled *The Politics of Social Administration.*

Ralph H. Kilmann is a professor of business administration and the director of the Program in Corporate Culture at the Joseph M. Katz Graduate School of Business, University of Pittsburgh. He received both his B.S. and M.S. degrees in industrial administration from Carnegie-Mellon University and his Ph.D. degree in management from the University of California, Los Angeles. Since 1975 he has served as the president of Organizational Design Consultants, a Pittsburgh-based firm specializing in the five tracks to organizational success.

John R. Kimberly is a professor of management and health care systems, chairman of the Department of Management, and a senior fellow in the Leonard Davis Institute of Health Economics at The Wharton School of the University of Pennsylvania. He received his B.A. degree from Yale University and his M.S. and Ph.D. degrees in organizational behavior from Cornell University. Dr. Kimberly joined the Wharton School faculty in 1982, following several years as a member of the faculty in the School of Organization and Management and Institution for Social Policy and Studies at Yale University. He has also held faculty appointments at the University of Illinois, Urbana-Champaign, and Cornell University.

Philip H. Mirvis is an author and a private consultant. His areas of study concern social and organizational change, with a particular emphasis on the changing characteristics of the workforce and workplace. Mirvis consults with organizations in the areas of mergers and acquisitions, large-scale change programs, quality of work-life surveys, and the implementation of social and technological innovations. He is the author of many articles on these subjects and of two edited books on organizational assessment and change. Most recently Mirvis has co-authored a book entitled *Cynicism at Work.*

Gareth Morgan is well known for his contributions to social research. A pioneer in developing creative approaches to organization theory, he has authored and edited a wide range of books and articles, including *Beyond Method, Sociological Paradigms and Organizational Analysis,* and *Organizational Symbolism.* He holds degrees from the London School of Economics and Political Science, the University of Texas at Austin, and the University of Lancaster. He sits on the editorial boards of the *Academy of Management Review, Administration and Society,* the *Journal of Management,* and *Organization Studies.* He has lectured at over forty universities in Europe and North America and has held a number of visiting appointments. He is now Professor of Administrative Studies at York University, Toronto.

Marshall Scott Poole is an associate professor of speech-communication at the University of Minnesota. He obtained his Ph.D. in communication arts from the University of Wisconsin at Madison in 1980 and taught at the University of Illinois at Urbana-Champaign from 1979 to 1985 before his present appointment. His current research interests are innovation and change in organizations, the role of information systems in group decisions, and organizational climates and communication networks. He is associated with the Minnesota Innovation Research Program, the findings from which he is co-editing with Andrew Van de Ven and Harold Angle into a two-volume research monograph entitled *Research on the Management of Innovation,* to be published by Ballinger Publishing Co.

Max Siporin, M.S.W., D.S.W., is a professor emeritus at the School of Social Welfare, Rockefeller College of Public Affairs and Policy, The University at Albany, State University of New York, where he continues to teach. His practice experience is in a variety of psychiatric facilities and social agencies, as well as in private practice. He has published widely in the areas of therapeutic methods, including works on marriage and family therapy. He is a fellow in the American Association for Marriage and Family Therapy and a distinguished practitioner of social work in the National Academies of Practice.

William H. Starbuck is the ITT Professor of Creative Management and directs the doctoral program in business administration at New York University. He received his M.S. and Ph.D. at Carnegie Institute of Technology, after receiving an A.B. at Harvard University. He has held faculty positions at Purdue University, the Johns Hopkins University, Cornell University, and the University of Wisconsin-Milwaukee, as well as visiting positions in England, Norway, and Sweden. He was also a senior research fellow at the International Institute of Management, Berlin. He has served as editor of *Administrative Science Quarterly* and on the editorial boards of several academic journals; he also chaired the screening committee for senior Fulbright awards in business management. He has published numerous articles on human decisionmaking, bargaining, organizational growth and development, social revolutions, computer simulation, computer programming, accounting, business strategy, and organizational design. He has also edited four books, including the *Handbook of Organizational Design,* which was selected as the best book on management published during the year ending May 1982.

Michael P. Thompson holds a Ph.D. in rhetoric from Rensselaer Polytechnic Institute. He is currently the associate director of the Public Service Training Program at the University at Albany. His research focuses on the evolution of the corporate classroom. He is also working on a competency-based introductory text for managers.

William R. Torbert has been graduate dean of the Boston College School of Management for the past eight years. He has pioneered a new "action effectiveness" model of M.B.A. education that implements the ideas in this book and has gained national recognition for the school. He was formerly an associate professor at the Harvard Graduate School of Education and an assistant professor at the Southern Methodist University School of Business. He also founded and directed two organizations—the Yale Upward Bound Program and the Theatre of Inquiry. Dean Torbert holds a B.A. degree in politics and economics and a Ph.D. in administrative sciences from Yale University and was awarded a Danforth Graduate Fellowship. He is a consultant for businesses and not-for-profits at all stages of development. He is the author of numerous academic articles on business and organizational behavior and the following books: *Being for the Most Part Puppets: Interactions among Men's Labor, Leisure, and Politics* (1972); *Learning from Experience: Toward Consciousness* (1973); and *Creating a Community of Inquiry: Conflict, Collaboration, Transformation* (1976).

Andrew H. Van de Ven is the 3M Professor of Human Systems Management in the Curtis L. Carlson School of Management and director of the Minnesota Innovation Research Program in the Strategic Management Research Center of the University of Minnesota. He received his Ph.D. from the University of Wisconsin at Madison in 1972, and taught at Kent State University (1972–1975) and The Wharton School of the University of Pennsylvania (1975–1981) before his present appointment.

Brian J. Westcott is a post-doctoral fellow at the Stanford Graduate School of Business. He received his Ph.D. from the Department of Industrial Engineering and Engineering Management at Stanford. Dr. Westcott also holds a B.S. in mechanical engineering from Lehigh University and an M.S. in mechanical engineering from Stanford University. His previous industrial experience includes positions at the Electric Power Research Institute, General Electric Corporate Research Center, and at Combustion Engineering.

RITTER LIBRARY
BALDWIN-WALLACE COLLEGE
WITHDRAWN